Cunningly Clever Entrepreneur

Shortcuts To Your First Few Millions

How to Start, Grow, Survive & Thrive in Your Own Business!

Andrew Wood

Legendary Marketing
www.LegendaryMarketing.com
800-827-1663

Price: $39.95
Published by Select Press
Novato, California
ISBN 978-1890777-12-8

10 9 8 7 6 5 4 3 2 1

Printed in Korea

Other Books by Andrew Wood

Cunningly Clever Marketing

Cunningly Clever Selling

The Golf Marketing Bible

Traits of Champions
(with Brian Tracy)

Making It Big in America

Summary Contents

(A detailed Table of Contents follows on page vii.)

Detailed Contents

Section 1

Section 2

CUNNINGLY CLEVER WAYS TO
HIRE THE BEST EMPLOYEES   55

Section 4

CHOOSING THE PERFECT LOCATION FOR YOUR BUSINESS

MARKETING FOR THE CUNNINGLY
CLEVER ENTREPRENEUR

GENERATING PRODUCTS, SERVICES, AND GROWTH THROUGH INNOVATION   165

CUNNINGLY CLEVER MANAGEMENT
193

Section 8

STARTING NEW VENTURES AND LAUNCHING NEW PRODUCTS   271

Section 10

SOLVING PROBLEMS THE CUNNINGLY CLEVER WAY

Section 11

Section 12

CUNNINGLY CLEVER SELLING FOR ENTREPRENEURS

Section 14

CRITICAL FACTORS TO OVERCOMING BUSINESS ADVERSITY AND MAKING MILLIONS

1

A Bulletproof
Blueprint to Set
Your Company Up
for Massive Success

CHAPTER 1

Critical Business Advice You
MUST NOT Ignore!

Rule No. 1: Never lose money.
Rule No. 2: Never forget Rule No. 1.
WARREN BUFFETT

The Department of Consumer and Employment Protection had heard that a farmer was not paying proper wages to his employees and sent an agent down to interview him.

"I need a list of your employees and how much you pay them," demanded the agent.

"Well," replied the farmer, "there's my farmhand who's been with me for three years. I pay him $700 a week plus free room and board.

"The cook has been here for 18 months, and I pay her $750 per week plus free room and board.

"Then there's the half-wit who works about 18 to 20 hours every day and does about 95% of all the work around here. He makes about $30 per week, pays for his own room and board, and I buy him a bottle of booze every Saturday night. He also has sex with my wife occasionally."

"That's the guy I want to talk to—the half-wit," said the agent.

"That would be me," replied the farmer.

Pay yourself first!

I know from firsthand experience how easy it is to go into debt, borrow money from your friends, and max out all your credit cards to meet payroll while taking nothing for yourself save the promise of sweat equity in the future success of the venture. Don't do it!

Don't even think about doing it!

Demand a paycheck for yourself.

Then demand profits. Do not just be satisfied with getting a paycheck. The opportunity cost will kill you if the work doesn't!

If you are not getting paid,
you are not in business!

CHAPTER 2

The Simple Paradigm Shift You Need to Create Massive Business Success

It will work. I am a marketing genius.
PARIS HILTON

In 1962, Thomas Kuhn wrote *The Structure of Scientific Revolution* where he defined and popularized the concept of "paradigm shift." Kuhn argued that scientific advancement is not evolutionary, but rather a "series of peaceful interludes punctuated by intellectually violent revolutions," and in those revolutions "one conceptual world view is replaced by another."

Now let's take all that mumbo jumbo and replace it with a simple concept that will make your business massively more profitable!

Most small business owners and service providers view themselves as doers of whatever it is those in their line of business are supposed to do. Chiropractors fix backs, financial advisors pick stocks, builders build homes, and lawn services cut grass. The cunningly clever business owner takes a different perspective, one that most doers find very hard to accept. The cunningly clever entrepreneur understands that the selling and marketing of the product or service is what produces superior financial results, NOT the doing!

The reason I was able to make large sums of money in the karate business is simple. I wasn't in the business of teaching karate like 99.9% of the others in that particular industry; instead, I was in the business of *marketing* "teaching karate."

Go to any business convention—take your pick of carpet cleaners, dentists, or golf course owners—and hang out at the bar. What you will hear is heated conversations on how to *operate* a business rather than how to *market* a business. The simple act of shifting your thinking from being in the jewelry business to being in the business of marketing fine jewels will have a staggering effect on your income. This is true no matter what business you happen to be in!

Once you start to accept that your primary business concern should be marketing your business, not operating your business, you enter a whole new realm of possibilities. You start to think in a different way; you start to ask better questions; you start to allocate your time in different and more productive ways.

The difficulty with this type of paradigm shift is that most people cannot move more than 10% from where they are in life and who they think they are. Builders build, that's who they are. They are managers of materials and tradesmen, usually with practical experience in at least one trade. They don't see themselves as marketers of the homes they build. Instead, they are likely to dismiss this critical function as the job of the Realtor or some untrained employee they have sitting at a desk in the model home.

Try this exercise in your workplace today and see what happens: THINK LIKE A MARKETER. Start making decisions as if your only job was marketing your business. Let's take a simple example of how a lawn care business might put this idea into action.

Knock on the door of every single customer's house on

your route after you have cut the grass and ask them two simple questions.

First, "Is there anything else in the yard that needs my attention?" (That's sure to amaze and impress anyone with lawn care service in your county!)

Second, tell them that you are trying to grow your business to put your son, daughter, or dog through college, and that you would like to know which neighbor or friend you could call on with the current client's personal recommendation.

On a route of 50 accounts, just asking those two simple questions and thinking like a marketer of lawn care service instead of a gardener could easily result in five successful referrals, or a massive 10% business growth in a single week!

NEVER let a single day go by without doing something to try to increase your business. Consider any day that you don't make sales calls, send prospecting letters, ask for referrals, or up-sell an existing client a dismal failure!

Let marketing, not operations, be your guide as to whether you have had a good day at the office, and you will quickly make the paradigm shift—or realize that the business you're in is not for you.

Change your primary mission in life to the marketing of whatever product or service you provide rather than operations.

CHAPTER 3

Develop a Sales Culture Early in Your Organization

Art is making something out of
nothing and selling it.
FRANK ZAPPA

The second most important paradigm shift most companies can make is to change their corporate culture for manufacturing, service, quality, or hospitality and get everyone from the receptionist to the truck driver involved in sales. As just mentioned, you have to market to generate leads, but then you also have to sell!

I was able to make millions in the martial arts business for one simple reason. I wasn't in the business for the love of the art. Sure, I liked it well enough. The hours were good, I didn't have to get my hands dirty, it kept me in good shape, and my customers bowed to me on the way in and out of the dojo!

But unlike 99% of the schools I competed with, who were in it because they loved martial arts, I was actually in it for the money!

Shock!!! Horror!!!

The majority of business owners end up in business because of a passion, a family connection, or by complete accident. Hardly any of these people see themselves as salespeople and so their businesses quickly hit a wall. Businesses seldom go broke because of bad service. Just think of the last time you were on the phone with your cell phone company, bank, or had a computer software problem. How good was that service? Yet they all make millions!

Businesses go broke, with few exceptions, for one reason—because they don't make enough sales.

Recently I finished a highly successful consulting visit with a leader in the equestrian industry. The company was doing over $20 million a year. But, like many companies, *sales* was almost a dirty word among the employees.

The best example I can give you is that they had over 130,000 people on their customer list but had NEVER once made an outbound call to sell anything to their own customers!

When we consult with clients, we meet with the client's staff to get them to understand that without sales, they don't have a job. Sit down with your staff and do the same.

Sales is everyone's job!

You must develop a sales culture in your organization if you're going to succeed. That culture should involve monthly, weekly, and daily sales goals. At the very least, you need a Monday morning sales meeting/training session. Doing sales training daily for 15-20 minutes will have an astonishing effect on your business—even if all you do is play some sales DVDs or audio CDs with information like what you are reading now!

DO IT WITH EVERYONE ON STAFF!

If the conversation about sales takes place only occasionally, very little will happen, so it needs to be an ongoing effort. On a daily basis, work with the people who are in constant contact with customers, no matter what their positions. Fifteen minutes at the start of EVERY day listening to sales audios or watching a sales-training DVD will pay lasting dividends. One of my clients did this just once a week, and their phone team increased sales by almost a million dollars!

By all means, preach customer service and product superiority, but don't buy too much into your own hype. Only by developing a culture based on a solid sales system can you succeed and grow in the long term, no matter what your business!

Every place where I have initiated this change in culture, two things have happened: "Dead wood" leaves the company and sales go up (and usually quite dramatically). The dead wood is usually the people who see sales as somehow distasteful, so you are better off without them!

**Develop your corporate culture early
and put a big emphasis on sales.
Getting every employee on your team involved
in sales will pay huge dividends!**

CHAPTER 4

Develop a Kaizen Culture Early

*Excellent firms don't believe in excellence—only in
constant improvement and constant change.*
TOM PETERS

Once you and your employees accept that your company should be all about sales and marketing, the final change to introduce is that of kaizen. Kaizen is the Japanese term for continuous, never-ending improvement. In today's fast-paced and ever-changing world, it's essential to your success that you and all your employees embrace this principle. Develop a company library of books, audios, and DVDs on sales, motivation, leadership, time management, and other key topics related to the success of your company. Reward employees for reading, watching, or listening on their own time.

If they don't read, they don't learn; and if they don't learn, they aren't worth hiring in the first place!

Now if you want to also develop a service culture, operational excellence, and product innovation, while being green, planet friendly, and people friendly, so be it. But make sure you have the three critical cultures in place first. You can make it without all the others, but you can't make it without the marketing and sales, or sustain it without kaizen. The others are optional.

Kaizen, of course, starts with you.

In the 1980s, it was said that if you didn't double your knowledge every seven years, you were lagging behind! Can you imagine what that number of years might be today?

At my peak, I was reading or listening to well over 100 non-fiction books a year! Now I'm down to about 50. How do you find time? Keep a book with you at all times. Read it while standing in lines, at the airport, on planes, or waiting for the kids. Turn off the radio in your car and turn your waiting time and travel time into learning time with audios!

Don't watch TV! There is an old saying that poor people have big TVs while rich people have big libraries. Commit the time to continued learning and improvement and lead your staff down the same path.

Develop a corporate culture of kaizen.

CHAPTER 5

Understand What Business You Are ACTUALLY In

It's the first company to build the mental position that has the upper hand, not the first company to make the product. IBM didn't invent the computer; Sperry Rand did. But IBM was the first to build the computer position in the prospect's mind.

AL RIES,
12 Immutable Laws of Marketing

Ask a golf professional, club manager, or golf course owner what business they are in, and 99 times out of 100, they will get it wrong!

They will say the golf business, the service business, the people business, the hospitality business, but rarely—and I ask this question to thousands of people a year—do they ever say what I consider to be the right answer.

They are, of course, in the entertainment business!

Their competition is not just other golf courses, but the NFL, soccer, baseball, basketball, NASCAR, Formula 1, movies, bowling, video games, sex, and just about anything else that can take a person's time, money, and attention somewhere other than their local golf club!

Ask a karate school owner what business he's in and only a slightly higher percentage will get it right. They will say the fitness business, the self-defense business, or the martial arts business. When I was running my schools I decided I was in the *personal development* business using karate as a vehicle to improve people's lives both mentally and physically.

Why does this matter?

Because it changes the way you market. It changes the way you present your product and run your operation, and—most important—it provides a clear competitive advantage for you in your marketplace!

Few people truly understand what business they are in. Make sure you do!

CHAPTER 6

Start with the End in Mind

Start with the end in mind.
STEPHEN R. COVEY,
The Seven Habits of Highly Effective People

Notice I didn't put this well-repeated piece of advice at the start of the book as hundreds of other authors of "success" books have done.

Why?

Because as important as it is, it's not nearly as important as the REAL-life stuff I just told you about: marketing, sales, and kaizen!

Most people would rather dazzle you with their visions than talk about boring stuff like training people how to sell, or profit and loss statements!

It *is* important to have a clear *vision* of what you want to accomplish. This should be written down and take no more than a single page. If it takes more to explain, it's most likely too complicated to succeed. That's why many of the world's best business plans were written on cocktail napkins!

The single-page vision statement should be backed up with some conservative assumptions and a pro forma to match. (A pro forma lays out the financial numbers of sales, expenses, and so on.)

Never start a business, expand, or start a new product line without a pro forma. It's astonishing how many people do!

Once you have done the math, double your expenses and triple how much time you think it will take to break even!

Now you're closer to reality!

Yes, reality often sucks, but it's still the best place to start!

Write it down; if it doesn't work on paper, it won't work in real life!

CHAPTER 7

Build Your Business on a Franchise Model Even If You Never Plan to Own More Than a Single Flea-Market Stall

Most entrepreneurs are merely technicians with an entrepreneurial seizure. Most entrepreneurs fail because you are working IN your business rather than ON your business.
MICHAEL GERBER

I read Michael Gerber's classic book, *The E-Myth*, a little too late for my first go round in the martial arts business. Actually I read it, but didn't realize at the time how brilliant a concept it was. Two years later at the insistence of a friend, I read it again. The next day—and I do mean the next day—I spent $10,000 with the company and eventually over $100,000 to learn how to systematize my business. (Read the original *E-Myth* book—it's better than the revised one.)

By this time I was trying to franchise my karate schools, but that's not the point. Gerber's point is that even if you run a flea-market stall, the business can NEVER run successfully without you unless you have *systems* other people can follow.

Yes, documenting systems is a huge time-consuming project. But just like eating an elephant, if you do it one bite at a time it will be easy. Start with whatever part of your business you know best. Simply list every single step that goes into doing a specific task critical to the success of your business. Write it down in a step-by-step manner so a 12-year-old could produce the desired result!

This won't solve all your problems, but the upside is huge. Every time you hire a new employee, you simply hand them a manual. This is how we do it at my company.

Phone calls to you on the weekend are replaced by a member of your staff actually looking up the answer in the systems manual. The customer's experience becomes more consistent because everyone on staff is working out of the same playbook. If it works for McDonald's, it can work for you!

The main theory of *The E-Myth* is simply this: To succeed, grow, and enjoy life by having your business serve you instead of you being a slave to your business, you must work *on* your business, not *in* it! In other words, spend part of your week working on all of your processes rather than simply serving customers and putting out fires! For a long time I committed half a day a week to this concept and it definitely paid off.

Spend some time each week working *on* your business, not *in* it!

CHAPTER 8

A Good System Consists of
Ten Major Elements, All of Which
Should be Present

*If you put good people in bad systems
you get bad results.*
STEPHEN COVEY

Make sure each system you develop contains the following ten elements:

1. The name and purpose of the specific system. Write a clear, concise statement of the result the system is intended to accomplish and give the system a brief, descriptive name. For example, the sales system should produce X number of prospects and sales per month.

2. A diagram of the system. The system should be presented in a diagram showing the sequence of steps and how they relate to each other.

3. Each step described in a series of clear benchmarks. Identify each action in sequence to create benchmarks that make the process clear and unmistakable to anyone who performs the work.

4. Assigned accountabilities. Accountability must be assigned for each step and for the overall system. Accountability should be identified by position, not by person. People come and go, accountability does not!

5. Time lines. Set specific time lines for when each benchmark needs to be performed. Time lines should be reviewed monthly, weekly, and, in many cases, daily.

6. Identification of resources required. Every system requires resources such as staffing, postage, supplies, and information. A detailed list of the specific resources needed to operate the system must be provided, along with quantities of each.

7. Measurement. Determine how you will quantify the system. You must set up a means of quantification so that you know you are getting the results you want from your system.

8. Established standards. A good system sets the standards for performance of the system and the behavior of the staff operating the system. Standards are most easily stated in terms of quantity, quality, and behavior. In many cases, like in sales, that's easy. In other cases that are more intangible, like how clean to keep your store, you will have to make up some subjective measure.

9. A documented system. It's not a system until it's documented. You cannot expect people to follow a system that is not documented.

10. Training in system usage. Management and staff must be trained in the proper usage of each system. Beyond systems training, more generic, ongoing professional training should also be included on topics such as goal setting, motivation, problem solving, presentation skills, and so on.

Developing and following a system takes more work in the short term. There are more steps to follow and more reporting than you are most likely used to doing now. Ultimately though, systems create less work as you become more efficient and make more money. In fact, you'll soon wonder how you ever got by without them!

See www.CunninglyClever.com for examples of complete business systems.

The sooner you start creating detailed systems for how you want your business to run, the better your business will perform and the easier it will be to grow!

CHAPTER 9

Why Ego Kills Most Companies

Don't let your ego get too close to your position,
so that if your position gets shot down,
your ego doesn't go with it.

COLIN POWELL

The number-one reason many companies fail is not what you think it is. It's not poorly thought-out campaigns, the wrong media, poor strategy, or lack of funds. It's EGO! That's right, ego. Pure and simple human ego destroys more companies, loses more battles, and kills more marketing campaigns than any other factor!

When people make business or marketing decisions that are based on ego rather than a proven plan for the orchestrated accomplishment of clear financial goals, they make poor decisions.

They make decisions based on what they like, not what works!

They make media decisions on what makes them look good to their peers, not what makes the phone ring. "Did you see our ad in such and such publication?"

They make misplaced decisions to keep poor-performing staff under the cover of "loyalty" and "caring." But really, they just want to look good.

They build corporate palaces, monster clubhouses, and ivory

towers rather than functional and creative working environments, burdening their organizations with mountains of debt they could easily have lived without!

They take the NOT-invented-here attitude to new heights and kill any program that doesn't have their own paw prints all over it!

When they do see an idea they like and can champion as "their own discovery," they bring it in as the flavor of the month citing their "open mindedness to new ideas," only to discard it six weeks later for a different flavor, instead of working the plan they have in place to its logical conclusion.

They hire people they like, people they can boss around, people who won't talk back or challenge their egos, not people who can quickly help them reach their goals.

Then they blame others for their failure, which, despite their bravado, inevitably happens when people make business and marketing decisions based on EGO rather than proven principles and the pursuit of a worthy goal.

Don't let ego ruin your business!

CHAPTER 10

Seven Resolutions for Superior Business Performance

A successful man is one who can lay a firm foundation with the bricks others have thrown at him.

DAVID BRINKLEY

Adopt these seven resolutions and watch your business grow and thrive.

Resolution Number One. Spend the first hour of each day on marketing. Send emails, write letters, make phone calls—do something that has a chance to generate business! I would credit this one factor above all others in business success. If you just get in front of the right people every day, you have a chance to make a sale! Too many business owners are so busy being busy that they never have time to market! How much time do you spend on marketing per week—*really* spend?

Resolution Number Two. Spend at least three hours a week (more would be much better) working *on* your business, NOT *in* it! That means taking the time to write procedure manuals, business plans, and the other cornerstones of duplication and long-term success. Few people enjoy this, but it is a very important factor if you are ever going to maximize the potential of your business. The more systematized your business becomes, the easier it is to run and the more time you can spend making money or playing golf instead of putting out fires.

Resolution Number Three. Outsource everything you can that is not critical to your core success. That means bookkeeping, cleaning, mailings, and so on. The more time you spend selling and marketing your business, the more money you will make. Look at Nike, a giant of a business success. They outsource everything, they make nothing. Instead, they focus on sales and marketing. There is a powerful lesson to be learned from this!

Resolution Number Four. Focus on your core business. Grow your business vertically, NOT horizontally. That means finding new products and services to offer to your *existing* market rather than trying to open up new markets. New markets are for the big boys with very deep pockets. For the small business owner or entrepreneur, the money is in your niche, whatever that niche may be!

Resolution Number Five. Try to add a residual income component to your business like service contracts or life insurance! Having your income 100% based on what you accomplish today gets old quick! How can you add something to your product or service so that customers pay you something every month? Even $5 per customer becomes your car payment pretty quickly!

Resolution Number Six. Find backup people! If you have five employees, you have five ticking time bombs! A good friend of mine recently had his friend and key employee of five years leave and start a competing business right out of the blue! Even I couldn't believe it, and it's happened to me more than once.

Always have a Plan B. It's the person who looks least likely to leave or cause problems who undoubtedly will! Don't get caught in the lurch. Make sure you can find backup people in a hurry! Your best people can fall in love, move, get arrested, and even die! Always keep resumes on file; you will sleep better at night: tick, tick, tick.

Resolution Number Seven. Set performance goals for yourself and your employees. Have something to aim at and keep it in front of you every day. This is Business 101 advice, but you'd be surprised how much more you can accomplish if you keep your goals for the year, month, week, or day right on your desk! Set up rewards for yourself and your staff for reaching goals! What gets measured gets done!

Live by these simple resolutions and you will be happier, stress free, and more profitable!

2

Avoiding the Big Mistakes

CHAPTER   11

Major Mistakes

I cannot conceive of any vital disaster happening to this vessel. Modern ship building has gone beyond that.
CAPTAIN EDWARD J. SMITH,
HMS Titanic

Like most successful entrepreneurs, I've made plenty of mistakes, some of them major, some of them minor. What many new entrepreneurs don't understand is that you learn much more from mistakes than successes. And you will make lots of mistakes. The trick is to expect mistakes and make them cheaply enough that they don't sink you. As long as you live to fight another day, you are succeeding and zoning in on where you'll make your profits.

Let's talk about the major pitfalls so that you'll be able to learn from my mistakes and avoid them. At the peak of my martial arts business, one of my clients broke away and started his own organization, one that mimicked mine but charged 60% less than what I was charging. I thought I could stand up to that since, despite his rhetoric, I knew he had no money to promote his product.

Then he made a backroom deal with the billing company that was billing my clients. Although the company vehemently denied this, every single client I had who was being billed through this company got a coupon for a free sample of my competitor's product. You don't need to be Sherlock Holmes to figure this one out!

This was not good since he got direct access to buyers with no list acquisition costs. But his masterstroke was to go to the industry's leading supply company and get them to sponsor him to the tune of $500,000! This was big. I had gone to them originally but they had turned me down, so I had made a small deal with their much smaller competitor. Once my program took off, they took notice and figured the best way in was to back a competitor.

I might have been able to handle a hit on any one of these fronts, but a cheap product, no acquisition cost to get buyers' names, and $500,000 in marketing muscle was a lot to go up against at once.

My business took a quick hit. Then a Korean company mimicked both of us and created their own offering. Other smaller groups sprang up with their own programs. A few years later the company that backed my competitor fell out with them, and started their own program. In the space of 24 months, I had gone from having little or no competition to ten businesses, including three or four major players competing with me.

I had made a critical strategic error, one I should have known from reading biographies of history's greatest generals:

NEVER underestimate the enemy. Over time, even an underfunded and undertalented adversary can erode your market share.

CHAPTER 12

Never Fall in Love with Your Product

*Experience is what you get when you
are looking for something else.*
MARK TWAIN

Mark Twain lost his entire fortune on a series of entrepreneurial ideas, most notably a typesetting machine that never actually worked. Twain, like many of us, fell in love with the idea and simply didn't know when to say stop.

I have a friend in the exotic car business whom I visit quite often. Every time I'm down at his house, he has a Ferrari, Aston Martin, Bentley, or some other beautiful car in the driveway. He lets me drive whatever he has, which for a car nut like me is heaven. Invariably I say, "Why don't you keep this one?"

His answer is always the same: "Andrew, you can't fall in love with the inventory, just move 'em down the line." And that's what he does, quickly moving cars for a $2000–$3000 profit in a day rather than holding out for the $7000–$10,000 profit they might bring later.

Too many people hold on to inventory to achieve a set price when the market wants to pay less.

Too many people fall in love with their products or ideas and refuse to compromise on price, terms, quality, or financing because of their company's value, reputation, or location.

Too many people fall in love with their products and throw good money after bad to make minor improvements in quality or functionality that the customer rarely notices or cares about.

GUILTY!

I spent three million dollars developing the **ultimate** golf website product, Marketing Commander, in a market that, to my dismay, turned out to be too unsophisticated to care. There are ten other companies in the golf website business now, all with products no better than what I had a decade ago and, do you know what? The market doesn't care. I could just as easily have tweaked my existing product for very little money and kept the three million. The market wants simple, easy, and cheap, not sophisticated reporting and powerful marketing tools.

Maybe that will change, but it will be a decade from now at best.

Never fall in love with your product, price, or idea for too long. The market will tell you what it wants.

CHAPTER 13

Don't Forget that Your Core Business Is Where the Money Is

*My success, part of it certainly, is that
I have focused in on just a few things.*
BILL GATES

Do one thing and do it well. Do it better than anyone in the area. Do it better than anyone in your county. Do it better than anyone in the state, or even the nation.

Most business owners make the mistake of being in too many different businesses at once, and for most of the 1990s I was one of them. It's amazing how easy it becomes to justify buying a $10,000 copy machine to cut down on your print-shop bills when the payments are just $89 a month. Or to expand the line of products you sell to your existing client base beyond the areas of your core business. While clients may trust you with their billing, they may not trust you with their office supplies or vice versa. Focus on being known for one concept and build your business around that core value.

When I was in my twenties, my friends and I used to frequent a certain hole-in-the-wall bar because it featured over 300 different brands of beer. It did not pretend to be a restaurant, a sports bar, or an Irish pub, just a bar that offered about every beer in the world at that time! Consequently, their overhead was low and their profits were high.

A friend of mine with a fairly large wholesale printing operation decided that he could make a killing in the copy shop business by using copy shops to feed business to his large presses. He opened three shops at once in nearby cities. The hours were brutal, the staff unreliable, and the jobs that came in were so small they were hardly worth running. Six months into the venture he sold them at a loss.

The following year, he refocused on the wholesale printing business. This was the business he knew inside out; this was the business he had made his living from for over a decade. He hired more reps, kept the presses running 24 hours, and tripled his business. By working with single-minded focus, he turned a modest enterprise into a multimillion dollar company in just over 12 months. He did this by focusing on his core strengths and expanding the one business he knew better than anything else.

When my Martial Arts America business was rolling, I decided to get into the student billing business. It seemed like a perfect product extension. I had four hundred schools under license that were using one billing company or another. To make it easy, I partnered with a small billing company looking to grow and branded it with a great name for the industry, "Black Belt Billing." While not a total failure, it never really worked. My clients liked the fact that I gave advice separate from billing. Many also had strong loyalties to other billing companies who had helped them get started. With me in the billing business, all the other companies tried harder than ever to stop their clients coming to me by copying my ideas.

While it cost me no real money, the time, effort, opportunity cost, and increased competition I created by stepping on the other companies' toes was huge.

Discover your core business, then work it for all it's worth without being distracted by every other opportunity that comes your way, even if they seem to make perfect sense. Any business can be a great business if you focus on it 100%.

It's amazingly easy to get distracted by other opportunities that are not your core business. Don't do it.

CHAPTER 14

Don't Put All Your Money in One Place

If you owe the bank $100, that's your problem. If you owe the bank $100 million, that's the bank's problem.
JEAN PAUL GETTY

One of my best friends lost $30 million to Bernie Madoff, just about every dime his family had amassed in thirty years in business. But you don't have to be a victim of the greatest fraud in history to get in deep financial trouble at the drop of a hat. It can just as easily happen at your local bank.

When I was in the martial arts business I had my personal account, my business account, a line of credit, and a credit card with Bank of America. When I moved back to Florida from California, I obviously changed all of my addresses. I was slowly winding down one business and starting a new one when, out of the blue, $30,000 vanished from my bank account, making it impossible to make payroll.

When I called the good folks at Bank of America, to my utter astonishment they told me they took it.

"You can't do that!" I stammered.

"But oh yes we can," they said. "You left the state of California and didn't tell us. Your line of credit does not allow you to move your business without telling us first, so we called it.

I pointed out that they had been sending my statements to my Florida address for almost two years but to no avail. They took the $30,000 and wouldn't give it back, even though I was paying the loan!!!

In another case, the credit card processing company I was using changed its rules overnight and demanded a $15,000 cash reserve that they could keep for up to six months. Not devastating, but painful enough at the time.

**Don't put all your money in one bank.
A bank's change of policies will screw you—
it's just a matter of time.**

CHAPTER 15

Don't Put All Your Trust in One Person

Put your trust in God, but keep your powder dry.
OLIVER CROMWELL

I had a good friend who had built a very successful carpet business from scratch. Twenty years later it was netting him over a million a year. This allowed him to open an art gallery, his true love.

Although his carpet business was a fairly large company, he had only one salesman, who was also his best friend. The trouble was, the salesman, as they often do, thought that he was not being paid enough. (He was making $250,000 in his late twenties, and this was 15 years ago.) One day he simply walked out; no comments, no arguments, no blow up, he simply left and started his own carpet business, taking half of my friend's clients with him.

It devastated my friend's business; in less than six months, he lost everything!

In the karate business, the same story was repeated weekly. The dedicated instructor who had been taught from childhood by the senior master walked out the door with half the students, leaving the senior master devastated emotionally and financially.

I can't tell you how many smart, successful people I know

who have had hundreds of thousands of dollars embezzled by their bookkeepers or managers. (All of which could have been avoided by a 15-minute weekly audit of the financials.)

People are people; they are motivated by love, hate, jealousy, pride, money, ego, revenge, and a million other petty vanities.
Never put all your trust in one person.

CHAPTER 16

Many Partnerships End Ugly

Do not trust all men, but trust men of worth; the former
course is silly, the latter a mark of prudence.
DEMOCRITUS

It's easy to take on partners or investors early in a business and give away small chunks of equity. I used to think this made perfect sense but it does not. Promise riches, promise bonuses, promise pay raises, cars, vacations, eternal gratitude, but try to keep ALL the equity to yourself.

Is this greed? No, it's simple self-preservation because when the partner, employee, or spouse goes south, the business often goes with it.

Think about your favorite rock band growing up. How many of them lasted a decade? Are they still together today? Probably not. There are invariably creative differences and the lead singer, drummer, or bass guitarist move on; often they are replaced, and rarely does it work. Instead, the "business relationship" usually ends in acrimony and legal wrangling about song rights, image rights, and who specifically owns the band name.

A little-known fact is that even a minority partner can essentially sue you for his share of the business at any time he decides to leave. The second (and last) time this happened to me, I ended up owing $300,000 to someone who went to work for a competitor.

If you do give equity, make sure you have an airtight buy-sell agreement in place for when it ends—one that is structured in a way that allows you to pay off the equity demand from a partner over time, without an instant demand for cash that can crush a business.

**Never give away equity if you can avoid it.
And always have an airtight
buy-sell agreement if you do.**

CHAPTER 17

Critical Lessons Learned Again and Again and Again... I Think I've Got It Now!

The greatest lesson in life is to know that
even fools are right sometimes.
HORACE,
ancient Roman poet

This chapter is an article I wrote a decade ago and, yes, I have learned my lesson—but at a huge cost. You can avoid these mistakes by applying the following five laws of business.

After 24 months and having spent over $250,000, my first catalog is finally printed. Now 100,000 copies sit in a Miami warehouse waiting for me to provide them with a mailing list of people I suspect will buy audios on how to improve their business or life. This will require substantial extra funds, testing, and time before I can determine which lists are good and which are not. At that point, it will be time to start the process over again and print new catalogs.

Along the way I have revisited first hand some of the universal laws of business and, although they are probably familiar to you, I think it's worth looking them over again.

1. However long you think your project will take, it will take twice as long. Having selected September of last year as my launch date for the catalog, here I am 12 months later ready to actually do it. How many times has that happened to you? Probably too many to count. We all get caught up in the excitement of a new project and somehow convince ourselves that this time it will be different. It won't.

2. However much money you think it will cost, it will cost twice as much. Originally I budgeted $100,000 for the project, which had a fudge factor of $20,000, double the 10% fudge factor that most business books suggest. The final cost was more than twice my initial estimate. Like the process of building a house, where you continuously add features as you go along, things got added that expanded the initial scope of the catalog. For example, we decided not only to produce audiotapes, but also to produce all our products on CD. This alone almost doubled our production costs and created the need for packaging in different sizes, doubling not only our packaging cost but also our printing cost since new cover artwork had to be produced to fit the different size.

3. Outside suppliers and vendors are subject to the same universal laws as you are and will constantly miss deadlines and exceed quoted prices. This third law is often overlooked because most of us like to take people at their words. Not that anyone means to screw up your schedule or your budget, it's just that stuff happens.

My recording studio had a pipe burst late one night, flooding the studio and putting it out of action for three months.

My catalog graphics person's father died, followed by his aunt. His wife lost her job and wildfires threatened to burn down his home, not once but twice. At one point, I flew him down to Florida for two weeks just to keep him out of harm's way and to try to play catch up.

The packaging company I used in Illinois was great – until the sales manager left for a better job. Then terms that had been agreed to were changed, turnaround time on my orders increased, and eventually I had to go to another supplier.

4. Simple things are never that simple. The fourth law is that things are never that simple. For example, it seemed obvious to me that once a particular audio program had been digitally mastered, it didn't matter much whether I wanted to produce audiotapes or CDs. So I ordered CDs and audiotapes, only to find that I had to spend an additional $5,000 having new masters made. CD masters are in fact different from audiotape masters. Apparently, you have to go back in and painstakingly put in all those little breaks so that you can skip to the exact spot you want to go to. Now you know.

Question everything, leave nothing to chance. Ask about the process, the design, the machinery, and anything else that could have an effect on the outcome of your project. Remember this: "There are no dumb questions, only people too dumb to ask them!"

5. Sales will be half of what you expected. The fifth law is one I am already prepared for, I hope. While the response rates in the catalog business can go as high as 3–4% for an established catalog, I am only figuring on generating a 0.5% response rate on my first attempt. Originally I had hoped to get a 1.2% response but these laws of business kept coming into my head again so while I am aiming for a 2–3% response, anything over 0.5% will be considered a success.

Due to all of the above factors, the final response was even worse than my worst estimate!

Take heed of these five laws—
they apply no matter what your business.

CHAPTER 18

Think Big—Rent Small

*First of all, I choose the great roles, and if none of these
come, I choose the mediocre ones, and if they don't
come, I choose the ones that pay the rent.*
MICHAEL CAINE

Thinking big while renting small is a rule I have always followed, thanks to a good mentor on this very important subject early in my career, but not heeding this maxim is a mistake I've seen hundreds of others make. Big buildings create big overhead, not just in rent, but also in taxes, insurance, maintenance, heating, cooling, and decorating.

For example:

- Developers build massive clubhouses before a single golf membership or lot is sold.

- Karate schools rent large warehouses when 1500 square feet produces optimum profits.

- Corporations build giant headquarters in anticipation of future growth, only to be caught out when the business or the economy falter.

Let your operation burst at the seams before you are tempted to get a bigger space and, even then, explore all options before committing.

For about 18 months in the late 1980s, my karate school

had been growing incrementally in a very steady and profitable manner. However, it got to the point where we had 250 students packed into a studio of just 1,148 square feet. That square footage included the office, the changing rooms, a bathroom, and some storage space, so the amount of space available for training was actually several hundred feet less. Over the previous few weeks we had gotten an increasing number of complaints from students and parents about overcrowding in the school. Luckily for us, the unit next door to my school, which should have been doing very well selling yogurt to my students and the students of the dance school on the other side of it, suddenly closed.

The landlord called me up and offered to lease me the additional space, which also happened to be 1,148 square feet. I was very excited and was looking forward to having the additional space, but that night I went home and started to think about the landlord's proposition in more detail. While on the one hand having the extra space would certainly come in handy, I started to think about the additional costs I would incur. For starters, my rent would essentially double. Then there was the additional expense of hiring another instructor. On top of that, there would be additional expenses of air conditioning, heating, and so forth. After some quick calculations, I realized immediately that I would need to sign up 100 more students just to pay for the additional space. Even with things going extremely well, that could easily have taken nine months, which would be nine months of less income with the eventual hope of making more in the future to cover the loss. I was in a quandary about what to do.

Having given the matter careful consideration, I suddenly came up with a plan. I decided that instead of taking the space next door and expanding my business, I would try instead to make more money from my existing situation. I then did something that few people would have the nerve to do—I doubled my prices overnight.

It should be said that I didn't double my prices on my existing clients. Instead, I offered each of them the opportunity to buy future months at their existing rate. The vast majority of my existing students took this option to buy six months to a year of lessons in advance. This provided a great deal of extra cash flow.

The very next person who walked into the school to sign up their child, having no previous knowledge of the old price, simply signed them up at the new rate with no questions asked. So did the next person and the next and the next. Within a matter of weeks I'd increased the school's income by over 50 percent a month with only a slight decrease in the number of students. Because we had slightly less students, classes were a fraction smaller. Therefore we were able to increase our service and increase our income at the same time. Now there's a thought. By the end of the year, with the natural attrition of some students and the influx of additional new ones, I had succeeded in doubling my income without doubling my space.

Never rent more space
than absolutely necessary.

CHAPTER 19

Timeless Business Advice
from Singer Kenny Rogers

To be successful, you have to have your heart in your
business, and your business in your heart.
THOMAS WATSON, SR.
founder, IBM

Although I was in the martial arts business for a decade, I physically taught martial arts for a living for only about four years. I enjoyed it for about nine months. Teaching seven-year-olds the same ten moves, three hours a day, six days a week, gets old fast.

I knew my time had come at Martial Arts America (my nationwide karate franchise) when I eventually wised up to the fact that despite a fantastic product, I could never realize my dream of 500 units operating under my banner. The churn rate was just too great. Instructors signed up and learned how to run their businesses better. Then when they thought they had all the answers, they quit and went back to being Joe's Karate. Some of them made it, most didn't.

I stayed in the business for another three years after I knew mentally that I was done, thereby wasting three years in limbo before finally pulling the plug and moving on to the next venture.

The opportunity cost of staying in a business beyond its "sell-by date" takes its toll physically, mentally, and financially.

As Kenny Rogers sang in the '80s hit song, *The Gambler*,

You have to know when to hold 'em.

Know when to fold 'em.

Know when to walk away,

Know when to run!

**When your passion is gone,
you HAVE to move ON.**

CHAPTER 20

Build Your Business to Sell It

I buy when other people are selling.
JEAN PAUL GETTY

One of the major mistakes I've made that has cost me millions is not selling a business at its peak. Or not being able to sell it at all, because the business was built around me and not around systems and staff.

There are only two things you can do with an existing business: Keep it or sell it. Let me explain this very important concept. If I walked into your business today, check in hand, how much would it take for you to sell it to me? What's the number that gets you to hand me the keys and ride into the sunset?

Okay, keep that number in mind. Knowing what you know about your business, would you be willing to walk into your business and pay me the exact same price to buy your business back?

If you said yes, then your business is most likely running well and doesn't need that much of your time and attention to make it work. Therefore you might as well keep it as your own personal cash vending machine. Unless, of course, you see forces on the horizon that could change things for the worse.

If you said no, then there is a good chance your business has problems or is consuming your life.

Too many entrepreneurs work ten or twenty years of their lives and have no business to sell at the end of the day. What they actually do is provide themselves with jobs; they do not really build businesses.

Your best strategy is to build your business in such a way that it runs without you because of the systems and people you have put in place. This provides you with a good living rather than sucking the living out of you.

Or build your business up to sell it for several times the income you currently generate as a nest egg. Then you can go do it again.

Anything else is just a job, no matter how well that job happens to pay. Plan your exit strategy early and, remember, the less your business is about personality and the more it's about good business systems, the easier it will be to sell. Or keep.

Either build your business to function without you as a cash vending machine or build it to sell for several times gross.

CHAPTER 21

The Scorpion and the Frog

The only thing to do with good advice is pass it on. It is
never any use to oneself.
OSCAR WILDE

Oh, how I wish I'd read this familiar tale earlier in my business life…

One day, a scorpion looked around at the mountain where he lived and decided that he wanted a change. So he set out on a journey through the forests and hills until he reached a river.

The river was wide and swift and the scorpion stopped to consider the situation. Suddenly, he saw a frog sitting in the rushes by the bank of the stream on the other side of the river. He decided to ask the frog for help getting across the stream.

"Hello, Mr. Frog!" called the scorpion across the water. "Would you be so kind as to give me a ride on your back across the river?"

"Well, now, Mr. Scorpion. How do I know that if I try to help you, you won't try to *kill* me?" asked the frog hesitantly.

"Because," the scorpion replied, "If I try to kill you, then I would die too for, you see, I cannot swim."

This seemed to make sense to the frog. But he asked, "What

about when I get close to you? You could still try to kill me and get back to the shore yourself!"

"This is true," agreed the scorpion, "But then I wouldn't be able to get to the other side of the river."

"Alright then...how do I know you won't just wait till we get to the other side and THEN kill me?" asked the frog.

"Ah..." crooned the scorpion, "Because you see, once you've taken me to the other side of this river, I will be so grateful for your help that it would hardly be fair to reward you with death, now would it?"

So the frog agreed to take the scorpion across the river. He swam over to the bank and settled himself near the mud to pick up his passenger. The scorpion crawled onto the frog's back, his sharp claws prickling into the frog's soft hide, and the frog slid into the river. The muddy water swirled around them, but the frog stayed near the surface so the scorpion would not drown. He kicked strongly through the first half of the stream, his flippers paddling wildly against the current.

Halfway across the river, the frog suddenly felt a sharp sting in his back and out of the corner of his eye saw the scorpion remove his stinger from his back. A deadening numbness began to creep into his limbs. "You fool!" croaked the frog, "Now we shall both die! Why on earth did you do that?"

The scorpion shrugged, and did a little jig on the drowning frog's back as he said, "I couldn't help myself, it's in my nature."

Then they both sank into the muddy waters of the swiftly flowing river and drowned.

Relationships that soured once almost NEVER get better the second time around. This goes for employees, partners, spouses, and customers.

Cunningly Clever
Ways to Hire the
BEST Employees

CHAPTER 22

Hire Slowly

The key for us, number one, has always been
hiring very smart people.
BILL GATES

In this section, you could easily get the impression I am an ungrateful ogre of a boss. I am not. I have had some brilliant employees without whose help I would not be where I am today.

I have helped many of my former employees (several of whom are now millionaires) in countless ways: from loans to buying them cars to paying emergency vet bills. I have paid many people very well, trained many in new skills, and been flexible with time off and bonuses—but that's for the good ones, the keepers. These will unfortunately be among the minority of people you hire. But if you heed my advice in the next few chapters, you can minimize your pain. You want to be careful when hiring as, make no mistake about it, the vast majority of your headaches will come from your employees' performance or lack of it, NOT YOURS.

One of the most common mistakes I see entrepreneurs make is hiring staff—before they are absolutely necessary. I know everyone keeps telling you that you need more office space, more people, or newer machines, but they lie!

- They lie because they are lazy.

- They lie because they think they are working "too hard."

- They lie because they sometimes have to stay past 5 p.m.

- They lie because they want bigger offices.

- They lie because they want newer, faster, trendier gadgets.

- They lie because their friends really need a job.

- Most important of all, they lie because they are NOT the ones paying the bills—YOU are!

It's not that they mean to mislead you; it's just human nature to want others to share in the work or to want new, bigger and better tools, offices, and equipment. Over the years at various times we have lost employees who moved, changed jobs, went back to school, or left for other reasons. In some cases more than one person left about the same time, and yet the work still got done without replacing them.

By all means start the hiring process, update resume files, and interview some people to get an idea who might be a good fit, but do not hire until you absolutely must.

Downsize quickly; upsize slowly.

CHAPTER 23

Fire Fast

*I could never have imagined that firing 67 people on
national television would actually
make me more popular!*
DONALD TRUMP

I've hired lots of people in my career that I wish I hadn't. But hiring them was never the problem — the problem was not firing them fast enough!

Your gut instinct will rarely be wrong when it tells you a person is not a good fit with your business or is simply not worth paying what you are paying them. In fact, I can't think of one case where I fired someone I shouldn't have. One of my weaknesses is not firing employees when I know it's time for them to go. I have waited weeks, sometimes months, to try to find the right time to part with the least possible acrimony. The truth of the matter is that this seemingly humane approach hurts both parties.

It hurts you by keeping incompatible or underperforming employees around who don't contribute to productivity (or worse, hinder it). Sure, these employees keep getting their checks, but it hurts them because they are working dead-end jobs with no future. It's far kinder to let them go so that they can find a compatible company and position where they can be happy and thrive. And the sooner you let them do that by cutting them loose, the better.

By all means, be generous with your compensation if you like.

Give them a month's pay instead of two weeks or keep them on part time as a consultant for enough time to get another job. BUT DO NOT PUT OFF THE INEVITABLE CONVERSATION EVEN ONE DAY LONGER THAN YOU HAVE TO.

Keeping people beyond their "sell-by date" (I am not talking age here) has cost me millions. Do not let it happen to you.

**As soon as you know,
it's time for them to go.**

CHAPTER 24

In Search of a Great Employee

You're only as good as the people you hire.
RAY KROC,
founder of McDonald's

I'm not sure if it's just me, but I just can't seem to find anyone who wants to work 70 hours a week for 40 hours pay and be on call when I need them on weekends!

I want to hire:

- someone who picks up a book or searches the Internet when they have a problem instead of bothering me by asking questions

- someone who is preemptive in solving customer problems, rather than reactive. Someone committed to quality and customer service

- someone who is still excited about growing and learning as a person.

People tell me my expectations are too high; I think theirs are too low.

I don't care if a prospective employee finished high school or college since I didn't either. I'd say that puts just about everybody in the ball game. For most positions, I don't care what experience they have had. Lots of people with twenty years' experience only experienced the same year twenty times; it's not like they kept reading, learning, and growing. Most golf club managers I meet are scared of computers. This severely limits their potential to do a great job. A simple night class at the local community college would fix the problem, as would hiring a personal computer trainer (anyone over 12) to help them out for two or three Saturday mornings. You see my point.

I'm not interested in resumes either—waste of paper. Most of them are works of fiction when it comes right down to it. "Experienced in *Photoshop*" can mean just about anything from they can do the cover of *Time* magazine on their own to they are really good at drawing stick men.

Have you ever seen resumes where the applicants say they are not great communicators but work well as members of a team? The only place my eleven employees in California acted like a team was passing the check around the table to me at our Monday-night pregame staff meeting at Daly's sports bar!

Maybe it's just me, but in the three years I worked as bag boy at a golf club when I was in my late teens and early twenties, I never ever showed up for work even a minute late or called in sick, despite making a heady $3.25 an hour. (Actually, the first nine months I worked 40–50 hours a week free in exchange for rounds of golf.) One of my current six employees is late for our staff meeting every day. The traffic on Rural Route 44 is just hell!

Maybe it's just unreasonable to expect that an employee might spend $20 of his or her own money on a book to improve skills in any given area; heck, I'd be glad to pay for it if they asked. That's all I really want in an employee: initiative and a little enthusiasm. I want someone who says I didn't know how to do this so I bought a book, enrolled in a course, or asked a friend to help because he happens to be good at this sort of problem. I want someone who looks for ways to improve the process instead of just punching in and out everyday. I want someone with the focus and commitment to stay with a job and finish it on time, even if it means taking it home with them.

In return for living up to my standards, I pay pretty well, I am flexible about vacations and time off, and we will name a fish in the koi pond after you. I mean, how many companies offer their employees perks like that?

It saves a lot of heartache to be clear and honest about what life at your company is like and what your expectations really are, even if it scares some good people away.

Employees rise to meet expectations— set yours high.

CHAPTER 25

The Perfect Ad for Finding the Perfect Employee

I hire people brighter than me and then
I get out of their way.
LEE IACOCCA,
former CEO of Chrysler

Are you running ads that target the right type of people for your company or are you just running ads for anyone who holds a specific job title? The difference can be spectacular as I will share with you from a recent personal experience.

A little over a year ago I ran an ad for an advertising copy-writer for golf courses. I got hundreds of responses, most from people who couldn't write a thank-you card. I also got a great many people who could write but could not write sales copy. That is to say, they could accurately describe what's in the picture but couldn't motivate a dog to lick a bone. They all thought they could write good copy, but I had high expectations. I play golf and at one time expected to win the Masters and I wanted a Masters-level copywriter.

So I designed a different ad, an exclusionary ad, an ad that would attract the right people and drive the rest away. Before you read it, I have to tell you that within minutes of posting the ad on Monster.com I got the following response:

Mr. Wood:

After reading your obnoxious ad, it's no wonder you can't get good people to work for a @#$^^& like you!

Followed almost immediately by:

Mr. Wood:

I don't know who wrote the copy in your ad but it's obvious you don't need a copywriter, whoever wrote it is a talented genius! I would be glad to work with such a master!

Please find my resume attached.

Interestingly enough, this ad produced ten talented applicants, nine more than my more traditional previous effort.

Here's the ad I placed:

I am looking for a Legendary, Direct Response, Golf Copywriter to Work for a Legendary Company.

I am tired of wasting my time with amateurs, so please read the following with care before sending anything.

If you do not play golf at least once a week and do not have an undying passion for the game, PLEASE DO NOT RESPOND.

If you do not have samples of direct mail sales letters that you can attach with your resume, PLEASE DO NOT RESPOND.

If you are not familiar with, and agree with the philosophy of at least one the following marketing pros (Jay Abraham, Dan Kennedy, Gary Halbert, or a similar direct-response genius), PLEASE DO NOT RESPOND.

If you are not willing to MOVE to the nicest county in all of Florida (Citrus County), PLEASE DO NOT RESPOND.

If you are not willing to do a sample project (for which we will compensate you) to DEMONSTRATE that your ability is a match for our needs, PLEASE DO NOT RESPOND.

If you are not willing to work your ass off, PLEASE DO NOT RESPOND.

If you are not FULL of piss and vinegar, PLEASE DO NOT RESPOND.

If you are still reading, I have an opportunity for you that transcends the ordinary.

We are not your typical company, we are LEGENDARY MARKETING, the world's leader in golf marketing. We are growing fast, very fast! If you're the right person, you can write your own ticket!

Current benefits include staring salary of $80K plus, with the potential for much more for the right person. We offer a flexible but challenging work environment, free golf on over 200 courses (courtesy of our wonderful partners), very low cost of living (no state taxes and you can buy a beautiful brand-new three-bedroom house with a pool on a huge lot for under $200K), and a great group of 18 dedicated, fun-loving employees.

I couldn't give a toss about your resume but send it anyway; what I want is:

1) Samples of your direct mail work. (Can you write copy that sells?)

2) Lighting-fast turn-around on a project I provide, to see if your copy can sell a dog a bone.

If I like what I see, I want you in our office within 48 hours to discuss things further, so don't bother sending anything if you are "tied up" for a while!

AND PLEASE don't tell me a good writer can write anything…they can't! Either you know how to do direct response or you don't! If you qualify, ACT NOW. It will be the BEST career move YOU EVER MAKE!

Life is short; say what you mean, mean what you say, and target those employees who are most likely to be a good fit for your company at the exclusion of all others. The more clearly you go after the people you want, the more of them you will get!

Taking the time to write great and specific ad copy for your position will attract far fewer—and far better—candidates.

CHAPTER 26

The Best Interview Question Ever for Finding Great Employees

The employer generally gets the employees he deserves.
JEAN PAUL GETTY

I love all these bestselling books by the CEOs of multimillion-dollar companies. I've read a bunch of them and when it comes to people, they all have the same advice: "Hire great people."

Okay, that's good, sage advice; let me write that down…

There's only one problem: They really don't tell you how to do it, especially if you are not paying six-figure salaries, with rock-star stock options, and cradle-to-grave health benefits.

Plus, if they make a hiring mistake, who ever hears about it? The mistake is easily lost in the thousands of people they employ. No one good or bad employee is going to make all that much difference to a Trump, Virgin, or GE organization, but to your business, it could be critical.

Here's the best question you will ever ask in an interview:

What were the last three books you read?

Or be more specific based on the job:

What was the last book you read on marketing or management?

The majority of the time that simple question will be met with an embarrassed silence. Some shuffling, some mumbling, and then perhaps the title of one or two pulp fiction books! Hardly ever will someone astonish you by reeling off a list of sales, marketing, management, and customer service titles. If they do, HIRE THEM!

If they cannot name one book, they had better have some amazingly good qualities that are relevant and obvious, like a giant database of customers from a competitor that just went under, or I wouldn't interview any further. Nor would I go any further if they read one book a decade ago.

The principle of kaizen—the continuous, never-ending search for improvement—is something you either buy into or you don't. It is not something someone is suddenly going to buy into when they get a job—it won't last more than two weeks after they're hired, at most.

I have read over 400 books on sales and marketing, but I still read three marketing books last month in the hope of gleaning just one or two good ideas. It's a principle my employees buy into—or they don't keep their jobs.

You should demand no less. People who like to learn and who look for ways to increase their knowledge on their own time MAKE BETTER EMPLOYEES. Insist that your people read (or listen to) audio books MONTHLY.

If you do this—and only this—your sales and service will improve, and I don't care how much of a veteran you are dealing with.

People who do not invest in their own skills will not invest in developing skills for you.

**If they don't read (or listen to) books,
they don't learn, and if they don't learn,
they aren't worth hiring in the first place.**

CHAPTER 27

The Ten-Dollar Interview

Great effort springs naturally from great attitude.
PAT RILEY,
NBA coach

I have found a great way of saving time with prospective employees. I quickly outline the positions we have open and hand them a copy of one of my books. If it's a sales position, I give them my *Cunningly Clever Selling*. If it's a marketing position or service position, I give them *Cunningly Clever Marketing*. I tell them to go read it and call me back when they have. It costs me about ten dollars and saves me hours of wasted time.

Rarely do they ever call back. If they can't be bothered to read a book in order to get a job, they sure won't be motivated to read after they've gotten the job.

You don't even need a book on your specific industry, just one you admire that espouses the general type of ideas, principles, and values that you do.

Another technique I use with our more technical jobs is to invite the prospective employee to go through our entire suite of online video demonstrations, which takes about two hours. More people do this than actually read but, again, few people call back. They either can't be bothered, think the job is too hard, or simply realize that they don't actually have the skills for the job.

A third and even more practical way of interviewing is to ask the prospect to do a small project: design an ad, write some copy, come up with a short sales script—whatever makes sense for the position you are offering. Many will refuse on "professional" principle, many more will never be seen again because they really can't do the job and they know it, and a few will comply.

Nothing is a better use of interview time than providing tools that allow candidates to disqualify themselves without spending your valuable time or money training them.

CHAPTER 28

Great-Employee Interview Question Number Two: Just How Much Experience Do You Have?

Boxing was the only career where I wouldn't have to start out at the bottom. I had a good resume.
SUGAR RAY LEONARD

I take a certain perverse humor in this second question because the response to it is usually so sad it's almost funny. Almost every resume you ever get touts experience, and the more senior the position, the more experience they claim to have, so here is the question I ask:

> *Do you really have 20 years experience, where every year you learned more, took on more responsibility, and grew personally—or did you more or less experience the exact same year 20 times?*

The look on their faces when they hear the second question is often priceless. There's embarrassment, stunned silence, babbling, and the sad realization for most of them that the latter is unfortunately true.

Most people confuse showing up for work for twenty years with actual marketable and useful experience, but of course it's not the same thing.

It also pays to really look at the time frame of their "real-world" experience.

For example, a real-estate marketing consultant whose claim to fame is how well they did in Hilton Head in the late 1980s (BOOM!) may well be a great find but is likely to be the top of the class in the "build it and they will come" marketing mentality.

Most people's ideas and opinions automatically default to the time period where they had their greatest success, regardless of current market conditions. This is a BIG problem in the golf business, where change comes slowly and the world ZAPS by.

Experience is great, just make sure you are hiring the right kind of experience.

CHAPTER 29

Deadly Interview Clues, Stories, and Circumstances from which You Must Run and Hide

Employees make the best dates. You don't have to pick them up and they're always tax-deductible.
ANONYMOUS

There are lots of little clues you can pick up in an interview which are clear signals to run and hide from the person in front of you as quickly as possible. For example:

- Employees who bad-mouth their former employers will bad-mouth you as well.

- Employees who complain about working conditions at their previous jobs will soon complain about yours.

- Employees who point out the rules their former companies broke will soon be turning you in for something.

- Employees looking after sick relatives are to be commended and will soon rope you into their aid one way or another.

- Employees who detail their various health problems or past battles with drugs, alcohol, the law, or family will continue to have problems.

- Employees who have had too many jobs or moved cities too often, or simply have too many stories (unless there's a valid reason like a spouse who was in the military).

These are all people to run and hide from.

A few years ago, I had a copywriter apply for a job and then vanish. A few months later he applied again, and even agreed to come down to Florida for an interview; he never came. A year or more later he applied for a job again. I should have run, I should have hidden, but his work was really good.

He came, I liked him, but I knew there was something wrong. Too many jobs, too many stories, a beat-up car, yet he needed $10,000 a month and he needed a cash advance for medical problems with his wife, mother, girlfriend—I don't remember. He was a pathological liar. For six months everything went well. Then he left abruptly, taking two of my biggest clients with him. One of whom advanced him $10,000.

The company computer, which he didn't take with him, made clear what I had suspected all along. The "something wrong" was a huge gambling problem that easily surpassed the ten grand a month I was paying him.

Recently I had a really nice guy in my office in his mid-fifties. He was smart and witty, and I liked him. He had a bunch of sales and management experience, but he admitted he was selling newspapers on the street corner to make ends meet. Jokingly, I asked him where it all went wrong.

The edited version was this: He had worked in his parents' successful insurance business and done very well in his mid to late twenties. Then he got married.

"Is that where it went wrong?" I asked.

"No," he said, "my wife worked in the business and we were

doing great. Then my parents got divorced.

"Is that where it went wrong?" I asked.

"No," he said, "they had a good working relationship for quite a while, even after my mother married my dad's brother. Then I got divorced," he said.

"So that's when it went wrong?" I asked.

"No," he said, "things really didn't fall apart until after my dad married my ex-wife..."

I didn't ask for any more details...entertaining though it was.

When interviewing, remember there is always a reason why people are where they are. And you may not want the exact same problems in your business or life.

CHAPTER 30

Eight Universal Qualities to Look for in a Great Employee

If each of us hires people who are smaller than we are,
we shall become a company of dwarfs. But if
each of us hires people who are bigger than we are,
we shall become a company of giants.
DAVID OGILVY,
advertising executive and author

Obviously the right qualities for different jobs vary tremendously, but here are eight qualities that should be regarded as universal:

1. Look for personality over formal education, but take both if you can get them. Most people coming out of college with a background in marketing know nothing. I have hired several young people right out of school and most tell me they learn more at our office in two weeks—honestly, TWO WEEKS—than they learned in college. (They have to read *Cunningly Clever Marketing* in week one.) A friendly, outgoing, enthusiastic disposition, and a desire to know more, is normally far more important than formal education. If they have both—great.

2. Look for positive attitude and positive body language. Positive thinking is so overused, it's a cliché; but its value is real so you should never discount it. The glass is either half full or half empty. Don't even bother trying to fill up the half-empty people, it doesn't work.

Body language is something that's not often considered, but is important. It not only affects your customers, it affects your other employees. I have heard that Ritz-Carlton won't hire people who can't make positive eye contact in an interview. If you can't sit straight, stand straight, and walk around with a smile, it's a problem that grows like cancer.

If they have both a positive attitude and personality, you won't have to worry about them being a "team player."

3. Look for people who are REALLY open to personal growth and learning new skills. Few people are interested in acquiring new skills. At least a dozen of our current clients have marketing people in place who are running on three cylinders and should be fired. Why? Because they are either "too smart" or "too busy" to actually improve their basic marketing skills. All have delayed our continuous offers of FREE training on how to get the most benefit from our website product. This would take about an hour and would instantly improve their communications, save them time, and make their companies more money.

I frequently interview people who profess their love of learning, but leave clues about their REAL attitude towards self-improvement by saying things like "I didn't take that course or buy that book because the company wouldn't pay for it." Anyone who would leave their personal and business development and long-term success to the whims of their boss is a moron.

4. Look for organized people. Look for people with excellent organizational and time management skills. Disorganized people simply cost you too much time and money. Look at their cars; if they're a mess, that's their general method of operation.

The number of people who show up to an interview having not read our corporate website in detail is astonishing and, once again, shows a lack of basic organization. The information is there for the taking; if they don't take it now when they are looking for a job, they won't bother later either.

5. Look for the right age group that fits your product or service. Obviously the ideal age for employees will depend on your business to a large degree (for example, 21 or older if you sell alcohol and perhaps over 55 if selling senior living). All things being equal, throughout my business career I have found the most productive employees are usually people in their late twenties to early thirties. By 28 or so most people are partied out and look-ing for a career, and people of this age are far more likely to take direction than older employees.

There are, of course, a ton of great people in their 40s, 50s, 60s, and beyond but...they have kids, spouses, pets, aging parents, prejudices, and physical ailments that 28–35 year olds simply don't have. They are also seldom willing to work all the hours God gave—including weekends and holidays—to get a start-up going.

6. Look for speed and a bias for ACTION rather than procrastination. In today's world, where everything changes fast, speed is of the utmost importance. It's not just speed you are after, but a predisposition towards action rather than inaction. You want people who will get things done and not agonize over each little decision.

7. Look for contributors, not takers. Regardless of the position, you want an employee who is willing to contribute ideas and answers for improvement, rather than just blindly follow the status quo. Ask questions about what they would do differently if they got the job. Employees who contribute to the process and actively participate in general office life are far more valuable than those who don't—and most don't.

8. Look for dependability—there is no substitute Last, and by no means least, great employees are always dependable. This means they are punctual. In the five years or so I worked at a menial job while in my early twenties, I never showed up late. I guess I just expect the same. Punctuality is nothing more than a form of courtesy and self-discipline, and you don't need people who don't have either of these traits.

Good employees have a strong commitment to finishing the job. The real world is not 9–5 and it never has been. If they are not willing to stay an extra 15 minutes to get a project completed on schedule or help a customer with a problem, they should be working for a big corporation, not you. Dependable people do the job they are supposed to do every time, and no one has to worry that they won't deliver the goods.

It will help your hiring process immensely if you list the qualities you are looking for in a new employee and stick to them when hiring.

CHAPTER 31

Use Position Agreements Rather than Job Descriptions to Get Superior Employee Performance

An ounce of performance is worth pounds of promises.
MAE WEST

Now comes perhaps the most important part of the hiring process—writing a position agreement for the new employee. The longer I am in business, the longer and tougher my position agreements get, as I find new issues that need clarifying. Issues range from the number of personal cell phone calls that come into my office, to the amount of time people spend instant messaging friends on their computers. I used to be a "get it done and I don't care how" kind of guy. In fact, I still am. But it's just no longer enough. If you don't spell out very specific standards at every level, you just don't get the performance you need or expect.

A position agreement is not a job description. Rather, it is a detailed document that quantifies performance at every level of an employee's job. This may seem like mere semantics, but it is not. The critical difference between a job description and a position agreement is that in a position agreement, the employee signs a RESULTS statement.

The quantification of these results has both hard measures and soft measures.

A hard measure is one where the required behavior can be quantified. A hard measure might include a line that tells salespeople the minimum number of sales, in dollars they should make in a month. But that's not where it ends. It might also state how many calls they must make in a day. Furthermore, it might specify the number of conversations that should be initiated to be deemed as living up to their position contract. It might even spell out how many new prospects are added to the database daily.

All position agreements should include daily and weekly reporting so that each of these measures is checked. Make no mistake about it, when the number of calls or conversations drop, there will be a corresponding drop in sales.

Simple questions should be answered, like how quickly should phone calls from clients be returned.

Why wait until the end of the month and there is no money in the till to discover that calls are not being made? A simple daily or weekly check will expose a problem long before the end of the month. This is true at almost every level of every company, not just in sales.

Soft measures require more of a subjective evaluation. A soft measure would be asking employees to deal with prospective clients in a courteous and professional manner, to display a positive attitude, and so on.

General expectations should also be covered, like acceptable clothing, showing up for work on time, and limiting personal phone calls on company time.

The more of your specific expectations you detail in the position agreement, the more likely you are to get the performance you want, and the more likely you are to avoid misunderstandings. Should it be necessary to terminate the employee, position agreements make it easier. If the agreement is well written and adequately discussed with an employee early in the process, simply showing the document to an underperforming employee is likely to bring an improvement in performance or they will quit.

Position agreements work both ways. The employee should be asked for input on what they expect from the company. This might include clean working conditions, fair treatment, and the chance of advancement based on performance. In might include specific holidays, flexibility on personal days, and the company's policy on continuing education.

The results of failure to live up to the terms of the position agreement should also be spelled out. And, last but not least, the position agreement should be *signed*.

Position agreements take a good deal of time to write, but the heartache they can save makes them more than worth the effort. In fact, I recently revised a position agreement for my new sales manager and it ended up being eight pages long.

Focusing on specific action steps and results rather than vague job descriptions produces significantly superior results. But a word of warning: If you are going to hold people accountable to a position agreement, you must provide them with the tools and the time to carry out their missions. You can't get someone to sign this agreement and then make them spend half a day stuffing billing statements because someone in accounting is sick.

Position agreements make hiring, firing, performance, and accountability simple.

Sample Position Agreement

Position Title: Membership Director

Manager's Position: CLUB MANAGER

Result Statement: I am accountable for producing the following results:

1. Growing membership at (Lonely Pine) Golf Club by:

    a. 20 Full memberships

    b. 15 Social memberships

    c. 10 Corporate memberships

2. I am also responsible for a new member satisfaction rating of 8 or better, measured by the new member satisfaction surveys.

Work Listing

Entrepreneurial Work

Makes recommendations to the General Manager for improving membership initiatives.

Managerial Work

1. Ensures all member contact is handled quickly and sincerely.

2. Oversees the meticulous recording of projects and tasks in the CRM.

3. Reports results on schedule.

Technical Work

1. Makes daily calls.

2. Handles information calls and scheduling.

3. Maintains personal event planner.

4. Attends staff training.

Position-Specific Standards

1. Delivers and promotes prompt, courteous, and friendly service to all members, guests, and employees.

2. Motivates, directs, and manages staff and outside vendors in matters of membership marketing on a daily basis.

3. Coordinates and promotes membership campaigns.

4. Prepares annual and monthly budgets for membership marketing.

5. Understands and keeps abreast of membership financial record keeping. Takes daily corrective action as required.

6. Maintains website regarding membership calendar.

7. Supplies timely and pertinent membership information to web provider.

8. Follows up on all inquiries within 48 hours.

9. Documents ALL LEADS and CONTACTS in the CRM and updates them after every action.

10. Fulfills all enrollment obligations of the club for a new member (orientation session, new member follow-up, accurate enrollment paperwork, etc.)

11. Asks each new member for a minimum of three referrals.

12. Contacts three new people per day with influence in the community such as Realtors.

13. Attends community events and Chamber meetings to meet and greet.

14. Schedules and conducts membership tours.

15. Provides manager with weekly, monthly, and quarterly membership marketing reports including leads generated, tours given, memberships sold, referrals provided, etc.

16. ASKS EVERY MEMBERSHIP PROSPECT TO JOIN.

17. Reads all pertinent publications and trade journals monthly.

18. Reads at least one sales or marketing book per quarter from the list of approved titles.

19. Pursues the enhancement of YOUR personal skills including time management, goal setting, communications, and any other skills pertinent to the position through an aggressive personal development program including, but not limited to, books, CDs, videos, seminars, webinars, and manuals. Provides details to manager monthly.

The statements contained herein describe the scope of the responsibility and essential functions of this position, but should not be considered to be an all-inclusive listing of work requirements. Individuals may perform other duties as assigned, including work in other areas to cover absences or relief to equalize peak work periods, or otherwise balance work overload.

General Standards

1. Performs all work according to company policies and

standards, as well as in the spirit of the company's strategic objective.

2. Treats all guests and employees with respect and consideration.

3. Holds in strict confidentiality, all proprietary information, both of the company and its guests.

Compensation

$_____ per year

Commission Schedule on file for monthly, quarterly, and yearly commissions amounts.

Discretionary (10%) Performance Review Bonus.

Failure to meet these standards will affect planned compensation and may lead to possible termination.

Signature Page

STATEMENT OF THE POSITION HOLDER: I accept the accountabilities of this position and agree to produce the results, perform the work, and meet the standards set forth in this position contract.

Signature _____ Date _____

Name (print) _____

STATEMENT OF THE POSITION HOLDER'S MANAGER: I agree to provide a working environment, necessary resources, and appropriate training to enable the accountabilities of this position (results, work standards) to be accomplished.

Signature _____ Date _____

Name (print) _____

CHAPTER 32

Offer Average Pay and GENEROUS Bonuses

If you pick the right people and give them the opportunity to spread their wings and put compensation as a carrier behind it, you almost don't have to manage them.
JACK WELCH

For a long time, like many businesses, I overpaid most of my employees. Few owners get anything but astonishingly average performance from their staffs because they do not have clear performance goals and only a tiered bonus plan attached to their successful accomplishment.

The most effective compensation plans offer average pay with generous bonuses for surpassing goals and may contain a number of other intangible factors. Defining performance is easy with sales positions but gets harder to define as you go to other positions. (More on this later.)

Money

There should be no limit as to how much you pay any of your key employees *if they perform*. Employees in performance-based positions (especially sales) WANT an incentive plan rather than a salary. They want to be in command of their "unlimited" earning potential. Bonuses should be tied to a tangible schedule of results and increase in tiers as specific marks are passed.

Gifts

Reward employees with bonus gifts and trips. Trips are especially good as they insure the employee gets a real break and something positive to remember, rather than just using bonus money to pay off bills. Reward them with cars, but make them sign the paperwork (you make the payments) so if they leave, the golden handcuffs are on them not you.

Time

Not everyone is motivated by money; a large portion of your employees will be motivated by flexibility. Flexible schedules allow them time to pursue their hobbies or family commitments. For this reason, I have always been flexible with days off and work hours. Many people will work for less IF they have the flexibility they desire.

Fun

It goes without saying that the more pleasing the physical work environment the better. It also goes without saying that the more fun the environment the better. Both these factor are definitely high on the intangible-compensation-factors list.

Personal and Professional Growth

One of the very best things I can tell prospective employees about working at Legendary Marketing is they will leave at least twice as smart as they came in. This is a tremendous asset that few companies can boast—offering rapid personal and professional growth. This is especially desired by younger workers (Generation Y).

Offer average pay and generous bonuses, augmented with flexibility and fun to attract and retain great employees.

CHAPTER 33

Ninety-Five Percent of Your Employees Will Steal from You Even if It's ONLY Your Time

Half the lies they tell about me aren't true.
YOGI BERRA

Let's look at just a few statistics on what the FBI reports is the fastest growing crime in the US—employee theft:

- The US Chamber of Commerce reports that $50 billion dollars are lost annually due to employee theft and fraud and that 20% of all businesses fail due to the same reason.

- According to an Ernst & Young's report, *White Collar Crime: Loss Prevention through Internal Control*, companies lose 1% to 2% of sales to crime—most committed by, or in collusion with, employees.

Believe it or not, I take most people at face value, despite a lifetime of disappointment to the contrary, especially when it comes to employees.

"I have to do what's right for my family," seems to be a catchall phrase (I have heard once too often) to disguise cheating, lying, and outright theft. Many of my friends and clients have experienced direct financial embezzlement, some major, some minor, all at the hands of trusted employees, or in some cases other family members.

I have lots of personal examples, but the all-time classic was my original karate instructor Ron. For several years he did a great job for me; he was well paid and there was mutual respect. When he got married, he started selling insurance instead of teaching. I wished him well.

Years later I hired him again to work in my franchise. A short time later I also hired his wife. They were both paid excellent wages, but several years later when I decided to move the company to Florida they both declined to move. I changed Ron's job so he could run one of my karate schools and stay in California. I even continued to pay him the same salary as before, although his new job should have paid far less.

I trusted him implicitly, so rarely checked on him. For about six months I could never seem to get hold of him, and the other instructor with whom he worked was evasive about his whereabouts. So one Sunday night, I flew back to California unannounced to check for myself. I sat in his office for a week before he eventually showed up on Saturday morning to "check" on the school.

I confronted him and he said he had taken another job because, "He had to look out for his family and he wasn't sure if I was going to keep the school." So in the meantime he cashed a check from me for $4,000 a month as well as a check from his new employer. I asked him if he thought this was stealing and he said no. I bet to this day he actually believes he wasn't stealing, but he took almost $30,000 from me while showing up for work 8 hours a month on a Saturday when he was being paid for a full-time position.

Last year, one of my long-term and key employees quit. She had been a great employee for over five years. I also employed her husband, and between them they took home a mid-six-figure wage. Her husband took a job with one of my clients, which I didn't mind because his performance was marginal. But then they dropped the bombshell that they were moving to another city, and gave me less than a week's notice while I was on my annual vacation in Europe; For continuity's sake, I let her work remotely and continued to pay her for six weeks until I got back and then at a far reduced rate for six months after that. Then she quit and went to work for my client, something that was expressly forbidden in her contract. Her response was, "You always said non-competes were not worth the paper they were printed on and I have to look out for my family." There it was again, justification for actions that were obviously not right.

I should have handled it better and not pushed the issue, but at the time I was angry about her up and moving in the middle of my vacation. Had she even stuck around till I got back, I might have handled it differently and not completely destroyed the relationship, but I'm not the one who left.

You don't have to get into outright financial theft to lose thousands of dollars HARMLESSLY. Loss of time is loss of money. I had some young employees who, even after repeated warnings, spent two hours a day or more playing video games instead of working. Updating personal Facebook pages, non-business Tweeting, and any gaming or personal surfing during working hours is theft. Time theft IS financial theft.

Eventually some employees will screw you, or at the very best leave bitter and ungrateful for the years of risk you took to build a company and provide them with a job. (I'm not usually bitter because I look forward, not backward.)

It's important that employees know your expectations for taking personal calls, sending and reading personal emails, and so forth (these limits will be in the position agreements), not only because it impacts your bottom line, but also because employees who play around at work decrease morale for the rest of the staff. Some of the other employees will start wasting time themselves thinking that you must not care. Honest employees have to pick up the slack for these time wasters. They become resentful of their coworkers, and their respect for you as boss declines.

Don't think it won't happen to you. Monitor all your people very carefully; the ones who are working actually appreciate it.

Choosing the Perfect Location for Your Business

CHAPTER 34

Do You Need to Rent at All?

There are times when a battle decides everything, and there are times when the most insignificant thing can decide the outcome of a battle.
NAPOLEON BONAPARTE

I said in an earlier chapter that I've never made the mistake of renting more space than I needed and that's true—but I did make the mistake of renting *at all*. When my martial arts consulting business took off in the mid 1990s I had four people working in the room above my garage. We suddenly went from making $30,000 a month to over $120,000. Drunk with our own success, I decided to rent a new 1800-square-foot office building.

This was stupid, since clients never visited us.

It cost us $20,000 to set up the office and $24,000 a year plus utilities for the next four years. A complete waste of over $100,000 in cold hard cash out of my pocket! Plus the growth I could have had on that money during the exciting run-up to the dot-com bust. Easily another $100,000, for a total opportunity cost of $200,000.

I should have stayed in the garage and had it air-conditioned. I'd have just about paid off my home with the money I wasted on rent!

But I learned from my mistakes. I started my golf marketing business a decade ago. I waited until I had four full-time employees and was doing over $500,000 a year before finally getting office space.

Five years ago I bought and renovated a nice building. Now there is nothing I'd like to do more than sell it, take the profit, and go virtual.

Don't let others—or ego—talk you into renting space you don't need. Go virtual whenever you can.

CHAPTER 35

Buying Your Building

*In a real estate man's eye, the most expensive part of
the city is always where he has a property to sell.*
WILL ROGERS

Sometimes buying office space makes more sense than renting. The way my company works, I'm able to consider a virtual off, but a lot of businesses need a space for customers to visit, or for manufacturing or storage. Buying a building *can* be an investment that grows in value, but it still needs careful consideration. I have often had clients tell me they are building more space than they need so that they can rent it out to others and essentially get their space free. Sounds great in principle and it can work, BUT...

It can also be a nightmare of empty units, broken leases, and terrible tenants.

Do YOU really want to be in the commercial real estate business? Because that's the business you are in when you own a building, even if you are the only tenant.

- Is there an excellent chance the value of the property will grow substantially?

- Are you located in a high-growth area where there is likely to be a buyer when you want to sell it?

If you can answer yes to both of the above questions, then

buying a building is probably a good idea.

If you do buy, seriously consider renovating the building (another HUGE hassle). With the right fix-ups, you can increase the value of your building to gain instant equity.

If at all possible, buy a property where adding space is an option so you can expand later as needed rather than overbuilding now in anticipation of future needs.

If you fancy trying your hand at the commercial real estate business, fine. But if not…use your home, patio, garage, trailer, handcart, table, tent, or the smallest possible space you can get away with before you even think about buying or building office space.

Buy smart; build small; expand only as needed.

CHAPTER 36

Finding the Perfect Location for Your Business

The three most important things about real estate are location, location, location.

VIRTUALLY EVERY REAL ESTATE AGENT ON EARTH

The oldest adage in real estate is that the three most important things are location, location, location. While the advance of computers and communications has given us a whole new segment of work-anywhere type businesses, for the majority of small business owners the same old adage holds true. The selection of the correct *location* is critical to all retail business success. It doesn't matter what you are selling. The more people who physically see your store or office, the more business you will generate.

I have owned small businesses where the walk-in traffic was zero and others where 50 people a day came through the doors. The difference in rent was staggering but so too was the amount of money that had to be spent on marketing to get traffic to visit the poorer location.

The importance of a great location cannot be overstressed; it will make you or break you. High-profile fast-food chains dealing in high-volume sales, such as McDonald's, Taco Bell, and Burger King, spend tens of thousands of dollars to research and choose high-visibility locations with the maximum level of foot and road traffic. Pizza Hut won't put a store on 4th and Main until they know "X" amount of people will pass by their doors each and every day.

When is the last time you saw a local premier fast-food franchise like Taco Bell or KFC bite the dust? It does happen, but rarely. The fast-food "kings" know that 15,000 cars drive by 4th and Main daily. Experience, plus careful research, has taught them that a minimum of 200 vehicles will drive past the drive-through window between 4 and 8 p.m. and their occupants will purchase a specific, average dollar amount of food and drink.

People volume is a life-and-death affair to a fast-food franchise. Can you estimate just how much the average franchise must sell to realize $1 in profit? In some cases it is as much as $20.00! What does this mean to a business located near a successful fast-food operation? Success by association—at least in traffic volume.

The more people who pass your business and notice it from the road or sidewalk, the less money you will need to spend on advertising or marketing. Over the years, this could add up to an extremely large sum of money.

Look for a retail location within direct view of a fast-food chain. It guarantees traffic volume.

CHAPTER 37

Will the Population Base Support Your Business?

*It's human nature to keep doing something as long as
it's pleasurable and you can succeed at it—
which is why the world population continues
to double every 40 years.*
PETER LYNCH

If your business is one where clients or customers come to your place of business, you need to make sure there's a large enough population base to support it. If you are located in a major metropolitan area, do some research to discover how many people live within a three-to-five mile radius of your operation or intended operation. (Your local library is a good place to start.) A population base of 20,000–30,000 people will provide a strong marketing base for most businesses.

In lightly populated rural areas, people are not averse to driving long distances. They do it every day to get to the store or to work or to school. In such an area, it's possible to stretch the population base to a 15–20 mile radius from your location to achieve the necessary number of people to sustain a profitable business.

If yours is the only business of your type in your chosen area, you have the potential to capture a 100% share of your available population base. For instance, if you were to open a golf instruction business in a town of 30,000 people, you would have close to 3,000 potential students since about 10% of the US population plays golf. If you were to open a martial arts school, you would only have 300 potential students since about 1% of the population is interested in martial arts. If you were to open a restaurant, your potential market share might be 2,400 diners.

What percentage of the population in your area has a need for, or interest in, your product or service?

How far will they be willing to drive to get it?

How much competition is after the same market?

Are there enough people within your area to provide you with a steady client base?

If your customers come to your site to purchase products or services, you must make these calculations to make sure your business will succeed at any given location.

To make a living, you need to have enough potential customers who will come to your business. Do the math for your business.

CHAPTER 38

Is There Enough Business to Go Around?

And while the law of competition may be sometimes hard for the individual, it is best for the race, because it ensures the survival of the fittest in every department.
ANDREW CARNEGIE

Once you have decided that there are enough people to support your business, you must then look at what competition already exists that might dilute your market.

Let's use a golf instructor as an example. What if you're planning to start a golf instruction business and there are already other golf instructors in your area? If so, you must share the pool of potential students with your competitors. If there are three competing instructors in your area, you have a problem. Unless your competitors are totally inept, your business, fourth in line for the pool of golfers, will have a tough time breaking even.

You may think there's still room for you to prosper, and for all four instructors to average enough students to make a good living. However, this is very unlikely. There's one elusive element that upsets the entire equation: the *establishment factor.* Your top two competitors may have been in business for more than five years, and may have established deep roots in the community.

Consider the following scenario. You have carefully researched the area. Of your three competitors:

Instructor #1 has an excellent location, good name recognition, and is very busy. He drives a new Corvette and just bought a big house on the fashionable side of town. He takes out full-page ads in the local newspaper every week and throws a major charity tournament and clambake every year (from which he receives tons of free press and TV/radio coverage). He appears to be smiling every time you see him.

Instructor #2 is making a fair living, but nothing to rave about; he's a die-hard who will grin and bear the financial ups and downs and never release his grip on his business or his students. His wife makes a decent salary as a local government officer; they live a simple, comfortable life.

Where does this leave Instructor #3? It leaves him, unfortunately, in pretty bad shape. #1 and #2 control the territory, leaving Instructor #3 with the scraps. He is open long hours and is frequently idle...not from choice. He seldom smiles! It goes without saying that his business won't survive and he'll eventually have to close down or move into his backyard. Unless the two top instructors start doing something incredibly wrong, your chances of running a successful operation in your selected target area are slim to none.

Numbers can be misleading. Sometimes you have to probe a little deeper to get the true picture. For instance, if you research your market and find that you share the territory with three competing instructors in a population base of 30,000, should you look for another area? Is there a reason to be discouraged?

Not necessarily. Let's say:

#1 is a no-nonsense, tough-as-nails instructor who enjoys teaching only pros and low-handicap players and doesn't give group lessons.

#2 is located on the local Air Force Base at a 'Military Personnel Only' club.

#3 is a retired deputy sheriff operating at a rundown range who made a lifelong career out of issuing parking tickets to everyone within a 60-mile radius!

To your amazement you discover that their combined active student base doesn't exceed 180 students a year. There is room for you to do business. The three instructors do not appeal to the general population base. It is possible for you to capture enough of the total target market to become the leading golf instructor in the area and a solid business success.

The key is to really do your homework. A few extra hours or days now can be critical effect to your future success.

Probe to find out as much as you can about your existing competition before deciding on a specific location.

CHAPTER 39

When Good Locations Go Bad

He who rejects change is the architect of decay.
The only human institution which rejects progress
is the cemetery.
HAROLD WILSON,
former British prime minister

You may already be in town when suddenly two other competitors show up. If you have established your reputation in the community, new competition may have little effect. On the other hand, it may be a warning signal that it's time to move on. Sometimes a seemingly perfect location can be rendered bad by competitors moving into your market and shrinking your potential.

For example, in my second and most successful martial arts school, I was the only martial arts business in an affluent town of 60,000 people. There were thousands of families the perfect age and the *Karate Kid* movie part two had just come out. Not only that, but the school was also located next to Irvine Dance Academy. This business would not have been considered an anchor except that it had been there for 15 years and had an active enrollment of over 1200 little girls. While the little girls were dancing, their little brothers were looking through the window of my karate school. I'd invite them in to kick and punch a bag. More often than not, as soon as their mothers came looking for them, they'd sign up their sons. On the strength of location alone, a monkey could have done well financially.

Three years later, the situation had changed. The city had grown, several new shopping centers had been built, and the city boasted no less than 23 other martial arts schools. We were still doing well but the glory days of easy income without competition were gone forever. So when someone walked in out of the blue and offered to buy the business for a fair price I sold the same week. I moved to a fast-growing town twenty miles south and started over again.

Locations and shopping centers can also go downhill when the anchor tenant moves out, when gangs start hanging out in the parking lot, or when a new Walmart center opens across town. When you see the writing on the wall, start looking for a new location fast.

Don't be oblivious to competition or changing conditions in your area.
Good locations can and do go bad.

CHAPTER 40

Consider the Basic Age Group and Socioeconomic Factors of the Area

I'd like to live as a poor man with lots of money.

PABLO PICASSO

Just because an area has a lot of people does not mean that it's a great area to do business. Big City, Michigan, has lots of people, but if you select a location on the wrong side of the tracks where unemployment is high and people can't pay their heating bills, your business will fail.

Such pitfalls are not entirely economic. You may open up in a ritzy quarter of Largetown, Nevada, and fail because the local population base with plenty of disposable income spends it all at the slot machines!

Beverly Hills has plenty of people and plenty of money, but it also has plenty of choices on how to spend that money.

Rancho Mirage, California, has one of the highest incomes in the world and yet it is also full of old people, and therefore not a great place to locate a fun zone, dance school, gymnastics center, or any other kids-based business. A jewelry store would do well there and fail miserably in East LA.

The key is to look beyond the basic numbers and break the data on age, income, profession, and other factors down to a level where you can use it to make an informed decision for your particular business. You must match the age and demographics of your customers with the number of people in that range—not the total number of people in the area.

It's not just about population; it has to be the right *type* of population for your business.

CHAPTER 41

Does Your Market Have the Necessary Median Income AND Discretionary Income?

When we got into office, the thing that surprised me
most was to find that things were just as bad as we'd
been saying they were.

JOHN F. KENNEDY

The population base and sociodemographic makeup is not the only statistic to consider. What is the median income of those living in your market area? (Median income is different from average income. It is the number that half the people fall above and below.)

For instance, if you had the choice of locating your golf business in the South Bronx (median income $20,000 a year) or White Plains (median income $100,000 a year), which would you choose?

Obviously upscale White Plains would be a wiser choice, not only in light of the heavily urban nature of the South Bronx, but because the population base of White Plains contains more people who can afford, and are likely to be interested in, golf lessons.

Discretionary income is of prime importance to most business owners. It's the amount of money remaining after expenses. If the discretionary income figure is very low in your area, you will be forced to sell a higher volume of product than in a more affluent area where you could charge more.

How do you determine the median income of a location? How do you discover the general age, sex, occupation, and income characteristics of your targeted population base? Current figures can be obtained from the Census Bureau and local municipal agencies. Discretionary income can be determined with the EBI (Effective Buying Income), a retail trade survey of buying power compiled by the US Census every five years. It includes information on areas of population with lots of discretionary income. The EBI is conveniently arranged by zip code so you can ascertain the ability of a given location to support your business.

If discretionary income is too low, there is a distinct possibility you might be well advised to pick up stakes and find a wealthier zip code. It may be no more than a few miles away. But don't overlook other demographic information. Palm Beach, Florida has a very high median income, but it's a lousy place to put a day care center for kids since the average age is 70 years.

Go to your library and study the data. A librarian will be happy to supply you with all the information sources you need. You will also find that most Realtors have this data along with other useful information like daily car counts.

Make sure your prospective customers can afford your products and services.

CHAPTER 42

Consider the Direction of Your Town's Future Growth

If you think the United States has stood still, who built
the largest shopping center in the world?
RICHARD M. NIXON

Consider the growth in your area. Most areas grow in one direction, while the opposite part of town tends to decline in value and in desirability. Some areas of the United States, such as Las Vegas, Nevada, Orange County, California, and Orlando experienced rapid growth before the crash. Other areas like Detroit have experienced a steady decline. The area where I lived in California grew from 300 to 65,000 in less than ten years. This type of growth provides a tremendous opportunity for an entrepreneur to go in early and establish his business as the one of choice. The first owner to be up and operating wins a grand prize: the opportunity to sign up hundreds of clients first. The down side is you can arrive ahead of the curve and many businesses don't survive until the critical mass of people arrives to push them over the edge of success.

Try to establish what the future growth patterns will be in your area. Talk with someone in the real estate business who is knowledgeable about future development plans so you can be sure to locate in an area of town that people are moving to rather than leaving. It's also a good idea to talk with city officials to see if there are any major works planned. I once rented a nice space on

Main Street only to have the entire road dug up for a new sewer line, basically putting me out of business for an entire year.

Try to locate where the growth will be.

CHAPTER 43

Parking and Traffic Flow

*In some neighborhoods, looking for a parking space is
not unlike panning for gold.*
GARY WASHBURN
sports writer

It is a remarkable—and sad—fact of modern life that people will fight, sometimes literally, to park near the place they wish to visit. Even the athlete going to the fitness center for a strenuous workout will park as near to the entrance as he can get, even circling for a while if he notices someone about to vacate a prime space.

Remember driving into a crowded movie theater parking lot on a Friday night and happening upon an empty parking space close to the box office? Did you experience a sense of joy, elation, and even victory? Did you feel special? Do not make the mistake of minimizing the importance of parking in selecting a business location. The public at large is very sensitive to this problem. They have to deal with it every day, almost everywhere they go.

In certain metropolitan centers like New York City, some businesses have limited options, and are forced to set up business in out-of-the-way locations due to ridiculously high rents in the more attractive areas. Big-city dwellers usually don't find this a major problem. They understand the business owner's dilemma because they are in the same boat. However, the drawbacks are still considerable. Unaccompanied women and parents of youngsters will be reluctant to use public transportation or to do business at a facility located in less-than-ideal surroundings.

Does the location have access from both sides of the street?

This can be a very important issue especially if it's a divided highway or a difficult place to make a U-turn. Access from only one side can cut your traffic count in half. Also, be aware of whether drivers are coming or going as they pass a specific location. If your business is located on the outbound side in the morning, it's not nearly as valuable a location as the other side of the street on the homebound journey—unless of course you sell coffee and donuts. Most people stop and buy things after work, not on their way to work.

All the visibility in the world may not help you without parking availability and easy street access.

CHAPTER 44

Consider Local Media Boundaries before Choosing Your Location

Advertising says to people, "Here's what we've got.
Here's what it will do for you. Here's how to get it."
LEO BURNETT,
founder, major ad agency

This may sound like an odd thing to consider when looking for a new location but it can mean a huge difference in your advertising costs, especially in large cities where several boundaries exist. I had a friend who opened a restaurant in Anaheim, California. He was on the corner of two major streets and to all intents and purposes it seemed like a great location. It was only when he started to look into local advertising that the gravity of his mistake hit home.

The Pennysaver, a local advertising publication and traditionally a great way to get business, had four zones—all of which divided at that crossroads. To Frank, that meant spending four times as much money just to get his message to the other sides of the street!

In another case, I had a client dependent to a large degree on *Yellow Pages* calls who located his business in such a way that his $600 *Yellow Pages* ad did not reach the homes directly across the street from his business. The only solution was to run ads in two books. Check with your local media reps where the dividing zones are for all major publications and media you might use. A little time now could pay off big for you later.

If you rely on local advertising, paying attention to media boundaries can save you a fortune when choosing a location.

CHAPTER 45

Look for a Center with a Major Anchor

As a rule, he or she who has the most information will have the greatest success in life.
BENJAMIN DISRAELI

A major anchor is a blessing for most small business owners. Anchors are stores that draw people to a particular shopping center. Any retail business that puts itself in close proximity to an anchor has a real plus. Anchors include popular convenience stores, supermarkets, or drug stores, such as Albertsons, Tesco, Winn-Dixie, Safeway, Costco, or Walmart.

Food market locations are safe bets; everybody has to shop for food. For the majority, a regular stop at the market is routine. The same people who buy food will see you. There will be a constant flow of people walking past your window. This visibility will bring you a substantial amount of new business.

Also good are national chains, fast-food places, and coffee shops. Large banks can attract good traffic, as do general retailers like K-Mart or Target. You will almost always pay more to locate in a center with an anchor, and if you are a retail business it will almost always be worth it.

A major anchor guarantees people will come.

CHAPTER 46

An Eight-Step Plan for Finding the Perfect Location

One of life's most painful moments comes when we must
admit that we didn't do our homework,
that we are not prepared.
MERLIN OLSEN,
former football star

When helping clients choose a great location I often find that they get stuck on a particular place. It's not always the best place, but for whatever reason they develop an emotional attachment to it very quickly. Rather than going straight for your first choice, here is an eight-step plan of action I suggest that you follow:

1. Buy a city map and drive to every shopping center in the area. Real estate agents very often only show you what they want to show you. Plus, by doing it yourself you will get a better feel for the area.

2. Write down the phone numbers of all the rentals in shopping centers that seem to meet your basic criteria for size, location, and visibility and circle them on your map. Give each a number and note one other key store in the center for reference. (After driving in circles for a few hours it's easy to forget which is which.)

3. Always find at least three or four options before calling

and getting prices. Remember to call centers you like that have no vacancies; they may well have a tenant on the way out. I have gotten many of my best locations from this simple tip.

4. Drive to each location at different times of the day and on weekends and note how busy the center is at each time. Some centers are day centers, some centers are night centers, some are weekend centers, and some are always busy. Which type is best suited for your particular business?

5. Watch the traffic flow of both people and cars. On more than one occasion I have seen business owners jump at a location because of a major anchor at one end of the shopping center, only to find people parking in front of the anchor and never even glancing at the far end of the center. Also important to consider, especially in a bigger center, is how the traffic flows. A store located right at the entrance to the parking lot will get far more attention and traffic. Best of all there is rarely a premium put on this space.

6. Perhaps the best test of all is to visit several individual businesses. Ask them how business is, how the landlord is, and whether traffic in the center is growing or shrinking. Ask how long the space has been for rent. This can be a big help in your negotiations with the landlord, especially if it's been around a while. Empty space generates no money.

Always take what they have to say with a pinch of salt but listen to what they tell you. Often you will uncover information that will help you in making a decision. Is the anchor tenant about to leave? Is the city about to tear up the road? Or is the shopping center about to be sold?

7. Look at who your neighbors would be in the specific space. If they attract your types of customers, it's a big plus. If they attract teenage boys, it may be a minus.

8. Finally gather all the data, pick the best one with a second as a backup and enter into the negotiation stage. Remember that you don't have to accept anything currently on the market if they are not winners. Maybe you can sublease space in an existing store while you wait for the perfect place. This also reduces your costs.

Don't get emotionally attached to a particular location. Follow this eight-step plan and you will choose a superior location.

CHAPTER 47

Five Timeless Tips on Negotiating a Lease

Negotiating means getting the best of your opponent.
MARVIN GAYE,
singer

Rates vary so much from place to place, even in the same city, that it's very hard to be specific about lease negotiations, but here are some general rules to keep in mind. First, let me say that the landlord or leasing agent will kick, scream, feign insult, and tell you about the three other prospective tenants bidding on the very same place you are interested in—despite the fact it's been empty for six months. But follow these principles and you'll get a good deal.

1. Everything is negotiable. I usually start offering about 25–30% less than the asking price per square foot and usually settle for a discount of about 15–20%.

2. Always ask for free rent to get started. It is standard policy in most places to allow one free month for every year of lease you are willing to sign. Therefore, if you sign a three-year lease, you can expect to get three months free rent, but always ask for more.

3. Ask the landlord to help you with the needed improve-ments. About half the time they will, or will opt to give you some other consideration instead. Ask for the walls to be painted or carpet to be put in before you take possession of the premises. In some cases where the landlord really needed a tenant I've even had them build out the entire space exactly to my specifications. The rule is simple: You don't get if you don't ask.

4. Always rent less space than you think you will need. It's very easy to be seduced by the vision of how wonderful your store will be and how much money you are going to make. Remember this: I've never seen anyone go out of business because they leased too little space! I can, however, give you hundreds of examples of small business owners who went out of business because they rented too much space.

5. Cheap rent is usually cheap for a reason. Like TV time at three a.m., cheap rent usually means little traffic in the center. Try figuring out in your mind what extra money you will need to spend to build up traffic at a less-than-ideal location. Sometimes it's worth it; many times it's not.

**You don't get if you don't ask.
Make the deal work for you.**

CHAPTER 48

For $99, Greyhound Will Take You Anywhere You Want to Go!

You ask any actor—they'll tell you
they'd rather shoot on location because you don't have
to invent the energy, the energy is there.
ADRIAN GRENIER

Several years ago I was doing a seminar where a young man in the front of the room kept saying, "That won't work in my town because [take your pick]…It's too small, too conservative, too many sign laws, bad zoning, not enough traffic, no good retail locations available…"

After my usual spiel on "Why most towns really aren't that different" (THEY ARE NOT.) I finally gave up and said, "For $99 Greyhound will take you anywhere you want to go!" (Which was a popular ad campaign at the time.) Everyone but him laughed.

While you may think this answer is a little trite, nasty, or obvious, believe me it is not. Many people simply do not consider the simple answers to their own problems because they place a great many mental constraints on their thinking.

"I can't do that because …[take you pick once more]… I grew up here, my friends are here, I like it here, my parents are here, I have family here, I know everyone here."

If you run the only coffee shop in a town of 1200 people, it may well be better than being one of ten coffee shops in a town of 50,000, but it's not nearly as good as being the only coffee shop in a town of 10,000 people.

As mentioned earlier, when I opened my second karate school, I was the ONLY karate school in an affluent town of 60,000 people. When I sold my karate school I was one of 23 schools and recreation center programs in the same town! Unless the market demand grew by 2000 plus percent, (it didn't) something had to give.

I was still the best school in town, and likely the most profitable, but business was getting much harder to acquire and would only have gotten worse. Even if I had wanted to stay in the karate business at the time, it would have made far more sense to sell that school and open somewhere else.

I am constantly amazed by the number of people unwilling to change locations to massively increase their opportunities for success, and by the number of people who expect the status quo to be maintained despite a massive increase in competition.

Even if you are not in any type of retail business, the location question can still raise a number of important issues. For instance, are you in the right part of the country? As a rule, in America, the South is a far cheaper place from which to operate a business than the North or the West. The middle states like Texas, Oklahoma, and Missouri are the perfect place to locate a business that ships nationwide. And the prospect of living a better lifestyle in the sun can attract workers to take slightly less pay in return for better weather and living conditions in places like Florida.

This country is a large and wonderful place. If you can't make a living doing what you want in one area, move closer to the major city in your state. Better still, move to a fast-growing area in the Sunbelt—like Nevada, Texas, Florida, or California.

There is no reason on earth why you can't do it, other than your own lack of desire.

It was this very location factor that a decade ago convinced me to move my business from California to Florida. The result was an immediate improvement in shipping time to my clients, since 90% of them were East of the Mississippi, decreased phone costs, and the beauty of no state taxes. As soon as my lease ran out in California, I rented a new office in Florida that cost $20,000 a year less. I bought a bigger house for the same money and generally improved my business and my life with the simple decision to relocate. While that's a step not everyone wants to take, it is something to consider.

You have to be willing to move where the opportunity is. Fish where the fish are and the other fishermen aren't.

Marketing for the Cunningly Clever Entrepreneur

CHAPTER 49

Before You Spend a Single Dime on Marketing, Do This First

The most important thing is not which system you use.
The most important thing is you have a system!
ZIG ZIGLAR

It amazes me that the vast majority of golf clubs, resorts, and real estate developments that I work with think that someone paid a modest salary has any clue how to sell a $25,000 membership or $500,000 villa without training—let alone memberships or real estate that are priced far higher.

Even if your product or service is cheap, allowing anyone to handle leads without formal sales training is not much better than just throwing them away.

Do NOT start ANY MARKETING campaign without a written sales system in place and the sales training to back it up. A sales system will take ONLY one sale to pay for itself and will keep on returning the favor with every employee you hire from now until you retire.

Even a small change, such as how the phone is answered or how an objection is countered, can have an astonishing effect on your sales performance and overall success.

Imagine if you closed two out of ten leads instead of one. You have just doubled sales at NO cost!.

Now think of this concept for telephone inquiries, referrals, or dealing with objections. Incremental improvement at each phase of the sales process leads to ASTONISHINGLY greater results.

This is why NO marketing campaign should ever be undertaken without first having a sales system and training in place.

The system should include:

- step-by-step instructions
- phone scripts
- qualifying scripts
- a presentation script
- objection scripts
- closing scripts
- a referral program

To go forward with any marketing campaign without investing in a written sales system is, quite frankly, insane. Just a 5% improvement in sales skills can easily increase your bottom line by 30% or more.

Countless millions are squandered on campaigns to generate leads, yet little to nothing is spent on the back-end sales system or follow up. Do NOT make this cardinal mistake.

Before you invest a dime in advertising or marketing of any kind, invest in a sales and training system to back up your efforts.

CHAPTER 50

The Critical Importance of Understanding Your Customer's Lifetime Value

Treat your customers like lifetime partners.
MICHAEL LEBOEUF

To run a successful business, you need to know exactly what a customer is worth to you. Knowing this not only helps determine how much money you should spend on advertising and marketing to get a customer but also how much time, money, and effort you should spend on trying to *keep* a customer! If your customers spend only a few dollars a year, then you certainly can't send them a hamper full of goodies at Christmas time. If, however, your customers spend thousands of dollars with you, then it might well be worth the extra goodwill.

I remember back in the mid-1980s reading Carl Sewell's book *Customers for Life*. At that time he found that the average Cadillac buyer at his dealership would eventually spend over $375,000 with him—as long as he kept them happy. It must be triple that now.

In my karate school, we figured out that the average student would spend about $1,000 over the course of his training. In my marketing business, the average client is worth far more than that.

Take a look at your top 20%—your best clients. What did

they spend with you last year?

Take a look at your bottom 20%. What did they spend with you?

After throwing out the bottom 5% and top 5% which might bias your results, what is your average client worth to your business?

You might be surprised by how much your best clients are spending with you in a year. Now project that number over five years, ten years, or perhaps even longer.

For example, I use a local limo service at least once a month to go to the airport at a cost of $75 plus tip. This means that, providing they keep showing up on time, I will be worth well over $8,000 in business to them over the next five years, and closer to $20,000 over the next ten when you take inflation into account.

That means that I ought to rate the occasional upgrade from a town car to their stretch limo. I should make their Christmas card list, and I might even get a small token gift now and then. Going the extra mile and spending $25 to $50 a year on me is going to be well worth the cost and will be far cheaper than finding a new client to replace me.

The value of clients cannot and should not be measured just in terms of dollars spent. There are other much more intangible measures of a client's worth that are equally important in terms of building your business. For example, I have several clients who don't do a great deal of business with me, but account for a large portion of my referrals. They are like sports fans, always telling others how my business has helped them. Their worth in terms of referral business adds up to far more than the dollars they spend.

Other clients are worth far more than the books show because of their marquee value or brand name. I just picked up the marketing account for a large and prestigious resort. Although the dollars involved are small, having their name on my list of clients will undoubtedly produce more business for me. The same will be true in your business. Certain clients or companies that you do business with add to other people's perception of your business expertise and quality. That makes those clients special.

As business owners, we get so caught up in looking for new clients and chasing new prospects that we can fail to properly service our very best and most profitable customers. Going through this process and figuring out just what your customers are worth, both tangibly and intangibly, on an annual basis, can go a long way towards helping you focus your efforts on the customers who most deserve your attention.

Determine your customers' lifetime value now!

CHAPTER 51

There Are Only Three Ways to Grow Your Business

You will either step forward into growth or you will step back into safety.
ABRAHAM MASLOW

Most people over-complicate marketing with talk of image, brand, feel, look, style, and culture. These are all important and relevant factors if you are a multinational company — and all are of *little importance* if you are not!

What is important for you is the simple fact that there are only three ways to grow your business:

1. Increase the number of clients. This is where most businesses focus their efforts, although it's very often the hardest of the three ways to increase income. A large increase in your number of clients or customers usually comes from a change in pricing or a change in marketing strategy. For instance, changing your focus from direct sales to building a database of prospects, backed up with multiple follow-up campaigns, always increases business significantly.

The amazing thing is that while you rack your brain to come up with a killer idea, the chances are the idea that will significantly increase your business will be simple and easy to copy from someone outside of your industry. You just have to do a little research. (For a great source of marketing ideas see www. CunninglyCleverMarketing.com.)

2.   Increase the average transaction value. How can you get customers to buy more of what you sell each time they call, visit, or click? If ten people stand at the counter to buy a widget for $15, the 80/20 rule says that if all were offered the chance to buy six widgets for, say, the price of five, two people would do it, increasing your income by almost 100%.

Simple, but most customers rarely receive the offer. While the customer is standing in front of them, daily-fee golf clubs sell one round instead of five. Shoe stores don't add socks or polish to a sale, hotels sell that night's stay in the summer without trying to sell a return stay in the fall, and so it goes. There's no cost other than the few moments of time it takes to make the offer:

> *Mr. and Mrs. Jones, have you ever had the pleasure of being up here in Vermont when the leaves are changing? It's stunningly beautiful. Our fall packages just came out this week but they sell out very fast. Shall I go ahead and reserve yours while you are here today?*

Most companies can increase transactional value astonishingly quickly with 15 minutes of sales training a day!!! (For a great source of cheap and potent sales training see www.CunninglyCleverSelling.com.)

3. Increase the frequency of repurchase (or the length of time they stay as a customer). How do you get customers to buy your products or services more often to get more total value out of each client? I helped a software company massively increase its income by simply changing to a residual pricing model. Instead of charging $4,000 plus a small annual fee for maintenance, they now charge a set up fee of $1,500 and a $400 a month license fee. Since their average customer stays seven to ten years, you do the math! A simple change of marketing strategy can turn a struggling business into an extremely profitable enterprise.

Of course, in an ideal scenario, you to do all three and enjoy exponential growth by increasing your number of clients, increasing the transactional value, and increasing the frequency of purchases.

**There are a thousand things you can do
in the name of marketing.
First, focus on increasing your customer base, your
average transaction value, and the repurchase rate.**

CHAPTER 52

He with the Biggest Database Always Wins

Don't water your weeds.
HARVEY MACKAY

Like it or not, the title of this chapter is a fact. This is something that most business owners are not happy about since the total sum of their data collection efforts over the last 20 years amounts to 750 names and addresses and the 113 emails they collected this year but haven't gotten into the computer yet.

This may not be you but—trust me on this—I talk to hundreds of business owners a month and this example is better than average.

The size and quality of your database is the foundation for the long-term success of any marketing campaign, yet the simplicity of this fact is lost on many. When I ask seminar audiences full of business owners and marketing executives what's the first thing they would do to market a new business, buying a database of contact information for people who have an interest in that product is rarely, if ever, mentioned. When it is, it comes way down the list of suggestions after running ads, going to trade shows, and even renting billboards.

Imagine two businesses in Los Angeles that sell parts and accessories for Corvette sports cars. One has a database of 600 Corvette owners while the other has a database of 6,000.

Who do you think is in the position of strength?

One can market to a large enough database of potential customers to maintain a healthy business while the other must run his business while constantly searching for more prospects.

It does not matter what business you are in. **You need a large enough database of people who have put their hands up as qualified prospects** so that you can sort through them to find an adequate number of actual customers. Most businesses do a terrible job of building their databases. Golf courses that have seen 50,000 people a year play their course for two decades have email lists that total 750 names (honestly, that's the average!). Car dealerships selling hundreds of cars a month can't find 1,000 good addresses to mail to. Local electrical, air conditioning, water purification, and lawn services do hundreds of transactions but never collect data on their customers. They are forced instead to run endless coupon ads looking for new customers when everyone they ever needed was already in their grasp.

If you are selling coffins, build a list of very old people. If you are selling video games, build a list of teenagers and young adults. If you are selling homes in Florida, build a list of affluent people who are about to retire. If you sell cigars, build a list of people who smoke them. If you sell stuff for weddings, build a list of people about to get married.

NOTHING is more important than building your prospect database.

**He with the biggest database of prospects wins!.
Not occasionally, not some of the time, but
all of the time, *every* time!**

CHAPTER 53

Preach to the Choir—Don't Try to Covert the Muslims

Don't try to teach a pig to sing...it wastes your time and it annoys the pig.
UNKNOWN

Before I get a bunch of hate mail, Muslims should be preaching to the choir too. Converting people from one set of values, beliefs, or vendors is a difficult, tiresome, expensive, and thankless task.

My first how-to manual sold a whopping 1,148 copies in its first year. Which at $150 each in an industry of 12,000 or so people was not half bad. Over the next decade I came out with over 50 additional products or services and for years I marketed them to the list of 12,000 business owners I had in that industry. Never, not even by accident, did the 10,852 people who did not buy my first manual ever come close to reaching the sales of the 1,148 people who did.

Eventually I resigned myself to the fact that, like it or not, my market in an industry of 12,000 business owners was in fact 1,148 people. It took me years to reach this conclusion and tens of thousands of dollars in wasted printing, mailing, and postage. Once I stopped trying to convert *more* customers and instead started to focus on what other products and services I could sell to my *existing* customers, I was able to quadruple the size of my company in a matter of months.

Focus your efforts first on existing customers, then on prospects, then on prospecting. The first will always out-produce the other two.

CHAPTER 54

For Instant Results and Long-Term Profits, Pay Someone to Write a Great Sales Letter for Your Business

Advertising is a business of words, but advertising agencies are infested with men and women who cannot write. They cannot write advertisements, and they cannot write plans. They are helpless as deaf mutes on the stage of the Metropolitan Opera.
DAVID OGILVY

Once you have amassed a large database of prospects, the single most important weapon in your marketing arsenal is a GREAT sales letter. This is a FACT lost on the vast majority of people who think that no one reads anymore (despite the fact that in the last decade, the size of the average bookstore has grown from about 3,000 square feet to 60,000 square feet).

Someone must be reading!

Top direct-sales copywriters don't come cheap. I charge a minimum of $15,000 for a series of single page sales letters or one long one. Others like Dan Kennedy and Jay Abraham charge far more. Of course, you can hire a cheap copywriter or one with no history of direct-sales success, but that's a big mistake. Ninety-nine percent of professional writers—people who may write excellent prose—cannot write sales copy. It's the difference between reading a travel magazine article and saying "That sounds like a nice place" and "Honey, bring my wallet. I'm going to book our vacation at this new beach resort right now!"

A GREAT sales letter for your business will pay untold dividends for years to come. I have sales letters I wrote 15 years ago that are as bankable as a vending machine. In other words, every single time they are mailed they produce many times their cost in profits for my clients.

A seven-letter "Thunderbolt Campaign" (a series of sales letters sent over a short time span) we designed for a resort doubled their income for five straight years, generating over $5 million in highly profitable sales. This from a total investment of well under $100,000 in printing, mailing, and copywriting fees.

Another single-page sales letter I wrote produced $1.7 million in sales for a sports organization and was sent to under 200 prospects. A four-page letter I wrote for a golf club in California that was dying on the vine produced 198 new members while *raising* the dues!

A great sales letter will also double as:

- website copy (most sites have impotent copy incapable of stimulating buying action.)

- great brochure copy (most brochures contain politically correct corporate speak—i.e., crap)

- a script for a video, audio, DVD, or webinar presentation

And last, but by no means least, as:

- a great sales pitch when you meet a prospect in person

By all means skimp on graphics, skimp on web design, skimp

on branding, skimp on print ads, but do NOT skimp of writing a great sales letter.

A great sales letter will ultimately produce more money for your business than any other single marketing investment.

CHAPTER 55

Simple Marketing from the Sign Man

Good advertising does not just circulate information. It penetrates the public mind with desires and belief.
LEO BURNETT

While driving home from a meeting in Orlando, I came off the I-75 exit at Wild Wood and was stopped at the light to make a left onto Hwy 44. As usual, there was a panhandler on the side of the road with a homemade sign begging for money. I have seen a person there a hundred times and, although it occasionally crosses my mind to make a donation, I seldom get past thinking about it before the light changes. On top of that I am a bit of a skeptic when it comes to beggars. On more than one occasion I have offered to hire a man holding a work-for-food sign, only to be turned down. This time, perhaps because it was the Christmas season, I not only stopped, but I gave and laughed as I did it. The difference was all in the man's marketing.

As I pulled up to the light, a thin man of perhaps 50, with a stubbled beard and shaggy clothes, stood up with his cardboard sign. As he did his face lit up into a smile, which despite numerous missing teeth turned his face into the face of a man who didn't seem to have a care in the world. As I made eye contact, he pointed at the sign and his smile grew, as his face lit up with the expectation of a child on Christmas morning. His smile and body language had already stirred my hand towards my wallet. When I read the sign it was a done deal. It said in large black letters: **"Why Lie? I Need Beer!"**

The honesty and simplicity of the pitch won me over and I forked over five bucks. I don't mean to trivialize the plight of this man or any other on the street, but it did reinforce some simple laws of sales and marketing that many of us miss because we make the process so complicated. The rules of sales and marketing are the same regardless of what product, service, or proposition you're trying to sell.

First, before you can sell anything, you must attract your prospects' attention with your ad, message, or sign. The combination of the man's location and sign must certainly have given him a lot of prospects the day I saw him.

Second, you must create an emotional desire for the product. This man's body language and smile gave me the initial connection with him and increased my desire to help. My wife responds better to beggars with animals than to pleas for beer. (She gives money to anyone with a dog.)

Once the emotional connection is made, a proposition must be clearly stated. What are you selling and why do I want to buy it from you? The sign man was not selling his plight, but instead was selling me a laugh and perhaps the feeling I would get from doing something good.

Finally, and most important, a sale must be asked for. In the case of the sign man, his sign said it all! Then he stood up and walked slowly and non-threateningly towards the car, certainly ready to ask for a donation had I not given it to him first.

These simple laws hold true with all sales and marketing propositions from selling cars to selling insurance, from selling candy to selling homes. We often lose sales and customers because we try to complicate this simple formula that time has proven works in making a sale:

- get your prospects' attention
- create the desire
- make the presentation
- ask for the sale

Never do anything in the name of marketing that does not contain the above four elements—NEVER.

CHAPTER 56

Spend Your Money Only When and Where It Can Produce Maximum Returns

Money is plentiful for those who understand the simple laws which govern its acquisition.
GEORGE CLASON

A common mistake I see is companies wasting money in an effort to give equal resources to different parts of their business that may NOT deserve investment.

For example, when I first took over the marketing for a big resort in Michigan they had two distinct seasons, summer and winter. In the summer they marketed golf, and in the winter cross-county skiing and snowmobiling. While the marketing budget for the winter was smaller, it was still significant. But there was a problem. In the summer, with room rates higher, and people playing golf and eating and drinking, the average guest was spending $300 a day. In the winter, with room rates at rock bottom and rooms filled with snowmobilers who were out on trails all day, the average take was less than $100. A $200 difference in income.

After using direct mail and print ads for the first couple of winter seasons, we decided that the winter market was best left to email and the website, and that all the print and direct mail money would be redirected to increasing the summer business where margins were massively higher. It was hard for the client to accept, but to their credit they went with the new strategy and it paid off. (Of course, summer visitors become prospects for the winter season as well.)

Another resort was losing money in the winter, so we told them to shut it down for two months in the winter. Again, a difficult decision for the owner but one that realized $300,000 to the bottom line with very little effort.

Don't spend time, money, and resources in relatively unimportant parts of your business.

CHAPTER 57

The Best Way to Use Local Publications and Media Is to Start a Relationship

We have a strange and wonderful relationship—he's strange and I'm wonderful.
MIKE DITKA

No, this is not a sales pitch for your local paper. In fact I am often critical of how people squander money in local publications. The upside is that local publications are...local. They have a loyal readership and you know that everyone you do reach is in your actual market area. The mistake many make is to run ads that basically say "here we are; stop by." or they use a discount-only mentality. That may work in some businesses, but it is by no means always the best way to reach your customer.

The best way to use local publications, indeed most publications, is to use them as lead generators. Think of them as the first stage of a two-step process, not a direct sale. In other words, instead of judging the response to your ad based on the actual sales you make, base it on how many new relationships you are able to start. Most sales these days are based on some kind of prior relationship and that takes a little time.

Gaining a new customer for most businesses costs a great deal of money. In my business I figure it costs me an average of $750-$1000 to get a new client. In some businesses, like car dealers, it might be $250, in others that sell high-end products like homes, it might be as high as $15,000 or more per sale.

Run an ad that makes it easy and painless to start a relationship with your company. Don't run image ads; run lead-generation ad.

Some of the ideas you might consider and adapt to your local business include:

Run ads that offer:

- free consultations
- free estimates
- free tax planning or investment advice
- free seminars by experts, designers, financial planners, etc.
- no obligation check ups
- free evaluations
- free tire changes
- free videos or audio CDs
- free booklets or planners
- contests of all kinds

Invite people to:

- a party
- a grand re-opening
- a fashion show
- a special tasting

- a factory tour

- free coffee

You can run coupons, but make sure that coupon use is always tied to the prospect parting with some information, not merely handing it over for a discount. Make sure that whatever your promotion you always get contact information, including a phone number and an email in return for your offer so that you can follow up with the lead and develop the relationship.

Once you have generated leads, don't squander them. You should become very focused on following up all leads so that a relationship with your company develops. Treat each piece of data like gold. Make notes on your prospective customers' likes and dislikes. The more you know, the easier it is to develop a relationship by finding common points of interest which ultimately turn into real business. The more people you meet, the more people you will get to know. The more people you know, the more people you will have as friends. The more people you have as friends, the more people will choose to do business with you. The more people who do business with you and are pleased, the more people will refer additional business to you.

It all starts with generating leads and the best place to do that is right in your own back yard. Just remember to put a clear call to action in your ads and offer some kind of clear benefit to the prospect for contacting you.

Changing the focus of your advertising from selling to starting relationships will produce huge gains in profits.

CHAPTER 58

Use Micro Sites and Vertical Websites to Massively Boost Online Sales

One reason so few of us achieve what we truly want is
that we never direct our focus;
we never concentrate our power.
TONY ROBBINS

The most common mistake I see in online marketing is people trying to make their website do too many things. Their theory is that if you put enough things on your site someone who comes is sure to want something, right?

Wrong!

In fact, the more focused your website is on a single product or concept, the more effective it will be in making money. Think about the last infomercial you watched on TV. Someone spent upwards of half a million dollars for you to see that super golf club, fitness machine, or kitchen aid. In the whole 30 minutes how many products did they try to sell you? Ten, five, even two? No, they tried to sell you one and only one. Because that's what works.

If you have five products you want to sell, you are far better off making five websites rather than putting all the products on one.

If you have multiple products or services, at least make sure people can choose quickly so that the information and products they are reading about are specific to what they want. For example if you sell home, life, and auto insurance, have three giant buttons on your home page so that visitors quickly get exactly where they have a need and so you can deliver information in a specific way rather than making wide generalizations.

Many large companies miss this and throw everything but the kitchen sink on their websites. Take for example a typical resort website. You'll see buttons for golf, tennis, spa, swimming, dinning, rooms, meetings, and other activities, but rarely will you see a large graphic on the home page that invites you to BOOK A ROOM. (Which once clicked actually makes a quick sales pitch as to why you should consider booking a room at that hotel.) What a concept, a hotel website that focuses on actually selling rooms rather than providing puff-piece copy and stock pictures of people having fun.

When designing or redesigning your website, ask this key question: **What do I want my visitors to do?**

Then design all the copy, graphics, and elements to make that happen. Remove everything that could distract your visitor from doing what you want them to do. Yes, get rid of the weather channel, stock quotes, and the links to your family-tree page. Only include elements that help you either make a sale, get the prospect to call you, or capture their email address so that you can follow up with them at some point in the near future via email. If most companies did this, they would have to start from scratch on their websites, but the upside to making this effort is more clarity in the minds of your visitors. Confused or frustrated visitors rarely if ever buy. So be specific, be direct, and be focused with your message. Tell them exactly what you want them to do and why, and you'll be pleasantly surprised by the increase in activity that your site generates.

This advice can also be applied to your off-line marketing, including brochures, direct mail pieces, and ads. The simplest way in the world to make more sales is to ask for the order. And the first place to start that process is to make sure you ACTUALLY ASK for the sale on all of your marketing materials because most don't.

The more focused your website,
the more money you'll make.

CHAPTER 59

Finding the Little Strategy that Gives You a Big Edge

All men can see these tactics whereby I conquer,
but what none can see is the strategy out of which
victory is evolved.
SUN TZU

Very often the breakthrough marketing strategy that vaults your business beyond all your competitors can be very simple.

I had a client in New York whose surrounding area suddenly became predominately Asian in its ethnic make up. He had the foresight to put up a Korean language page on his website. (While many Koreans can speak English, far fewer read it well.) By being the only business of his kind in the area with information in Korean, he captured a huge share of this lucrative market while his competitors were sleeping.

Most golf clubs up North hibernate in the winter, doing nothing to stay in touch with their customers while there is snow on the ground. Hence it's an excellent time for the cunningly-clever entrepreneur to steal large chunks of their business. At one club in Ohio we emailed everyone in the club's database to receive their first round of golf free after the snow melted. The campaign went viral with almost 19,000 people filling out 22 questions to get a free round of golf. The ten other clubs in the area combined couldn't come up a database that large or that good and we did it while there was snow on the ground This one promotion and the huge database it produced set our client up for several years.

Another one of the key strategies I try to employ is forming strategic alliances or affiliate relationships to distribute my clients' messages to a target market for free. It could be the local dance school or hairdresser promoting a karate school, a major association sponsoring my seminars, or a win-win affiliate email from someone with a good list willing to do it for a share of the profits. You will always win when the prospect group is targeted, the message distribution cost is FREE, and you get a built-in testimonial from the affiliate.

When business is slow, most businesses consider discounting but I have many success stories where I have done just the opposite. For instance, last year we added over a million dollars in income to a horse training business by adding two additional levels of prestige and value at much higher prices.

A small change in marketing strategy, pricing, or packaging can produce amazing financial breakthroughs. Keep experimenting with new marketing strategies.

CHAPTER 60

The 60-Minute Marketing Plan

Make no little plans; they have no magic to
stir men's blood.
DANIEL BURNHAM

Many business owners never develop a marketing plan for their companies, usually because they are too busy. However, armed with a pen, paper, and the right questions you can give yourself a huge edge in an hour or less by creating a simple marketing template.

Step 1: Determine where your business is now.

- How many clients do you have?

- How much money did you make last year?

- Gross?

- Net?

- What is the size of your potential market?

- What did you spend on marketing?

Step 2: Write down your goals.

- How many clients do you want?

- How much money do you want to make?

- Gross?

- Net?

Step 3: Determine how much you are willing to spend on marketing. The typical answer I get to this question is "as much as it takes," which of course is never true. Other answers include "I don't know" or "I'm willing to spend it if I get a return." However hard it is to come up with a marketing budget, you have to do this in order to have any chance of measuring your results. Despite what you may have read, there is no typical percentage or formula. Budgets should be based on what you want to achieve. If you want a 50% increase in business, it's not going to be achieved from a percentage of last summer's miserable income.

Step 4: Gather marketing materials. You might have brochures, sales letters, testimonials, bios, history, and past newspaper articles. Collect the marketing materials of three competitors. Collect materials from three companies in your industry that you most admire regardless of where they are located. Get together anything you can draw on for inspiration in your new campaign.

Step 5: Define your perfect client. The better you are at defining your customers, the easier and more effective your marketing will be. What do you know about your top twenty percent? Write down what they all have in common. They are the people who pay the bills so they are the people you must design your marketing effort around, not the customers who spend only a few dollars a year. Get the name, address, and email of everyone who ever walks through your door, visits your website, or calls on the phone. Offer special discounts, free cruises, or whatever it takes, but collect that data; it's more precious than gold.

Step 6: Re-design your brochures, flyers, website, and collateral materials. These should be more focused on attracting your perfect clients, the people with whom you most want to do business in the future. They should be full of BENEFITS to your customers. (Better still, you took my earlier advice and had someone write a great sales letter.) Okay, this part takes more than an hour if you do it yourself, but the rest doesn't.

Step 7: Focus first on increasing sales and referrals from existing clients. Many people are so eager to pursue new clients that they often forget that the greatest and quickest sales gains always come from within. Mail and email your existing customer base more often. Ask for referrals at every contact and offer upgrades in service to all you already do business with.

Step 8: Find mailing lists that match the characteristics of your perfect clients. The more specific that group is, the more effective your marketing will be. Direct mail still offers the most tangible form of marketing. Email marketing can also be effective when it's targeted.

Step 9: Set up the criteria by which you will measure response to your efforts. There is an old management maxim that says what gets measured gets done. In marketing what gets measured gets rated for effectiveness and then is either increased or dropped depending on the results.

Step 10: Start implementing the new campaign. Choose the right timing for your campaign so that it can be kicked off with maximum effectiveness. For example, if you live in Florida and own a golf course, you probably won't want to do this in August.

Just one hour spent developing this simple plan can pay huge dividends for your business.

CHAPTER 61

Entrepreneurial Marketing

*Cunningly Clever Marketing made me laugh,
wince, nod in agreement, howl, point out a statement to
my wife, and become wiser in the ways of
both marketing and reality. A superb read!*
JAY CONRAD LEVINSON,
author, *Guerrilla Marketing* series of books,
Over 20 million sold in 57 languages

Invest in the future of your business—buy
Cunningly Clever Marketing**!**

In this section, I have provided you with some of my most valuable marketing concepts, but since I can only devote one section of this book to this critical function you must go further. You must invest in Cunningly Clever Marketing. Yes, this is a shameless ad for another one of my books right in the middle of this one. (I did not include this page in the page count.) But it's a book you will thank me for a million times over, once you read it and instantly profit from it's advice.

Generating Products, Services, and Growth through Innovation

CHAPTER 62

Spotting, Creating, and Capitalizing on Opportunity

Opportunity is missed by most people because it comes dressed in overalls and looks like work.
THOMAS EDISON

To quickly get ahead in business and life, have a keen eye for spotting opportunities. If only we had the foresight to register a domain name in 1993—any domain name—because back then they were still all available. If only we had bought land on the river or where the mall now stands. If only we had unloaded all our stocks in early 2007 instead of 2010. Hindsight is always 20/20. But the question is: How can you spot the next great opportunity for your business?

I'm not talking about you having to predict major national and international trends like the price of gold or the stock market. I'm talking about not getting so caught up in your day-to-day work that you miss simple opportunities. It's about you working *on* your business, not just *in* it.

The first step to inviting opportunity into your life is to be on the lookout for it. Seek it out by looking, listening, and constantly analyzing how you do business. The question "What can I do better?" should always be at the front of your mind instead of being locked away in a vault at the back.

Your business and life ultimately are determined by the quality of the *questions* you pose and answer.

I find it useful to specifically schedule a formal time in the week to work *on* my business. I normally hold meetings with my key staff at my home on Monday nights. Over drinks and appetizers, the agenda is not about day-to-day minutiae or problems of the hour. Instead, it's specifically geared towards innovation and ideas.

- How can we add value?

- How can we keep customers longer?

- How can we convert more leads?

- How can we get more referrals?

- What ideas can we bring in from outside our industry?

- Are we making the best use of new media?

- How can we capitalize more on social media?

- What was the most interesting trend spotted this week?

- How can we do it faster?

The more often you ask these and similar questions, the more frequently you engage your employees (and even clients in some cases) in the discussion, the more quality ideas and innovations you will generate.

Always be asking how you can do "IT" better.

CHAPTER 63

The Power of Problems

Your most unhappy customers are your
greatest source of learning.
BILL GATES

Listen to other people's problems because problems are often opportunities in disguise—especially the problems of the customers and clients you serve. In every problem there is an expression of a need. Needs can very often be translated into additional products and services for your business.

For example, many of my golf course clients in Florida were asking where on the Internet they could advertise their websites to golfers in the Northeast so they could persuade them to visit their courses in the winter. At the time there were no good options, so I created some by building an Atlantic City Golf portal, a New Jersey Golf portal, and others. This allowed me the opportunity not only to help my clients, but also to sell them ad space on my Northern sites to help them drive traffic back to their sites.

The idea for a golf portal developed further when I talked with one of my neighbors about his attempts to sell his home in a golf development. He was frustrated that no one had even come to look at his home in the several weeks it had been on the market. That prompted me to add a real estate option to all of my golf portals. For a small fee, people in any golf community in Florida could run an ad for their home on my Orlando and Palm Beach Golf portals, as well as several other Florida sites, which would get it in front of 100,000 golfers a month. Best of all, we also ran the ad at no additional charge on all our other city golf sites including all of our sites up North.

As a young man, Ross Perot (one of the richest men in the world) was working for IBM. He noticed that his customers who were buying IBM computers needed help in processing their data. He went to IBM with this idea. They said they weren't interested, so he started his own business. He eventually sold it for $2.8 billion dollars. He found a need and filled it!

Over the years, the majority of the product or service innovations we have come up with have either been customer suggestions or customer problems. Your business will be no different if you listen carefully.

Your customers' problems are the keys to your next innovation, product, or service.

CHAPTER 64

Ask Ridiculous Questions

The power to question is the basis of
all human progress.
GANDHI

Two decades ago, I had the opportunity to spend an entire morning with one of the highest-paid marketing consultants in the world. For three hours over coffee and breakfast, he barraged me with questions about how I did business. Each question was followed by another and then another at an exhausting pace. He then offered a suggestion or comment. As it happened, each thing he suggested for three straight hours was something I was already doing. Finally, almost in exasperation, he asked, "What would your clients pay three times as much for?" I told him I didn't know.

Now he urged me to think, pointing out that if I charged all my existing clients three hundred percent more, I wouldn't need to worry about attracting a bunch of new business. In one fell swoop, I would have reached my financial goals. I thanked him for his time, picked up the check for breakfast, and began to drive back home.

On the way, I chatted with the friend who had accompanied me and, I admit, we more or less made fun of the guy. After all, raising our fees three hundred percent seemed like an outlandish idea. It had taken three years to painstakingly build the business to its present state. Somehow increasing prices by three hundred percent didn't seem like a very realistic or useful idea.

That night over dinner and throughout the following few days, we kept repeating the question over and over, hoping the creative solution to our financial problems was really as easy as figuring out what we had to do to justify raising our prices three hundred percent. One idea followed another, until we truly had a package that would add value to our monthly consulting service. A couple of weeks later we rolled out the new program at our customer convention with nothing more than a logo and a verbal description of the new services we planned to offer, together with the three hundred percent price hike. Within an hour our clientèle had grown 25%.

Within three months, we had not only increased revenue by 300%, but also had increased our client base by 300%, leading to even greater rewards than we had initially hoped for. All this because we were willing to actually keep asking the same stupid question: **How do we rationalize a 300% price increase for our clients?**

Make a habit of asking yourself ridiculous questions and then actually go through the process of finding the answers as if you were solving real problems. This technique can lead to major breakthroughs.

The more ridiculous the question, the more powerful the right answer will be.

CHAPTER 65

How Jumping the Lines at Disneyland Could Provide the Innovation You Need to Triple Your Profits

Innovation is the specific instrument of entrepreneurship. The act that endows resources with a new capacity to create wealth.
PETER F. DRUCKER

When people think of growth, they usually think in terms of new locations or more products and services to reach more customers. There is nothing wrong with this approach, but this should be the last way you consider growing. The first is to look at your existing market and figure out what else you can sell them. What other product or services are your existing customers willing to buy from you?

If you have ever been to a Disney park in the height of summer, you are in for a long wait at just about every ride, sometimes an hour or more in the dripping heat. But you don't have to wait in lines anymore. As long as you are willing to pay a substantial extra VIP fee, you can go straight to the front of the line. Not only do you see more, do more, and sweat less, you also can't help getting that smug sense of satisfaction from looking at the poor people in line who you've just usurped with your VIP pass.

Going vertical by offering more to customers you already have is the fastest and most profitable way to build a business. My basic clients pay $295 a month, but I have some who pay $3,000 a month, and every dollar amount in between. By offering add-on services to existing clients, I can double, triple, or even quadruple the amount of money I make without spending a dime to find a new client. It's very possible you could do exactly the same thing.

Last year, I was able to go into one company in an industry in which I had absolutely no experience and, without adding customers, I increased their revenue by over $1 million in residual income. I simply added two higher price options by offering additional value. While their profit at the base level was $8 a month, at my new higher levels it was $40 and $80 respectively.

From VIP parking to velvet rope seating, from queue jumping to adding value, every business has between 5% and 30% of their customers who will pay more for premium services. You just have to offer it.

Developing premium products or services to offer existing customers is the quickest and easiest way to increase profits.

CHAPTER 66

Look Outside of Your Industry to Find Innovation

There's a way to do it better—find it.
THOMAS EDISON

Ninety-five percent of your competitors in any city or industry will be manufacturing, selling, and marketing in exactly the same way as you are. That's why it's so important to look beyond your locale and your industry for ideas and opportunities.

In the late 1990s I enjoyed tremendous success by looking at what type of business-to-business services were available in the "real" world and then adapting them to the martial arts business. At that time very little information existed on how to run a karate school as a profitable business. I combined a little multilevel-marketing philosophy with the boom in personal development to create a boxed package of sales, marketing, motivational, and training materials specific to martial arts school owners. The boxes were shipped out monthly and automatically billed to customers' credit cards. This was nothing particularly original, BUT no one had taken the concepts that were working in the rest of the business world and customized them to the martial arts world. Later, when working with the PGA, I did exactly the opposite. I took all the information I had gathered on how to run a martial arts business and applied it to the golf business.

Since almost every business runs on the same basic principles, you will often find new and innovative ideas outside your field that can easily be adapted to your situation. All you have to do is look.

When Southwest Airlines was looking for ways to turn their planes around faster (they are now the fastest in the industry), did they look at all the other airlines, most of which are lame anyway? No, they went to Indianapolis and studied how race car pit crews changed four tires and gassed up a car in under ten seconds.

Step Outside Your Normal Group

By the same token, you will often find that going outside your own organization or circle of friends to consultant colleagues in totally different industries can pay interesting dividends. Ask them to offer suggestions about your particular problem. They won't be burdened by your emotional attachment to the problem or share the same baggage or mental constraints, real or perceived. You will often see approaches to solving problems that are totally different from those used by people in your particular circle. Sometimes this produces instant results. In other cases, even though it doesn't produce the exact result you want, it does stimulate a new line of thought that ultimately yields the answers you sought.

You might want to take this a step further by forming a brainstorming or mastermind group. These groups are usually made up of friends, associates, and suppliers from different walks of life who meet casually once a month for the mutual benefit of offering solutions to each other's specific business challenges.

There is a great idea right now in another industry just waiting to be adopted by yours; what is it?

CHAPTER 67

Look for Holes in Your Market

Opportunity is a haughty goddess who wastes no time
with those who are unprepared.
GEORGE CLASON,
The Richest Man in Babylon

Sam Walton became the world's richest man in the 1990s using one fundamental strategy. He built his stores in smaller towns where his competition didn't go because they thought there weren't enough people to support a store. (Which just shows how wrong you can be.)

Southwest Airlines used the same initial strategy in building their company on less-traveled routes and secondary airports, where the gate fees were less.

I built a multimillion-dollar business in an industry no one had thought about—the karate business—that at its peak had 20,000 schools in the US alone. Earlier in my martial arts career, I had the only karate school in two different cities.

Apple Computer has specialized in developing products that no one asked for in focus groups, because people can't ask for what they don't know. The products usually weren't completely new; rather, they combined existing elements and great designs in new ways.

The Body Shop, Tom's of Maine, and many other companies created new environmentally friendly products long before the interest was obvious to big companies.

Netflix developed the idea of mailing movies to you because people didn't like the pressure of having to rush back to the video store. Yet Blockbuster and other stores missed this market because they were entrenched in real estate.

Similarly, Amazon.com captured the online book market that was missed by Barnes and Noble. And physical bookstores seem to be going the way of video stores.

As a small, nimble competitor without a big investment in stores and infrastructure, you have the chance to think outside the box and do things differently. As the famous consultant (and author of 40+ books) Peter Drucker said, the railroads missed dominating the airline business because they thought of themselves as in the *rail* business, not the *transportation* business. Work to find those niches where you'll have a big advantage over entrenched competitors as you establish yourself.

Where are the holes in your market?

What business does not exist in your town?

What markets have you failed to fully exploit?

What veins of gold could be mined deeper?

There is money in holes.

CHAPTER 68

Mix It Up to Stimulate Innovation

We are always saying to ourselves…we have to inno-
vate. We've got to come up with that breakthrough. In
fact, the way software works…so long as you are using
your existing software…you don't pay us anything at all.
So we're only paid for breakthroughs.
BILL GATES

Most innovations are not the invention of something completely new, but rather an improvement on something in
existence.

Change the Color

When General Motors offered cars that were any color you
wanted, rather than Ford's "any color as long as it's black" approach, they immediately and critically dislodged Ford's firm grip
on the automotive marketplace. As fashion changed, Levi's blue
jeans had a hit on their hands when they went black. When SKYY
vodka went to an unusual blue bottle, their distinctiveness soared.

How might you change the color of your product, packaging,
logo, clothing, or appearance to create something new?

Change the Material

When Gary Adams of TaylorMade Golf produced his first
metal driver, or the "Pittsburgh Persimmon" as he called it, he

revolutionized golf equipment and enjoyed huge success. Later, other innovators would switch from stainless steel to titanium, and then to exotic combinations of metals. Big or small, companies that innovate can find a position of leadership in their industry.

How could you innovate by changing material?

Make It Bigger

In the early 1970s, Prince revolutionized the tennis world when they introduced the oversized racket. The racket had a bigger sweet spot and was easier for the weekend warrior to hit.

Karsten Solheim did exactly the same with Ping golf clubs. By introducing the cavity-backed club, he completely changed the traditional weight distribution and made the sweet spot much bigger. This enabled him to capture the lion's share of the premium golf club market for 20 years. Two decades later, Ely Callaway would move the very same concept up a notch with the introduction of the Big Bertha driver, profitably followed by even larger models called the Great Big Bertha and the Biggest Big Bertha.

One of the large US hotel chains scored big with NBA teams in a cunningly clever but very simple move. They added longer beds. Can you imagine how hard it must be sleeping in a six-foot bed if you happen to be a seven-foot basketball player?

Could your product or service benefit from being bigger?

Or Make It Smaller

While Callaway convinced the golfing world that bigger was better, Barney Adams introduced Tight Lies fairway woods and Orlimar introduced the TriMetal wood. Both were small companies, both produced small-headed clubs, and both chose to innovate by marketing via infomercials rather than through traditional channels. Orlimar went from grossing $2 million a year to $70 million, while Adams went even higher in the space of a little over a year.

Apple changed the computer business from a world of large mainframes to small desktop models.

The Japanese auto industry changed the American family car from very large to rather small. Later, smart cars took it to a whole smaller level.

Could you make something smaller but better?

Very often a small, seemingly insignificant change in your product's color, size, or material can have a profound effect on sales.

CHAPTER 69

Add Features or Services to Create an Innovative Market Advantage

*If the only tool you have is a hammer, you tend to see
every problem as a nail.*
ABRAHAM MASLOW

Bartles & Jaymes found a whole new market for their wine simply by mixing it with soda and fruit juice, creating a whole new segment of the beverage market (wine coolers).

Snapple did the same thing with iced tea, while Jolt did it in the cola business by adding caffeine when the rest of the world was taking it out. Jolt has since been surpassed by energy drinks like Red Bull and Monster.

How could you change your mix? What could you add to your existing product or service to create an even better product?

Offer Value-added Services

When American Airlines started their Frequent Flyer program in the early 1980s, they instantly caught the attention of the frequent traveler. Hotels like Hyatt offer desks, business centers, Wi-Fi, and a host of other business services to specifically attract business people to their hotels.

Rental car agencies like Hertz and Avis offer pick-up and

drop-off right at your car's parking space, bypassing the normal check-in lines. Enterprise and National took it a step further by picking you up and dropping you off at home.

Charities offer special recognition for their leading patrons, as do churches and hospitals. How could you offer more recognition, publicity, or rewards to your clients?

What can you add to your existing product or service to change the value proposition to your customers?

CHAPTER 70

Take Away Features or Services to Create an Innovative Market Advantage

When you innovate, you've got to be prepared for
everyone telling you you're nuts.
LARRY ELLISON
CEO, Oracle Corp.

In the airline industry, pioneers like Sir Freddie Laker (Laker Airways) and Herb Kelleher (Southwest Airlines) were entrepreneurs who innovated, not by adding or mixing but by taking away. By removing frills like meals and movies, and charging extra for everything except the seat you sat in, they lowered ticket prices dramatically and created a whole new segment of the industry—"the discount airline." Incidentally, Richard Branson named one of his first Virgin planes "Spirit of Sir Freddie" in recognition of Laker's advice and inspiration to him.

Today, Ryan Air has taken this concept to a whole new level in Europe, with fares as low as one pound. In fact, the last few times I flew with them, the cab fare from the airport to the hotel was double the price of the flight! They make it up with add-on charges for everything.

Ugly Duckling and Rent-a-Wreck did the same thing in the rental car business. By buying used fleets instead of new fleets, they were able to offer their cars at substantially lower rates.

Rent-A-Wreck was originally founded in early 1968 as Bundy Very Used Cars by Los Angeles entrepreneur Dave Schwartz. His pioneering concept was renting used cars for less at neighborhood locations. Airport-based car rental was typical in the 1960s, and most renters were business travelers. As the brand exposure of Rent-A-Wreck grew, so did the recognition of a new market as they tapped into the vastly underserved market of value-conscious customers who didn't want to pay the high rates of the "traditional" car rental companies.

Motel 6, the hotel chain, offers a clean, comfortable room at the lowest price of any national chain. (Don't expect a flat screen TV in your room.)

Supercuts hair salons offer eight basic cuts at one low price.

How might you remove something to become a low-price innovator in your industry?

What can you subtract to change the value proposition for your customers?

CHAPTER 71

Innovation from Below

Opportunities multiply as they are seized.
SUN TZU

Creativity and problem-solving ability are essential talents for any entrepreneur, but as every entrepreneur knows, no one person has a lock on innovation. Creativity should also be encouraged and stimulated at every level of your organization, for creativity very often comes from below — from people in the trenches, or factories, or on the front lines with the customer.

Take the case of Bette Nesmith, a freelance artist working as a lowly secretary, who used her natural creativity to solve a problem. Before the days of computers and word processors, when you made a mistake at the typewriter it often meant starting again at the beginning of the page. One day, Bette's background in art came to the rescue. She suddenly realized that whenever she made a mistake while painting, she simply painted over it. With this in mind, and after several failures, she produced a strange concoction in her kitchen. She named it "Mistake Out."

Many of the other secretaries she worked with used the product, and a local office supply store asked her to make some for them to sell. No one, however, was willing to give her a dime to help expand her little business. She finally hired a college student to help her and went ahead on her own, still working part time as a secretary. A single parent, her road to success was a rough one.

At first, she went from one office supplier to another, selling a few bottles at a time. Her first year's profit amounted to just over $200. Thirty years later she sold her little company, which became the Liquid Paper Corporation, for 50 million dollars.

Empower Others to Innovate

Empower your staff to solve problems creatively. Make it known that in your company there are no bad ideas. Offer rewards for creative ideas that save time, money, and manpower. Reward creative ideas that increase sales or customer awareness. Conduct one major promotion a year with worthwhile prizes for the best ideas generated during a month of internal competition. Or put into effect a permanent system of rewards for employees, with rewards based on the amount it saves or the extra profit it produces.

**Empower everyone on your staff to innovate.
A lot of the best innovations come
from the front lines.**

CHAPTER 72

Use Speed as Your Strategy

Ready, fire, aim is better than ready, aim, aim, aim.
TOM PETERS

Speed and creativity are the entrepreneur's greatest weapons. I have a passion for fast cars, but my passion for speed is not limited to pleasure behind the wheel. It includes my business because speed is an important strategy in business.

Two people whose books influenced my early career and made me err on the side of speed were Brian Tracy and Mark McCormick. Both men believe that most great ideas are killed or copied by others while people pursue perfection in developing them. I fully believe that a good idea executed quickly—even if it is less than perfect—will massively outperform a perfect idea that is implemented six months later. In addition, you'll get months' worth of leads that much earlier.

Hey—if you can be fast and perfect, so much the better. Just be FAST first. Let me give you a world-class example of this theory in action.

Microsoft NEVER releases a perfect product; in fact, far from it. Instead, it works quickly to develop new technologies it then releases to John Q. Public and lets him find all the bugs so the company can fix them. That's even cheaper than outsourcing the debugging offshore because it's FREE! Now, I am sure that Microsoft wishes it could put out a perfect product, but it also realizes that being ahead of its competitors in launching products is far more important than having a perfect product.

The bottom line is this—if you have a good idea or a need for new clients, get in gear and get something going. Do it on a small scale if you have to, so you can make changes inexpensively later if need be. BUT don't drag out the process for weeks in search of perfection. Innovate, but don't overbuild. Good is usually good enough to succeed and takes less time, money, and effort to achieve. While others are busy working on choosing the perfect type font, you will have already licked the stamps on your latest campaign and be heading for the post office.

At every stage of your business life there are people looking to slow you down, people looking for perfection in an imperfect world. Let others struggle with the vice of perfection.

In today's fast-paced world, people are rarely prepared to wait for anything very long. Instant food, overnight delivery, and 24-hour shipping is the norm.

How can you offer your product or services faster than your competition?

CHAPTER 73

The More Creative You Are in Accepting Payment, the More Money You Will Make

If you're attacking your market from multiple positions
and your competition isn't, you have
all the advantage and it will show up in
your increased success and income.
JAY ABRAHAM

It's a fact of business life that very often the people who want to do business with you don't actually have the cash, or at least are not willing to part with it. They are often, however, willing to part with services, or leverage other items of value they may have to get what they want.

I have been paid in cash, diamonds, land, cars, paintings, carpentry, room nights, gift certificates, vacations, golf clubs, advertising, and professional services, to name just some of the creative ways I have accepted payment for my services.

I sat on the land until it went up in value, gave the diamonds to my wife, and used the services for things I would have had to pay for anyway. I used vacations for employee motivation and customer incentives and sold the rest of the stuff on eBay at a discount, but still at a profit.

Yes, it's far more hassle than just banking a check, but if you are willing to make the effort on both ends of a deal, provide the service, and help the customer pay you, you'll be amazed at how much more business you can close.

Often you can get a higher value in trade than you would have gotten in cash. At the very least, most customers are willing to pay a higher fee in trade than they would expect for cash.

People are fundamentally lazy.
Be creative, assume the work and risk of
getting paid, and you will close and profit from
far more deals.

7

Cunningly Clever
Management

CHAPTER 74

Helping Your Employees Be Great

God must have loved the common man for he
made so many of them.
ABRAHAM LINCOLN

At a seminar last year, a business owner attending the event with his staff stood up and announced that he just couldn't get the performance he needed from them. In fact, he said that every one of them seemed to lack motivation. I immediately asked what type of staff training he provided them with, to which he replied, "a staff meeting once a week." As it turned out the staff meeting was not used as a training opportunity, and it degenerated into a gripe-fest. I pushed on and asked what training he had given his staff in the arts of goal-setting or self-motivation. The answer, of course, was "None."

This provided me with the perfect moment to recite one of my favorite maxims. "If you keep on doing what you always have done, you will keep on getting what you've always got."

If you want your staff to be motivated, you have to help them advance *their* personal goals, and you have to help them understand what motivates *them*. More importantly, *you* have to understand what motivates them. Is it recognition, money, fear, or pride? Each person is uniquely different in this respect.

Their personal goals and motivations are usually easily uncovered with a few simple questions. Armed with that new knowledge, the astute business owner can develop an empowerment strategy to help his employees become better at their jobs.

Employees of your business should understand that continued learning is expected and required, no matter how simple or mundane their jobs might be. A person can always become better. Teachers should strive to be better communicators or presenters. Retail staff should learn more about body language and building rapport. Auto shop mechanics should learn more about follow-up and better customer care.

Every organization should share this maxim with everyone, from the janitor to the brain surgeon, "Get good, get better, be the best." Now that's easy to say, but it doesn't happen by accident. You must take charge and be the catalyst to get employees, who are perhaps not in the habit of learning, to get involved in making themselves a greater asset to your organization.

One way is to hold a training session during regular business hours, and simply open an hour later. That way everyone shows up and no one begrudges the meeting. Another way is to hold it during lunch hour and spring for pizza.

Back up your training with ongoing support. Provide your employees with an audio to listen to in their cars on the way to or from work. Each month you can focus on a different skill to bring out the best in your employees. Include a worksheet to be filled out and brought back as a means of checking their comprehension. Offer them a small reward to encourage their willing participation.

Recommend a book each month and offer incentives to those who can answer a few simple questions on its content. Hand out the rewards at your regular staff meetings and compliment your employees on their efforts to make themselves more valuable to your company. Encourage all your employees to attend seminars and allow them some time off to do so. In fact, as I write this, two of my staff are in Orlando at a professional seminar.

The bottom line is this—stop looking for super-employees—in reality they rarely exist. Instead, take the responsibility to inspire and empower ordinary employees to become exceptional. People are people; the difference is in the efforts you make to bring out the best in them.

Take the lead in inspiring
ordinary employees to greatness.

CHAPTER 75

Are Your People Doing What They Should—OR What They Want?

Excellence is the gradual result of always striving to do better.
PAT RILEY

Back when I was in the karate consulting biz, I hired a guy to sell. He had been one of my customers and he told me he was great at sales. For a couple of months he did okay. Then he found out he liked creating the content we were selling far better than actually selling it. Slowly but surely he made fewer and fewer sales calls until he was spending almost all his time creating content. Sad to say, I let a couple of months go by before I asked him why we had no sales. He made a passionate plea about why he needed to be creating content and that he was just TOO BUSY to make sales calls. Great, but we already had someone on staff who produced the content rather well—ME!

I have a number of clients who have someone on their staff who insists on writing their monthly e-newsletter because "they are the only ones who can do it right." Now, there is certainly nothing wrong with this if that person's job is MARKETING. But if that person's job is sales, then it's not a task they should be doing. They should outsource it to my professional copywriters, and give them some input and direction if needed.

Why is someone in sales spending two days writing an e-newsletter rather than selling? Simple—they would rather be creating than cold calling. You see this a lot with "salespeople." They offer to do the newsletter, the e-blast, and stuff envelopes, and pretty soon they are too busy doing just about everything else to actually sell.

Selling is hard, selling is measurable; most of this other stuff is not.

This scenario is by no means limited to sales. Just this week one of my new employees spent the entire day correcting typos on one of our information sites. When asked why, she said because a customer had taken the time to write in and point out the mistakes. Great, but I couldn't care less if there are a few typos on a site with 10,000 pages of content. I am selling ideas and solutions, not English grammar!

Some golf pros love teaching and are never in the shop, others hate being out in the sun and are excellent in the shop. This might be a problem, or it might not, depending on the club. The fact is, people gravitate to what they like to do (or feel most comfortable doing). And they do it very quickly, without telling you or anyone else. Heck, sometimes they don't even notice it themselves.

Unfortunately what this also means is the job they were hired for—their core function—is running at half speed, and that's at best. This means something critical is NOT getting done in your business.

This gives you two choices if you want to get the most from your employees:

1. Assuming that position is open, allow them to do the job they gravitate towards, although it's rarely the one they have been hired for. In some organizations,

usually larger ones, this can work out and at least they will be doing something they are passionate about. In smaller organizations it will usually leave a gaping hole.

2. Manage your expectations with a brutally detailed position agreement that leaves no wiggle room for wandering off in another direction. If they want to volunteer to do something else, add it to their position agreement.

People quickly gravitate to doing the work they like. You must continually make sure that's the work *you need done*.

CHAPTER 76

The Cunningly-Clever Retro Management Tool That Will Work Wonders for Your Productivity

I wouldn't say I was the best manager in the business.
But I was in the top one.
BRIAN CLOUGH,
legendary English football manager

My company has a sophisticated ticket system for monitoring customer requests and a sophisticated CRM for tackling leads and follow up. We also have a number of internal Google docs, spreadsheets, and shared intelligence. But you know what seems to work even better than all of the technology that I have eagerly committed tens of thousands of dollars to? A blackboard! That's right, a blackboard—actually it's a whiteboard, but the very act of gathering my staff around it each day works wonders.

On it are listed major projects in progress, sales, leads, and a list of problems or out-of-the-norm requests that need solving. Nobody can say they didn't see it or that it got lost in hundreds of tickets because all the major stuff gets put on the board. At various times we have abandoned this method and relied on technology, but we always go back.

An added bonus is the clapping, cheering, and camaraderie developed when erasing something from the board. You just don't get that feeling from a shared spreadsheet.

In my karate school days, I printed out a list of all 250 clients and kept it stuck to the back of my desk. Each month, as soon as I had talked with a student personally, or talked with the parents, I highlighted that name. Towards the end of the month I had an instant visual snapshot of what clients I had not seen or talked to that month and made additional efforts, including calling their homes, to let them know they had been missed. This did wonders for my cash flow and retention.

Yes, even back then I could have tracked this on my computer (and you should do that as well), but there is something more powerful about a bit of paper stuck to the wall that all of your staff can see.

Put your numbers, projects, progress, and problems up on the wall every day where everyone can see them and contribute to moving things forward and solving them.

CHAPTER 77

Do You Know Your Three Critical Sales Numbers and What They Instantly Tell You about the Health of Your Business?

He who asks a question is a fool for a minute; he who does not remains a fool forever.
CHINESE PROVERB

Do you know your numbers—I mean really know your numbers? Most businesses do not. Even more troublesome, a great majority of sales and marketing people seem oblivious to their value as well. The numbers I am talking about are not found on a lotto ticket—I guess if they were, more people would know them.

I am talking about the number of inquiries, number of prospects, and number of sales. These three numbers are critical to your marketing success, critical to your sales success, and critical to the success of your company.

In the karate business, I knew the numbers inside and out: Forty inquiries produced 32 appointments, which in turn produced 25 trial lessons, which in turn produced 20 signups, 18 of whom made it past the first month. Those numbers, when hit, produced $120,000 a year in profits. I always hit those numbers because

I looked at them every day and held myself accountable for reaching them.

Selling real estate is no different. I have a Realtor client who turns 6% of her leads into prospects and then closes 25% of the prospects. Good second number, poor first number. By increasing her leads-to-prospects ratio from 6% to 12%, she would double her sales. That's an incredible number. The truth of the matter is that she gets more than enough leads to double her sales, but she fails to convert them to prospects.

A low leads-to-prospects ratio indicates one of three things:

- a poor marketing program that generates too many unqualified leads

- a poor sales process (directly related to a poor sales training program)

- a poor follow-up procedure that allows good leads to slip through the cracks

That's how powerful numbers can be. You can troubleshoot a multimillion-dollar operation with just three numbers.

When I ran a telemarketing operation selling business books and tapes the numbers once again were key. Each salesperson called 60 people a day, talked to 18, and sold $800 worth of product. If they did not call 60 people, they did not talk to 18, and therefore did not sell $800 worth of product. It sounds simplistic and it is, but day after day, week after week, the numbers held true. (They could have made more than 60 calls a day if their job descriptions didn't require them to do other things as well.)

I just hired a new salesperson; his job is to make no fewer than 250 calls a week. From that we can extrapolate the number of people he should talk to and the number of sales.

That's the power of numbers: They lead to a logical result.

Last week I was incredibly busy. I had several very large proposals that had to get out, and several in-house projects that had to be finished. Because of this I did not send out my regular weekly e-zine. By not sending out my e-zine, I have thrown off my numbers. Every week that my e-zine comes out, I get at least two calls. Not surprisingly, this does not happen when I don't. So now I have to make it up somewhere. I also didn't make my regular five outbound calls a day to warm up a few prospects—another strike against me. But I'll make it up somehow next week because I KNOW if I call 10 people a day next week, it will put my numbers more or less back on track.

The numbers don't care what I do, and the numbers never lie.

Make sure you know what your numbers are telling you about your business.

CHAPTER 78

Measuring the Intangible for Tangible Results

No snowflake in an avalanche ever feels responsible.
GEORGE BURNS

There are lots of concrete things business owners can do to measure the performance of their businesses. You can measure profit and loss, the number of clients you have, your market share, or the number of widgets that you can produce in a day. These are all important measures that can be seen in black-and-white reports, but there are other less tangible items that should be also be measured.

Most business owners have a feel for how some of the more intangible factors are helping or hindering their performance. The problem is that a *feeling* is not an accurate enough measure of important factors like:

- brand/name awareness in the community

- customer satisfaction

- employee morale

- systemization of your business

- cutting edge ideas

All of these factors are vital to the long-term success of

your business. It is not easy to quantify some of these subjective categories, but think of yourself as a judge in an ice skating event. There is no black-and-white measurement of performance on ice, —a bunch of judges hold up numbers and --the other competitors can be judged plus or minus that score. You must do the same for your business.

Take a topic like employee morale and score it from minus ten to plus ten with zero being neutral—where you have as many unhappy as happy employees. Where do you stand right now? If you are not well into the plus side, you have problems.

Let's take a statement that might be part of our strategic plan like, "We are a cutting-edge company in our industry" and try to measure it in a way that makes it more tangible.

Here are a few of the questions we ask at Legendary Marketing to measure that intangible statement on a scale of minus ten to plus ten.

- Do we visit our competitor's websites once a week and look for new products or services?

- Do we scan the trade magazines and trade websites to look for mentions of what they might be doing?

- Do we attend industry trade shows and events?

- Do our people attend seminars and conventions to increase their knowledge?

- Are our staff reading books and listening to audios that increase not only their job-specific skills, but more general skills like time management and communication skills?

- Do we look outside our industry each month for ideas

that we could apply to our business?

- Do we come out with new products and ideas at least once a quarter?

- Do we effectively communicate our forward progress and leading-edge status to our employees?

- Do we effectively communicate our forward progress and leading-edge status to our clients?

- Do our clients and prospective clients view us as a leading-edge company based on the comments and emails to or about us?

- Do we upgrade our internal technology every quarter to improve the speed and performance of our employees?

By reviewing each of these questions each month, we can come up with a number and measure our relative performance as a leading-edge company. There are lots of other areas in which we try do exactly the same thing. Tracking and measuring these intangibles will only make your business a better place to work and a better functioning, more profitable business.

Think of all the factors in your business that would be good track, then follow this system for doing it. You will quickly discover that what gets measured gets done and that it quickly gets done better.

What gets measured, including the intangibles, gets done—better.

CHAPTER 79

Manage by CRM

*Good management consists in showing average people
how to do the work of superior people.*
JOHN D. ROCKEFELLER

For most of the past decade there has been an enormous amount of hype about CRM (customer relationship management) software. While I am sure the majority of *Fortune* 500 companies have now found one they like, many smaller businesses have not.

A good CRM should:

- put all your key data in one place

- be available to your entire staff

- have contact history on all prospects and customers

- track and predict sales

- tell you which employees are productive and which are not

- allow you to continue seamlessly serving a customer if an employee leaves

If you have a good CRM in place and use it, you will save yourself hours of wasted time a week. What's more, your employees who have to log their activities on a daily basis will become astonishingly more productive.

A good CRM, used daily and to it's full potential, is worth it's weight in gold.

CHAPTER 80

Why Most Business Contracts
Are Worthless

Always do right. This will gratify some people and
astonish the rest.
MARK TWAIN

For most of the 25 years that I have been in business, I have done business — including some really large deals — without contracts. At various times I have tried contracts, or others have insisted upon them against my wishes.

I tried them in the karate business when I was selling licenses. I had what I thought was a simple yet complete five-page contract drawn up at great expense by a contract-law attorney.

The majority of people signed it without any fuss, but about a dozen sent it to their attorneys. All of these came back with numerous paragraphs they wanted changed on the advice of counsel. But you know what's really funny? None of the 15–20 paragraphs in question were the same.

After trying to appease a couple of potential licensees whose attorneys were doing nothing more than TRYING to justify their fees, I finally just said to sign it as is or don't, I am not making any changes.

Eventually they all signed.

My web business took off no upfront fees or contracts, I began to use contracts as my product became more and more powerful it took far longer to set up, so I changed to contracts again. People signed them, dated them, faxed them back, and then completely ignored them five months later when a new manager showed up who demanded a cheaper solution.

In my experience it just doesn't make a difference having or not having contracts, as the results are the same.

FACT: When someone wants to break a contract, they will lie, steal, cheat, dream up nonexistent problems, and blame you and your staff for every ill in their lives.

This person is not someone who will bring joy or prosperity to your life. Forget the indignity of it. Forget the lies. Forget the fact that you are 100% in the right and the contract breaker is wrong. It simply doesn't matter. If you sue them, you MAY win. (The lawyers always win!) It will cost you a large amount of time, money, mental energy, and lost opportunity, and even if you win that's just where the fun starts.

IF you win, you then have to collect. Ask the Brown family how much they ever got from multimillionaire and "presumed" double murder O.J. Simpson and you will begin to get an idea of what chance you have of ever seeing a penny from your judgment. Yes, you should have things spelled out in as much detail as possible to avoid confusion down the road. You can even go to the trouble and expense of having an attorney draft a solid letter of agreement so you both know what you should be doing, or just write something up yourself so it's clear to both sides what the deal is. Just don't expect it to mean much once a person has decided to no longer do business with you. If you have a good attorney — and I have had a few — they will give you exactly the same advice as above when it comes to pursuing contract settlements through the courts. People who want to screw you will try, and people who don't won't. A piece of paper, no matter how well written, won't stop either party from acting the way they act.

Contracts kill more deals than they save; use them only when you have no choice.

Please consult your attorney before following this sage advice (LOL).

CHAPTER 81

In Search of Prime

They say Rome wasn't built in a day, but I wasn't on
that particular job.
BRIAN CLOUGH

In every business there is an optimum place to make money. Go beyond that place, and there is a big gap between where you are now and your next growth in **net profits**. It's often best to stay where you are successful rather than expanding, diversifying, buying competitors, etc.

You will most likely ignore this advice, as the majority of entrepreneurs confuse growth with profits, but let's give it a shot anyway.

In order to grow your business, you need more staff.

In order to grow your business, you will need extra space.

In order to gear up as a manufacturer or enjoy greater volume discounts, you must also order greater quantities of materials in advance.

All of these things cost you more in cash outlays with little or no guarantee you'll actually see a return.

Which business do you think makes more money, a karate school with 250 students or a karate school with 300 students?

All things being equal, the karate school with 250 students

wins. I was involved with hundreds of karate schools of all shapes and sizes, from 900 square feet to 15,000 square feet, and the most profitable model I ever saw was a studio around 1,200-1,500 square feet with 250 students. It was the optimum size to grab the cream of the market in any area while being run by one full-time and one part-time instructor to keep the overhead low.

There is a prime size for your business where it will produce maximum revenue in its current form; find your prime.

CHAPTER 82

Outsource Everything

If it flies, floats or fornicates, always rent it...
it's cheaper in the long run.
FELIX DENNIS,
billionaire publisher

In this day and age, the more you can outsource the better. Outsourcing reduces fixed overhead for wages and space. Outsourcing allows you to change vendors quickly and easily if they are not meeting expectations or deadlines. Outsourcing allows you to gear up or gear down easily. Outsourcing allows you to get specialized help rather than forcing your existing staff to do things they are ill trained or ill equipped to do well.

Outsourcing usually costs more per hour than doing it in-house, but overall you will save money. For example, a lot of my clients try to do telemarketing in-house, especially when things are slow in the winter. The employees they reassign to make the calls are usually untrained, hate it, and generally fail without finishing the job. It would be far cheaper and more effective in the long run to outsource this to a telemarketing company and let them deal with the headaches.

The same can be said for a thousand other tasks that you might let staff do because they volunteer or have nothing better to do, like building websites, designing brochures, or writing sales copy. These are all highly skilled jobs when done properly and should be outsourced to experts. The fact that an existing employee can design a website that looks nice means nothing if it doesn't have all the elements or functionality that a professional website designer and marketing person would include.

My favorite example is from a seminar I did in Atlantic City, New Jersey. A business owner at the seminar got up and announced during my segment on sales that, "I don't like selling, I am no good at selling, and so I hired this lady to do the selling for me."

Great I said, "Who's training her how to sell?"

"I am," he says, oblivious to the giggles around him.

Use your existing staff for what they do best, and outsource the rest.

CHAPTER 83

Carefully Evaluate the Opportunities that Come Your Way

Opportunities are like buses; they all take you some-where, just not necessarily where you want to go!"
JOHN SUNNUNO

Throughout your business life, opportunities will come and go like the wind. Partners, competitors, spouses, clients, friends, and perfect strangers will cross your path with new ideas, markets, products, and can't-lose schemes. Some will be good, some will be bad, but most will be somewhere in between.

All will steal your focus.

Some will steal your time.

Others your resources, and

The majority your money!

The greatest skill in management is not knowing what opportunities to take, it's knowing which not to take.

CHAPTER 84

How to Always Make GREAT Decisions about the Future of Your Business

Be willing to make decisions. That's the most important quality in a good leader.
GENERAL GEORGE S. PATTON

Over the years I have had thousands of business owners call me up and ask any one of a hundred different questions about how to run their businesses:

- What should I charge?

- How big should my space be?

- How many staff should I hire?

They should already know the answers because they should have started with the end in mind, but few do. So how do you go about making good decisions that will affect your future and your income?

First, define the criteria you will use to make your decisions by answering some version of the following questions (the questions will vary depending on your business).

Here is an example of the questions I used to ask when I was consulting with karate schools:

1. What business are you in?

2. How many clients do you want?

3. How big a school must you have to teach that many students?

4. How many employees must you have to teach that many students?

5. How much do you want to NET?

6. How hard are you willing to work? How many hours per week? And I mean really work, not just show up?

As an example, here are the answers you might get to these questions from a savvy karate school owner:

1. I am in the personal development business. I use martial arts to maximize my students' physical and mental potential.

2. I am aiming for 250 students.

3. I have only 1500 square feet of space.

4. I have only one full time and one part time employee.

5. I want to make $25,000 a month and net $12,500.

6. I will work 10 hours a day, five days a week.

Now, based on the above core criteria let's ask a few questions and use the criteria as our guide in coming up with answers.

How much should I charge?

Given the above criteria (make $25,000 a month from 250 students) you must average $100 per student so, any way you get to that number will work. For instance, $70 tuition, $20 average testing fee per month, and $10 merchandise; or $100 tuition, no merchandise, no testing; or $80 tuition, $20 merchandise, no testing fee.

Let's take another popular question:

Should I give family discounts?

You can, but if you make them too large you will have a problem.

1. You can lower your average student fee but our core criteria is that it should be $100.

2. If you lower your average student fee, you need more students to hit your numbers. More students means more space and more employees.

Now I am not saying don't give family discounts, but take into consideration what effect it will have on your overall plan and charge accordingly.

Let's look at adding an after-school program:

1. It educates my students and helps them develop, so it makes it on those criteria.

2. It brings in over $100 a month from each student who signs up, so it's a winner there.

3. With that extra income, I really don't need more space because I get to my financial goals quicker with fewer students.

4. More staff? Maybe, maybe not.

Based on these criteria I could add this sort of after-school program and not break any of my core criteria.

Should I use a billing company for my tuition payments or should I do it in-house?

1. Using one works because the school in question has determined it's in the personal development business and not the billing biz.

2. It works because billing companies do provide support and motivation to help you grow.

3. It also works because you don't want to add more staff.

4. It works because they want to help me make more money and, although they charge a fee, it's more than worth it.

It takes discipline to sit down and design your core criteria, and still more discipline to stick to the plan and use it as your guide when opportunities come along. What it will do for those who have discipline is save thousands of dollars by keeping you focused.

Take the time to write down your goals and the criteria by which you will make decisions to help you reach them.

CHAPTER 85

Suspects, Prospects, Customers, Clients, and Partners

*Surround yourself with only people who
are going to lift you higher.*
OPRAH WINFREY

I group people with whom I do business into one of five categories. I am interested in all of them since you need all to succeed,
but I am most interested in the last category because it's not only
the most profitable, it's the most personally and professionally
satisfying.

Suspects

These are people you *suspect* might like to do business with
you. You identify them because of some factor: They may live
in your local area, receive a certain magazine, or be on a list that
might make them look like possible prospects. Online , they might
frequent the same chat rooms and discussion boards you do.

Prospects

Prospects are people who essentially put up their hands and
say, YES, I'm looking for a new place to eat, a carpenter, dance
school, or new car. They have the need for whatever product or
service you might provide.

Customers

Customers are people who buy from you occasionally, maybe even quite often, but they see you primarily as a vendor. They have no special connection to you or your business and might just as easily shop down the street.

Clients

Clients are people who buy from you repeatedly. They like you. They may be interested in your advice or comments on how to best use your product, or form a deeper relationship with your company. They will most likely refer you to others and some should be cultivated further into partners.

Partners

Partners work for the good of both parties. I call all of my customers partners because that's really the only type of customer I want. Truly though, only a handful really are partners. Few of your customers and clients will ever become true partners either. They will say they are, they may even want to be, but they are not.

In my marketing business, when a partner is truly involved with us it results in the mutual success of both businesses. We refer business to them, and them to us. The success of our campaigns helps us generate more clients as much as it drives more revenue for our partners. When things don't go as planned, both sides identify shortcomings rather than point fingers. Partners are engaged in the process of coming up with great offers and executing the programs. They understand that generating leads is only half the battle and that THEY must be responsible for lead conversions (sales).

Most people would rather this was not so. They would rather take all responsibility for success, but blame the "marketing" when things don't go well. Every one of my partners has my cell phone number. Every one of my partners can call me seven days a week, but few ever do because when they do, they often find out that they have to work—that there are a great many things on their end that remain undone. They have to make decisions about offers, timing, and planning. They have to engage in SALES TRAINING to increase their staff's performance, and I guess that most would simply rather not. Like most business owners, they are already up to their arses in alligators and they would rather have someone else just fix it.

I will go above and beyond in investing my personal time and effort, as well as leveraging all of my resources and connections, to help a partner succeed. Great partners stimulate each other. They share success stories, ideas, and leads. These are the type of "customers" you must strive to reach and it really doesn't matter if you are in the marketing business, the restaurant business, or the flower shop business.

Look to cultivate your customers and clients to become partners. That's where the money and satisfaction will come from.

CHAPTER 86

Up-size Slowly—Downsize Fast

Nothing is more difficult, and therefore more precious,
than to be able to decide.

NAPOLEON BONAPARTE

The biggest mistakes I have made in business have not been growing too fast—up-sizing—although I have done that plenty of times. In no case was the growth decision fatal. The real opportunity to make a BIG mistake is in not *downsizing* fast enough when things start to go bad.

There are a great many factors in business and in life that will always be beyond your control: commodity prices, competition, production problems, terrorism, natural disasters, sickness, accidents, or the economy in general. But whatever causes the slowdown doesn't matter. What matters is that you move fast to compensate for the loss of sales and income.

Very few businesses act fast enough when, in hindsight, the writing was always on the wall.

They act slowly because (take your pick):

- They are optimists in general and expect things to get better.

- They feel a moral responsibility to their staff and keep paying them, although they can't afford ALL of them.

- They don't actually look at their numbers or they don't look often enough..

- Pride, ego, or stupidity gets in the way.

- It's easier to do nothing than act.

Do not go into debt to finance operations of an established business. Downsize and downsize fast to make expenses less than income.

Don't ignore facts, downsize fast.

Cunningly Clever
Service

CHAPTER   87

Does Your Business Have a Good or Bad Reputation for Service?

A business exists to create customers.
PETER F. DRUCKER

One of the very best ways to differentiate your business is by offering legendary service. While a reputation can be built, enhanced, and even achieved with sales and marketing, at some point your reputation is going to be put to the test. You may be the fastest gun in the West on all the wanted posters, but when the other guy staring you down draws, that's not going to count for much unless you really are fast. When you can back your reputation up with legendary service you immediately vault yourself to the top echelon of whatever industry you are in.

It's a funny thing, but in all my years in the karate business—a business that is not noted for any of the values it espouses such as self-discipline, loyalty, and integrity—I have never met an instructor with a *bad* reputation. This is an interesting fact only because every instructor I meet can name several people just down the street who have *terrible* reputations. The instructor talking, of course, always has a good reputation—at least he thinks he does. But then again so do some of the instructors down the street! It's pretty much the same when talking with mechanics, chiropractors, real estate agents—in fact, just about everyone.

So how are reputations, good or bad, formed in the minds of the public? How much of any person's or company's reputation is true and how much is hype? The fact is it really doesn't matter because in the minds of the public, *perception is reality*. If we see someone stepping out of a limousine in front of a ritzy hotel, we automatically assume that the person is rich, successful, and perhaps even powerful or famous. If we see a company whose stock is rising, we assume it must be doing well; if it's falling, we assume it must be doing poorly. If other people tell us a particular restaurant is good or bad, we are inclined to believe them. The fact that our taste may be totally different from theirs doesn't really enter into it; a good reputation is good and a bad reputation is bad. Most people won't take the time or effort to confirm either way; instead they will just accept things as they appear to be right up until something happens to change their minds to the contrary.

This is the point at which the hype, the posturing, the positioning, the marketing, the promotions, and the advertising must take a back seat to good old-fashioned service.

- Can you deliver the goods?

- Can you back up the position you claimed?

- Are you who we think you are?

There is already a buzz out there about your business; what is it saying...?

**When it comes to customer service,
customer perception is reality.**

CHAPTER 88

On a Scale of One to Ten, How Good Is Your Company's Service?

It is not the employer who pays the wages.
Employers only handle the money. It is the
customer who pays the wages.
HENRY FORD

If you asked each of the following—all very nice people—whether they feel they have a good reputation for service, each would unequivocally say yes. Each would tell you how they love working with people, how they are excited about their jobs, and how everyone who deals with them has good things to say about them. All would be wrong, because the service, or the follow-up service I received from each will forever brand these people in my mind as also-rans.

The first house I bought in Florida generated a very large commission for the real estate agent who was both the listing and the selling agent. She spent a grand total of one day with my wife and me before we bought it. Now, admittedly, for one reason or another we didn't move in on time, but the fact remains she spent less than eight hours on a deal that made her firm tens of thousands of dollars. Did we have fruit waiting in the kitchen, a bottle of Dom Perignon, or a thank you card? NO! In fact we got nothing—way to build your reputation lady.

When I bought my first Ferrari several years ago from a very nice salesman in Newport Beach, California and referred him to a friend the following week who bought a Porsche, how did he thank me? Actually, he didn't—well that's not quite true. He did thank me when I dropped my friend off to pick up his new Porsche—when I was standing right in front of him. After that, no card, no wine, not even a $15 Ferrari key ring. Translation: Ralph I love you, but I'm not going to buy another car from you.

I have been a loyal Avis customer for about 20 years but I'm ready to try someone else because, despite a great slogan—"We try harder"—they have disappointed me too many times recently. Like on vacation in France when I lost my key to the rental car. Nine hours later, after taking a $200 cab ride, I had a new car. It took five hours for them to send a tow truck, break into the car, deposit my belongings on the side of the road, and leave me there. Seriously—to my utter astonishment they drove off! When I got back to the airport, they then charged me $150 for losing the key. Trying to fight it in my limited French was just not worth it, but they will lose $10,000 a year worth of business because of it.

The service provided by most companies (including yours and mine) is NOT nearly as good as they think it is.

CHAPTER 89

Wonderful Service Attracts Business Like a Magnet

Give the public everything you can give them, keep the place as clean as you can keep it, keep it friendly.
WALT DISNEY

We all have stories about people from whom we thought we would get superior service, but in the end were disappointed. Then, at the other end of the service and reputation spectrum, there is Rolls Royce.

The Legendary Rolls

Back in the early 1950s there was a legendary tale of service told by a new Rolls Royce owner who decided to travel on the Continent. While motoring through Switzerland in just his second week of ownership, his car broke down. He called the dealership, who called the factory. He was immediately put up at the very best hotel, given complimentary champagne, and fed the most wonderful food imaginable. In the meantime, a factory mechanic left Crewe and was flown by private plane to the Swiss Alps. It took almost a day for him to reach the car and two more days to fix the problem, but they were enjoyable days since the owner had been provided with additional transportation befitting a Rolls Royce owner. Several years later the same problem occurred again and the owner explained his previous problem to the dealership, along with a wonderful tale of how the problem was solved. The dealership called the factory. They categorically denied that a Rolls Royce had ever broken down anywhere, let alone in Switzerland, but were glad to fix the problem.

Apple Magic

I bought one of the first iPhones. The sound didn't work; they overnighted me a new one and a package in which to send mine back. A couple of days later, they told me just to keep the new one. A few months later, I broke it; they were just as quick to replace it. In fact, I was so impressed with their service I switched my entire company to Macs when it came time to buy new computers.

Legendary Club Service

Despite the fact that the golf industry prides itself on service, I have only been blown away by service twice in over thirty years of playing golf around the world. Once was at the Robert Trent Jones Golf Club playing in an event and the other at Trump National. The event at RTJ was the best-run event I ever played in. The staff remembered my name from a year previously. When I left my golf shoes in my locker with a missing spike, the following day my shoes had been polished and given a NEW SET of spikes. All the competitors were given lockers with their names on them, and the club gave out pin-location sheets even for the practice rounds. There were a host of other little details, like great food and wonderful course conditions, all of which produced a memorable event.

At Trump National the first time, I was impressed that I was greeted then led to the locker rooms and introduced to the attendant rather than being pointed in the general direction as is usually the case. I was given a locker, a towel, and a bottle of water, then driven to the range to warm up and wait for my host. After my round, when I walked out of the clubhouse, my car was already pulled up and running, "Since it's such a hot day, Mr. Wood, we took the liberty of bringing the car up and getting the A/C cool for you." Nice!

Wonderful service attracts attention simply because it's so rare.

CHAPTER 90

Why Your Service Probably Sucks

A satisfied customer—we should have him stuffed!
BASIL FAWLTY,
in the classic BBC series *Fawlty Towers* with John Cleese

No business wants to give bad service, but most do an alarmingly average job at best.

Why?

Take your pick:

- Most businesses don't have enough staff to give great service.

- You haven't defined what great service is.

- Staff are not trained on how to give great service.

- Staff are not rewarded for giving great service.

- Staff are not empowered to give great service by making their own decisions to quickly resolve issues in the customers' favor.

- You don't charge enough and therefore don't pay enough to attract great talent to your business, or people who care.

- Customers' expectations are unreasonable to begin with.

Did I miss anything?

So what should you do, just give up?

No, of course not. But the first step to better service is an HONEST and independent evaluation of your current service.

Ask Your Customers

Ask customers for honest and critical opinions on your operation. Do not argue or try to defend your points, just shut up and listen. Use surveys, telephone interviews, and idea boxes to solicit and generate ways to improve your service. Almost every innovation we have added to our consulting services over the years has been born out of a client's suggestion for improvement.

Ask questions like:

- How do you think we could improve the appearance of the business?

- How could we have a better merchandise display?

- Do our hours of operation suit your lifestyle?

- What specific improvements or additions could we make to serve you better?

- What do you like best about our service? (When people are slow with these responses, you have lots to do.)

- What do you think is worst about our service?

Hire a Consultant to Help You
Make Amazing Discoveries

In addition to direct customer feedback, another invaluable tool is to get a different pair of eyes examining your business, even if they are from a totally unrelated sector. You are never the best person to judge your own operation. Quite simply, you often can't see the forest for the trees. Sometimes you need to have an outside consultant come in and point out the obvious things that you can't see.

If you can't use a consultant, solicit opinions from friends, colleagues, and peers. Invite them to ask dumb questions about your sign-up procedure, sales pitch, follow up, and service. By encouraging them to do so, you will often discover areas that could be improved. You will make amazing discoveries such as that your office smells funny or that what you think is a clean bathroom doesn't cut it. You might discover that you confuse your clients with too many choices during the sign-up conference. You might find you are charging too little for your service, as is often the case when I consult with a business.

Not all of this feedback will be useful, of course, but it really does pay huge dividends to have outside people come into your operation and open your eyes to what is going on around you.

Step one to better service is an independent review to benchmark where you are now.

CHAPTER 91

Quantifying Superior Service

A satisfied customer is the best business strategy of all.
MICHAEL LEBOEUF

Goals are a great place to start when it comes to improving service, but what exactly is good service? Ask that question of most people and the net result of your answers will be, "I can't quite describe it but I know it when I get it!"

Good service is like good taste; it varies in the eye of the beholder. However, a major reason that poor service happens in most businesses and organizations is that good service is not *quantified*. Sure it's talked about, talked about, and talked about again, but rarely is it taken to the next step and quantified in a host of different ways. As you no doubt already know from other areas of your business, what gets measured is what gets done.

With that thought in mind, I suggest that you sit down with your staff and identify as many areas as you can in which service is given. For example:

- How quickly will the phone be answered—how many rings are acceptable?

- How quickly will customers entering your store be greeted?

- How quickly will you take their order?

- What extras do you offer your best customers? Others?

- How often will you send follow-up cards, thank-you cards, or reminders?

- What's the first thing to say when you have a complaint?

- How quickly will you resolve any billing problems?

- How and when will you thank people for their referrals?

- What level do you want to keep your number of monthly complaints below?

- What can you do in response to a complaint?

- What are ten examples of things that make great service?

The above are just a few examples. Your business will have other criteria specific to your industry or service. By specifically quantifying how you intend to measure performance, including measures for intangible things, you take a quantum jump in your ability to achieve higher levels of service performance.

Quantifying service criteria produces instant improvements.

CHAPTER 92

Make Employees—All Employees—
Service Oriented

*Do what you do so well that they will want to see it
again and bring their friends.*
WALT DISNEY

A fact that often goes unnoticed by executives in ivory towers is that, despite the best advertising, media relations, and
good intentions in the world, reputations are generally won and
lost on the front lines.

An airline is not judged by the quality of its captain or
management, but by its flight attendants and its ticketing agents.
I do not use a certain major airline (American) because their
ticket lady called me an idiot when I asked her to sign me up for
their frequent-flyer program and she found that my travel agent
had already done it automatically. Then she told me to make sure
I had the second number removed when I got off the plane in
Dallas. Despite my better judgment, I asked her to do it for me.
She refused, saying she only had thirty minutes before the flight
took off and had to deal with other passengers.

Now that may have been an isolated event, but the following
week when my Delta flight was canceled due to an equipment
problem, I was forced to fly American again, and I found myself
once again standing in line with the same lady at the counter.
This time it was the person in front of me who suffered her wrath.

Now it's unfair, irrational, and silly that I would judge the entire company of American Airlines on just two incidents with one unhappy woman, but I never flew them again.

A car dealership, copier showroom, or electronics store is only partially judged by the models it sells; its salespeople and customer service staff are more important.

The best way to get all employees into a service mode is to simply tell every new employee that their number-one job, regardless of position or job description, is customer service. Let them know that if they cannot answer a question or help a customer, they are to help that customer locate someone else who can.

Or take that customer's name and offer to have the correct person call them back later that day. Like anyone else, employees will rise to the level of your expectations only if they are given clear directions.

The very best move you can make to improve service is simply to empower your employees to make customer service decisions on the front lines. Small problems handled quickly stay small problems. Small problems referred to a non-present supervisor or manager fester and grow larger quickly.

Customer service is everyone's job.

CHAPTER 93

Why Customers Leave

*There is only one boss. The customer. And he can fire
everybody in the company from the chairman on down,
simply by spending his money somewhere else.*
SAM WALTON

Because of the nature of business, it's easy to forget that if we do not meet the needs of customers, they will simply leave. If they leave with an unsolved problem, they are liable to tell a whole bunch of people about their problem.

According to various studies, here is a breakdown of why people stop doing business with any particular person or company:

- 1% get injured, ill, or die

- 2% just disappear or get lost in the shuffle

- 4% move away from the area

- 6% change activities because of friends

- 9% leave because of cost

- 10% of people just love to complain

- 68% of customers leave because of indifference to them.

Let's take a moment to look at that last statistic. Almost two-thirds of all lost customers leave because of perceived indifference to them.

Perceived indifference is the leading reason customers leave.

CHAPTER 94

Existing Customers Are
More Important Than
Ones You Don't Have Yet

There's a place in the world for any business that takes
care of its customer—after the sale.
HARVEY MACKAY

Don't treat new customers or prospects better than old customers. It is very easy to fall into this trap and it's a surefire recipe for the destruction of your reputation and your business. For example, it's not unusual for a business to cut prices for new customers to attract their business while charging established accounts more money. All the explanations in the world are not going to change the mind of the existing customer that he is getting a raw deal.

A great way to make sure you are doing your best is to always act like your client has just told you she is considering another service. What would you do differently to try and keep that client from leaving? Well, first of all you would try to find out what was wrong, right? But let's suppose there is nothing in particular, or at least nothing the client is willing to share with you, then what?

In the karate business, we developed a five-step process for increasing customer loyalty when their interest started to wane. You should consider developing a similar system to aid in getting your clients back on track. Let's say that a ten-year-old child has expressed to us that he is losing interest in taking lessons; here are the steps we would then take:

- First, we are going to make sure he has extra fun over the next few weeks.

- Second, we are going to make sure he feels special. We might have him help teach the class to make him feel important, or have him help with a new student.

- Third, we are going to set up a test date just beyond his renewal date, which will encourage him to stay and reach his next goal.

- Fourth, we are going to provide him with encouragement and small rewards, perhaps a patch for his uniform.

- Fifth, we are going to contact the parents and let them know just how proud we are of Johnny's progress and all the things he is going to achieve in the future.

In short, we are going to go out of our way to do anything in our power to make sure Johnny doesn't quit. But you know as well as I do that most clients do not give warning before riding into the sunset, never to be seen again. The solution is to simply treat each and every client as though they were thinking of quitting. When you do, you will soon see a dramatic improvement in your customer service and retention.

Treat each and every client as though they were considering quitting.

CHAPTER 95

The Customer Is *Not* Always Right

The Constitution only gives people the right to pursue
happiness. You have to catch it yourself.
BENJAMIN FRANKLIN

Customers can be jerks who don't deserve your service at all. I recently found myself in the Denver airport waiting for a flight back to Orlando. At the last minute they announced a gate change followed by the dreaded announcement that the flight had been canceled. We were instructed to go across the terminal to American Airlines Gate 26 where we were told some of us would get a seat.

Being pretty quick on my feet, I was the first one from our flight to make it over there, only to find that 50 American passengers were already in front of me. I took my place in line and prepared to wait. A few minutes later the rest of the passengers from my original flight showed up and groaned at the sizable line. One man had no intention of being put out. He was a large man wearing a white suit with matching hat and carrying a large leather bag. He marched right to the front of the line waving his ticket in his hand.

"Young lady, I want a first-class seat on this plane and I want it now!" he said. The attractive young blonde looked up at him and politely pointed to the line suggesting that he take his place at the rear. On hearing this, the man, already flushed from the long walk, announced in a voice bordering on rage, "Do you know who I am?"

Cool as a cucumber, the woman picked up the PA microphone and spoke softly into it: "Ladies and gentlemen we have a large man in a white suit who seems to have forgotten who he is. If anyone knows his identity please check with an agent at Gate 26."

Moving at a surprising speed considering his girth, the man quickly vanished and, for the record, did not board the plane.

At Los Angeles Airport last year, I was on a Southwest flight bound for Las Vegas when the woman in front of me started to give the ticket agent a hard time. I'm not sure what it was about since I wasn't paying attention, but the woman was getting increasingly angry while the agent was obviously trying her best to be nice. Finally the agent decided that she had had enough abuse and taking the ticket from the woman, credited back her charge card and invited her to fly another airline. The woman was shocked. "You can't do that!" she said.

"Oh, but I already have," came the reply.

Herb Kelleher, co-founder and former CEO of Southwest backed up his employees when it came to unreasonable customers, as this passage from the book *Nuts! Southwest Airlines' Crazy Recipe for Business and Personal Success* shows:

> *Herb Kelleher [...] makes it clear that his employees come first—even if it means dismissing customers. But aren't customers always right? "No, they are not," Kelleher snaps. "And I think that's one of the biggest betrayals of employees a boss can possibly commit. The customer is sometimes wrong. We don't carry those sorts of customers. We write to them and say, 'Fly somebody else. Don't abuse our people.'"*

If you follow conventional wisdom, you probably bend over

backwards for your customers, even when they are obviously in the wrong. I, however, have a different view. Contrary to popular belief, I think that the customer is not always right; in fact they are very often wrong.

Letting overbearing customers walk over you or your employees can have a very poor effect on morale. That's why Southwest Airlines gives its employees the power to refund tickets to obnoxious passengers. They don't expect their people to take abuse and they are rewarded with exceptional employee loyalty.

In small matters, allowing a customer to take advantage of a situation might work out for the best. However, in larger matters or matters of basic human politeness it pays to stand your ground. For example, in one of my karate schools the parents supposedly watching their children from the lobby made so much noise that it was impossible to teach class. After asking for their co-operation for a couple of weeks with little success, I simply eliminated the waiting area entirely. They complained, they grumbled, but classes were much better, students were not coached from the bench and several parents privately praised the decision.

Eliminating bad customers early in a relationship will save you a lot of heartache and your employees will thank you.

CHAPTER 96

Why Pan Am Went Bankrupt, and What Delta and Others Learned From Their Mistakes

Care more than others think wise. Risk more than oth-ers think safe. Dream more than others think practical. Expect more than others think possible.
HOWARD SCHULTZ,
CEO, Starbucks Coffee

If you ever watch any spy movies from the 1960s or 1970s, or for that matter any movie from that era depicting a flight over-seas, you will see an almost identical shot of a Pan Am 747 taking off and touching down with a little puff of smoke coming off its tires. Ever since Pan Am went bust 20+ years ago, I have been a loyal Delta flyer. Yep, they accepted my Pan Am frequent flyer points! Since then I have flown half a million miles and reached Silver Medallion status. In other words, I am one of their best customers. So naturally they treat me as "special"! They charge me $400 a year to access the Crown Room lounge. They provide me with a special Frequent Flyer 800 number that gets answered more slowly than the DMV, and instantly try everything to ac-commodate me when my travel plans change, including advising me to fly a different airline. (More on that later.)

I recently booked a flight from Tampa to JFK for $400.50. No sooner had I booked it than the phone rang and a prospect, two hours further out on Long Island than JFK, called and said he'd give me his business if I came to see him. I called Delta back to change my flight to Islip instead of JFK. I was told it was no problem and that for an additional $497 I could make the change. I confirmed this fact not once but three times; such was my disbelief.

I hung up, went online, and found that I could book the new itinerary from scratch for just $333. Added to the cost of my original ticket, this priced my two tickets at $733 or $164 LESS than calling Delta and asking them to change my ticket. I got busy, waited an hour and called Delta again. By this time the price of the ticket I wanted had dropped to $315! I asked them to cancel my original non-refundable ticket and help me apply the balance towards the purchase of a new ticket. This done, I was able to pay the $100 fee and buy the cheaper ticket to Islip, keep the same return flights, and only be out $14. All it took was one hour, three phone calls, and an eternity on hold. In fact after holding for 15 minutes to complete the change, I held for 10 more minutes before the re-ticketing agent could come on the line and confirm what the first agent had already done…And remember, I am one of Delta's best customers! The third agent even suggested I call Delta's web help desk to see if they would waive the $100 fee since I had bought the ticket so recently. I declined because it would take more time and several more phone calls. And the airlines want to know why their business is so bad and why they are losing millions a month!

Running a major airline is complicated…BUT should it be so complicated that buying a one-way ticket on a competing airline (the Delta gate agent's advice) makes far more sense than paying double to fly on a half-empty flight because I wanted to get back to my family a day earlier on a 10-day business trip?

Anyway, the answer to the riddle in the headline, "Why Did

Pan Am Go Bankrupt & What Did Delta and Others Learn from Their Mistakes," is amazingly simple.

Obviously, they learned nothing. And on top of it, you now have to show up two hours early for every trip even if it's only a 50-minute flight. Then you get to wait another 30 minutes for your luggage to saunter down the final 700 yards of an 800-mile trip. What's truly amazing about the airline business is not that they are hurting, but how any of them actually stay in business. Can you run your business like that? I know I can't.

Eliminate poor pricing strategies from your business; nothing infuriates customers more.

CHAPTER 97

Golf Course Dress Codes, Cell Phones, and Snobs

There is more stupidity than hydrogen in the universe,
and it has a longer shelf life.
FRANK ZAPPA

Every industry has their stupid, unfriendly, non-customer-centric policies, but the golf industry in which I often work has more than most. Following are just a few shining examples.

At North Berwick Golf Club (Scotland) on a damp and foggy morning, I was asked to remove my $100 navy-blue, water-resistant sleeveless sweater with the logo of a very high-end club on it as, according to the steward, it constituted rain gear which was not allowed in the clubhouse. I had just stepped out of my car and I protested that it was my only sweater, that it was dry, and that I was cold. To which came the reply, "You'll warm up in a wee minute as soon as ye get yer coffee in yea." Which, loosely translated means "I don't give a damn. Take it off if you want to come in!" I did take it off, but was cold for 15 minutes while I waited for my coffee to arrive and warm me up. Yes, I know I was a guest and should just be delighted to be there, but instead I was cold and irritated.

Gullane (Scotland) is a monster of a course at almost 6,200 yards with the fairways hard as rock after weeks of high temperatures and no rain, thus ensuring that even a missed hit went

300 yards. We were forbidden to play the back tees (very typical in England and Scotland, as they consider it a privilege for the members, and, even then, only in tournaments). So we played Gullane at 5,800 yards or less with a driver and a sand wedge. If I had wanted to play pitch and putt, I could have done that on the free course at the Gullane village green. I felt cheated!

My club bans jeans (as most clubs do), a policy that costs my club about $3000 of my business because I can't be bothered to change to go to the club for lunch. (Besides, I look better in a pair of $150 Armani jeans than Bob Lynch looks in his 1978 brown polyester Sears slacks!) Some clubs allow black denim jeans, but no blue jeans.

Now I'm not asking to play in jeans, but how about you let me go in the club restaurant for a burger at lunchtime? At most clubs I have to wear shorts to my knees which makes it hard to walk, especially when it's dripping hot. What is wrong with tailored tennis shorts to play golf in? I've seen Jack Nicklaus play in them several times, and if it's good enough for Jack, it ought to be good enough for everyone else. I'm not asking for jogging shorts—I just want to be able to walk in comfort. Besides, the people who make these stupid rules are not the ones walking in 90-degree heat and carrying golf bags.

Let's take the tee-time reservation policy, which at most private clubs is that reservations cannot be made more than seven days in advance. What if you have a guest coming from out of town and you want to make sure you can get a tee time that coincides with his flights in and out four weeks from now? At a private club, why should that be a big deal? Isn't it member-centric to take care of situations like this for the enjoyment of the member and the traveling guest? Try doing it most places and you get the old "my hands are tied story." Or they will do it but only after the director of golf, club manager, or club secretary has stepped in to help.

At a private club why does the driving range close at 5 or 6 PM? What difference does it make (except the day the range is being cut) if I want to hit balls until dark? I really don't need any supervision. At my club, they leave all the balls out six nights a week, so it's not an issue of theft.

I could go on and on but I won't... Slay some scared cows in your business to make doing business with you fun, easy, and customer centric.

Eliminate STUPID, non-customer-friendly policies from your business.

CHAPTER 98

Usurping Murphy's Law

The more durable your equipment is, the further away
from civilization you'll be when it fails.
UNKNOWN

Murphy's law pretty much guarantees that if you have a problem with a customer that you resolve to fix, something will also go wrong with the planned fix, adding insult to injury. Here are some ways to help fix customer problems:

1. Listen to the problem in its entirety without interrupting.

2. If necessary, clarify the exact nature of the problem by asking questions.

3. Acknowledge the problem and show you understand it.

4. Apologize.

5. Propose a solution to the problem.

6. Give the solution a timeline.

7. Log the entire conversation, proposed action, and timeline in your CRM system (failing that, at least write it down somewhere).

8. Schedule a follow-up call to make sure the fix is to the customer's satisfaction. (Schedule frequent benchmark calls if it's a large project.)

9. Apologize again, and assure the customer of superior performance going forward.

10. This is the point where I also give them my cell number and tell them if they are not happy for any reason to call me personally. People like it when they think they have the owner/boss's ear.

11. Depending on how large the problem was, you may want to offer some additional value to help smooth things over. Always offer additional value rather than discounting.

12. "Red flag" the customer to let everyone on staff know that this customer needs additional TLC.

When fixing problems or responding to requests, you must always have a failsafe system to ensure that the actual requests, however simple, were carried out. Nothing damages a reputation more than a few simple promises not carried to their successful conclusion. People then start to wonder: If he can't take care of such a little thing, how can he take care of the bigger problems I entrust him with? Never promise something you cannot deliver, however small an item it may be. Always underpromise and overdeliver.

Easy to say, harder to do.

A system to follow up on complaints will always produce superior results.

CHAPTER 99

The Beauty of Accessibility

There are no traffic jams along the extra mile.
ROGER STAUBACH,
Hall of Fame NFL Quarterback

Go to any large company and try to find a phone number you can call and actually speak to a human being. Most hide behind FAQ pages that seldom seem to answer YOUR UNUSUAL QUESTION. They hide behind "contact us" with a drop-down menu of choices, none of which actually matches your issue. If you do find an 800 number to call, it's usually a voice mail sending you back to the website or an endless loop of choices you can't actually execute because you don't have the 15-digit code they want (in fact that's why you're calling).

When clients want to get hold of you, they want to do it now. Few things are more irritating than calling a service provider and being shuffled to voice mail automatically, with little or no indication whether the person you are looking for is in the office or traveling through Kenya on safari. I made a huge leap in business and customer service at my karate schools when I bought a cellular phone and answered my phone sixteen hours a day instead of eight.

I do the same thing now; I answer my phone sixteen hours a day. Any one of my clients can get me almost around the clock. Those who can't find me get a detailed voice mail that lets them know exactly when to expect a call back, or asks for a specific time and number where I can reach them after seven o'clock, in the evening, or on weekends, as the case may be.

If nothing else, tell your receptionist *when* you will be returning calls so that the person waiting for the call can continue with his or her daily life. Nothing irritates most people more than being told they would be called right back, only to be hanging by the phone for hours waiting for the call.

Don't hide on your website: put up pictures, short bios, contact emails, and phone numbers for all your key service staff.

Accessibility is a simple advantage you can offer that others won't.

CHAPTER 100

The Power of Personal Information

All things being equal, people will do business with
people they like; all things being unequal, people will
still do business with people they like.
MARK McCORMACK,
founder, IMG

Many business relationships today come down to just that—the relationship. The deeper you understand your clients' wants, needs, prejudices, and personal interests—above and beyond the actual business—the greater the chance you have of serving them for the long haul. Simple touches like birthday cards, Christmas cards, and anniversary cards go a lot further than the dollar you spend. Keep credit card numbers and customers' sizes on file so you don't have to continually ask for them. Keep notes on their favorite beverages, cigars, or foods so that you and your staff can access them. Developing a customer profile is a must to legendary service.

The profile I use has over one hundred questions about my clients that I fill in over time, through various conversations. This includes where they were born, where they went to school, what their parents did, what sports they like, what teams they support, which cars they drive, what religion they are, and so on. Some of these things I ask point blank, others my clients tell me over time in the natural flow of conversation. All of this information is deeply valuable in building a relationship and turning conversations toward *their* areas of interest rather than *mine*.

After each visit, my dentist calls my house that evening to make sure I feel alright. Not only that, but after he referred me to a physician, he found out when the surgery was scheduled and called me that night to see how it had gone. When my child was born, I was sent a bottle of wine with his label on it. This is someone whom I only see every six months, yet he acts as if he was almost part of the family. The result of this dentist's attention to service: Even when I moved my business over fifty miles away, I still drive to his office for appointments. He had backed up his reputation with service.

Most people have a relationship with just one person at a company, or within a specific family. When that person moves on (new job, divorce, etc.), it can create real problems. Go deeper into the company (or family) than just the person you happen to be dealing with. Make friends with the secretary or whoever answers the phone. Ask to be introduced to other members of the company or family. The deeper you go beyond your primary contact, the longer you will keep the business.

The more you know about your customers, the deeper the bonds between you will be.

CHAPTER 101

Keep the Tiger Behind the Bamboo

Silence never yet betrayed anyone!
ANTOINE DE RIVAROL,
French writer

Often, especially in situations where you spend a lot of time with a particular client, there is the temptation to cross the boundary and share personal information or problems. In the course of normal conversation, they may even ask questions or probe about your personal life.

You need to be open, but in reality they are not interested in your problems. Do not be conned into sharing them. Find out everything you can about your customers, while saying little or nothing about negative aspects of your own life. As the Chinese say, "Keep the tiger behind the bamboo." This will only add to your sense of control. Since you seem to be in complete control of everything, it will also help build your reputation faster.

Never tell your customers about your problems; they don't care.

CHAPTER 102

Training Your Customers to Receive Great Service

No matter what your product is, you are ultimately in the education business. Your customers need to be constantly educated about the many advantages of doing business with you, trained to use your products more effectively, and taught how to make never-ending improvements in their lives.
ROBERT G. ALLEN

A large part of *delivering* great service is to get your customers to take advantage of your various services and systems. Often customers blame suppliers for their own problems or shortcomings. Here is an entertaining and informative letter we sent to our golf course partners trying to engage them in helping us help them. Apart from anything else, just letting your customers know on a regular basis that you are committed to great service will help your reputation and gather more input.

Dear John Sample:

George Pye, former greenskeeper at Lilleshall Golf Club, in Shropshire, England, could have been the brother Humpty Dumpty never had, so close were they in physical appearance.

I recall as if it were yesterday, him gazing down at me from the seat of a tractor looking every bit his fifty years in his one pair of oil-stained overalls. His round, toothless face bore the look of utter disgust as he watched yet another of the accursed members take a shoe-sized divot from the middle of the 9th fairway. "Wack," he said loudly. He always called me "Wack" although for the life of me I have no idea why. "This would be a great course if it were not for the golfers!"

George Pye hated golfers with a passion. They took chunks from his beloved grass, left trails through his hand-raked bunkers, and yelled at him to get out of the way when he was trying to cut the fairways with his ancient lawn mowers. More than once I saw the wicked gleam in his face as he swerved those mowers to send a Titleist (golf ball) clattering through the blades to its death. I knew full well he would have preferred instead to have the guest, who had just left a putter-sized dent in the 10th green, writhing in agony beneath his mower blades!

Fortunately we don't feel the same way about the people who pay our salaries.

Our goal has always been to give you, our valued partner, 'legendary' service. Over the last few months of our rapid growth that has not always happened.

In the last two weeks, we have taken the following steps to ensure that our service not only meets—but exceeds—your expectations.

1) We have expanded our technical service department from three to seven people.

2) We have added a second shift and are now open seven days a week from 8:00 am to 8:00 pm for customer support.

3) We have added 8 people to our telemarketing staff, bringing the total to 16 full-time, in-

house representatives. We have also designed a custom software system that allows all 16 to work on a single project at once for faster results.

4) We have added two new marketing-success specialists both of whom are PGA professionals with a host of in-club experience. One of them will contact you in the next 30 days to proactively solicit your feedback and make suggestions about how you can better use your SmartSite or our other services to increase your business.

5) Service tickets are printed out and reviewed daily at 8:00 am by both the service department and management.

6) We have invested in a web-based media and traffic-management program that allows our partners to view the progress of all their print ads, telemarketing, and mailing campaigns, from scripting to media placement. Susan Winter, our Project Manager, will be contacting these partners over the next 30 days to provide login and training.

7) Perhaps most notably, we have put a temporary moratorium on accepting new clients in order to put our full resources into servicing our existing partners.

That said, delivering Legendary Service is a two-way street. To get your service requests handled quickly and accurately, you and/or your staff MUST use the Service Request Ticket System.

In order to provide you with Legendary Service, we request that all service requests are made through your SmartSite ticket system found on your SmartSite home page immediately after you login. If you follow the service request process, then your request will be routed to the correct department and you will be contacted about its progress.

If you simply email your request to a specific person—say me for instance—and I happen to be traveling, that can sometimes cause delays for days in handling your request.

Although we are glad to take both email and verbal requests, they ALL have to end up in the ticket system before the work gets done. We have found that quicker, error-free responses are more likely to come from tickets entered directly into the service system from the person making the service request.

How to Enter Service Requests

If you need help from our staff, whether it involves a change of a page or the creation of a new email account, the most efficient way of communicating your request is through a **service request.** By entering a service request, a communication path is established. We will notify you either by phone or email with questions we may have regarding your service request. We will also notify you directly upon completion of your request.

Please submit a separate service request for each request, problem, or issue. Be as detailed as you can in your request regarding the page, problem, or request.

Service tickets will be generated by each request and responded to as completed.

You can access **Service Request** from your SmartSite home page by clicking on the Service Request area, or you can gain access in the Help section by going to Common Tasks and clicking on "New Service Request." When you click on "New Service Request" a form will appear. On this form it will be necessary to complete all of the fields. The fields on the form are as follows:

- Your Name—the name of the person entering the request.

- Your Phone Number—The best number where we can contact you if questions arise regarding your request.

- Your Email address—The email address that we will use to correspond with you about your service request.

- Email—You may choose to copy anyone you would like on this service request.

- Notify me by—the best method for us to reach you with questions about your request or upon completion of your request.

- Request Type—Enter the type of request this is.

- Priority—When do you need to have it completed by?

- Request Subject—If you were to give a title to this request, what would it be?

- Request Description—Enter a detailed description of your request; you want to be as specific as possible when entering this information.

You may view your service requests at any time by visiting your Help Center and clicking on "view service request" on the sidebar. From here you may view either closed or open tickets.

Please share this procedure with ALL of your staff.

How long should service requests take to complete? That of course depends on the nature of the request. Seemingly insignificant changes like altering the flash show can take hours, while other seemingly difficult requests can be done in minutes. Most simple tasks are done in 24 hours. If your request will take longer than 48 hours, you will be notified.

Thank you for your time and your business. Please let us know if there is anything we can do to help us deliver Legendary Marketing, Service, and Results to you!

All the Best,
Andrew Wood
President
Legendary Marketing

Explain to your customers just how they can get the best service from you.

9

Starting New Ventures and Launching New Products

CHAPTER 103

The Importance of Perfect Timing

Life is all about timing.
CARL LEWIS,
Olympic gold medal winner

I was incredibly fortunate in that fate lead me into the karate business right about the time the second *Karate Kid* movie came out. As Warren Buffet is fond of saying about great companies like Coke, "A ham sandwich could have run a karate school at this time and made a living." Mine was the first karate school in an affluent city of 60,000 people.

My friend Jeff Cohen was fortunate enough to get into the licensing business in the early 1980s before it really exploded. He had the rights to the Farrah poster that adorned every teenage boy's room, but as huge as that was (the best selling poster of all time!) it paled in comparison to his next venture. He took a risk and bought the rights to a very strange looking doll for which he paid $40,000 and 10% royalties. Ten days after the movie opened, he wrote his first check to Stephen Spielberg for $990,000. The movie was *E.T.*

In his book, *How to Get Rich*, billionaire British entrepreneur Felix Dennis, founder of *Maxim* magazine and current publisher of *MacUser, The Week,* and many other publications, tells how luck in timing jump started his career. After seeing some Kung Fu movies, he and a friend decided to write a biography of Bruce Lee. They talked someone into lending them the plane fare, flew to Hong Kong, and showed up at Bruce Lee's apartment unannounced. He graciously talked to them for several hours.

They started writing and tried to interest publishers in their manuscript, but had no luck finding a publisher for their yet unfinished work. Then came an amazing twist of fortune or misfortune, depending on your point of view: Bruce Lee died. The book from two unknown authors became the number-one best-selling book in the world a few days after its publication.

The best businesses in the world can fail if the timing is wrong. While all of these examples have a component of luck, it really does pay to painstakingly research *when* might be the best time to open a new business or introduce a new product.

For example, the worst months for a karate school are the summer months, so you'd do far better opening in September rather than June. There is no point in paying three month's rent to sit on your hands while the kids are on vacation. The very best month to sell any type of health and fitness product is January. Opening an ice cream store in November won't make much sense most places unless you live in the Sun Belt. People read more in the winter than the summer, so January is by far the best month to sell things by mail and August the worst. Think very carefully about your timing when launching anything new, it can make or break a venture.

Get your timing right.

CHAPTER 104

Pioneers Get Shot

When I was a kid I never learned to play.
I actually got in bands through
watching people play and copying them.
CHARLIE WATTS,
Rolling Stones

If you watch any of the old western movies, there is a common theme in all of them that's just as true today. Pioneers often get arrows in the back. Among Silicon Valley high-tech firms there is a variation of this that says there is a dangerous *bleeding* edge beyond the cutting edge of innovation.

Yes, pioneers have the greatest opportunities to stake a claim or find the mother lode, but they also take the greatest risks. Once they have found gold, oil, or water it's all too easy for someone to set up shop right next to them and tap into the same source from an adjoining field with none of the risk or cost associated with the pioneers' venture.

Being in any market early is risky and costs twice as much as it will cost the next guy to enter the same market. Far better to be the settler who comes along and enjoys the fruits of the valley *after* the pioneer has rid it of dangers.

I was not the first person to put together a monthly package for martial arts school owners, but I was the first guy to get it right and charge a premium fee. Later several other people came into the business, all with shameless copies of my product and all at a lower price. I am sure they made every bit as much money as I did and without any of the development costs.

I created the market; they exploited it.

The same thing happened to me in the golf business. There were a couple of companies doing websites but I was the first to jump on it and create an easy-to-use premium product. Once my approach was proven successful, a whole bunch of people copied my product exactly. They had prices you can afford to charge when you copy, not innovate. While their products were inferior to mine, the majority of the business is unsophisticated enough not to care.

Lots of other companies have failed with the best product early. Sony beta was a better product than VHS, but failed because the other manufacturers had better marketing. Apple's original product was a better product than a PC but had to be bailed out years later by none other than Bill Gates before it succeeded. Lots of people delivered pizza before Domino's perfected that as their marketing strategy. A great many hit shows like *American Idol* were not original, but copied from hit formats in other countries.

Contrary to popular belief, most great products or companies are not great because of an original key idea but because someone has taken a good idea and made it cheaper or marketed it better.

Leveraging off an existing business, product, or idea is far less risky than being a pioneer.

CHAPTER 105

Finding Your Right Niche

I carved out a niche with the Wagnerian repertoire
since I am attracted by its theatrical intensity.
PLACIDO DOMINGO

It is a thousand times easier to make money in niche markets than it is in large or general markets.

I made millions in two niche markets, the karate business and the golf business. Both markets had mailing lists of between 12,000-18,000 prospects and so were easy to reach by mail. Both markets had limited competition when I entered and I had a knowledge of, and a passion for, both businesses.

I have written over twenty books. The two most profitable ones, one making $150,000 the first year and the other over $200,000, were written for these specialized industries. The ones written for mainstream consumption took far longer to reach any kind of critical mass. The bigger the market, the harder and more costly it is to reach.

My first two martial arts schools were both the only schools in town. If you wanted to take karate, you had to take it from me. As various fads such as fitness kickboxing and karate aerobics came and went, I resisted the temptation to offer these and stayed focused on basic martial arts. Many of my friends in the industry did not and, while it helped a few, it hurt the majority of them by shifting the core focus of their business from martial arts to fitness.

It was a different client; they typically paid half of what a karate student paid and stayed involved an even shorter time.

Given the choice to compete with all the national chains and open an auto parts store selling everything, or an auto parts store that specializes in vintage Jaguars, the choice is easy. There are mailing lists and even magazines dedicated to the vintage Jag niche market, and because it's a niche market you will be able to charge more.

Be sure to remember that if you get into the model train business because you love model trains, you are now in the business of SELLING model trains, not merely collecting and running them.

The more specialized your market, the greater your chance of success.

CHAPTER 106

Matching Your Passion to Your Niches

If you work just for money, you'll never make it, but
if you love what you're doing and you always put the
customer first, success will be yours.
RAY KROC,
founder, McDonald's

Make no mistake about it; running your own business is hard. The hours are long, staff unreliable, and customers fickle. The road to success is fraught with red tape, setbacks, and disappointment. That's why you HAVE to have passion for your business. If you are simply interested in a business because you think it might make money but have little real interest in the product or service you provide, you are on a risky path.

You will need all the passion and motivation you can find to deal with the normal roadblocks and stay motivated in the face of adversity. It is very hard to do this in an industry for which you have no passion. Indeed, when I personally lost interest in the martial arts business it immediately started to go downhill, even though I had a staff of twenty people. My lack of passion quickly filtered down.

The more passionate and knowledgeable you are about your product, the more chance you have of success. People can feel passion and enthusiasm in your voice and mannerisms. This goes a long way to helping you attract customers and make sales.

Look at your hobbies—which hobby would make a good business?

Look at your interests—which sport or pastime might you turn into a business?

What do you like to read about or watch on TV?

What do you find yourself talking about that excites you?

What are you naturally good at—what comes easy for you?

When taking a couple of years off after selling my martial arts business, I looked around for what to get back into and the choice was simple. My two biggest passions were golf and marketing, so I opened a golf marketing company.

One word of caution. Don't let your passion cloud your judgment. Just because you have a passion for cooking Italian food doesn't mean you should go right out and open a restaurant without first doing some research. The restaurant business is really tough—the hours are brutal and you can lose money even with great food. You need passion and persistence to survive.

Whatever business you start, it needs to be fueled by passion for that product, service, or industry, not just the desire to make money.

CHAPTER 107

Look for Opportunities with Residual Income Potential

Captain Kirk has been a source of pleasure
and income for a long time.
WILLIAM SHATNER

If at all possible look for a business that has residual income or try to add a component of residual income to your existing business. By residual I mean that people have a reason to keep paying you money, such as a magazine subscription. At the very least find a business with a large group of easy-to-target repeat customers.

It takes just as much time, effort, and money to attract a customer who buys once as it does to attract a customer who keeps buying. Therefore it makes far more sense to get involved in a business where the customer keeps buying on a regular basis.

The number of golf courses that operate as daily-fee (pay as you play) operations rather than operate on a membership basis amazes me. Even those that offer both often favor the daily-fee player since he pays a higher green fee. But, and it's a BIG but, the daily-fee player has to show up 20, 30, or maybe even 40 times before he spends the same amount as a yearly member. If it rains he may not show up. If his buddies are playing another course, he may not show up. If the course down the street offers a deal, he may not show up at yours. It makes far more sense to lock that player into your club with a membership, an annual pass, or a frequent-player card.

When I started in the golf marketing business, I built and sold websites for a fixed fee. This was okay to get started but a bad idea in the long run. Eventually I changed it from a fixed fee to a small setup and a monthly service fee of $295. This gave me less money up front but quickly built my residual income and actually increased my sales since clients no longer had to come up with $5,000 or $6,000 up front. Over time I added services, so the residual went from $295 to $495, to $795, to $1595, and eventually $3,000 a month for larger clients.

You don't have to be a math genius to figure out how much more profitable and predictable this business model is over the one-time sale model. If you sell water conditioning, add a monthly service fee. If you sell air conditioning, add a yearly check-up fee. If you sell estate-planning advice, add a yearly update fee. Even if you sell pizza, sell a card for ten or twenty meals so you are guaranteed more than one night's income immediately.

Whatever type of business you have works better with some kind of residual income component.

Without residual or repeat business, life is hard.

CHAPTER 108

Become a Business Sponge

Invest three percent of your income in yourself
(self-development) in order to guarantee your future.
BRIAN TRACY

Before you start your new venture, commit to becoming a business sponge. Soak up every bit of key information you need to rapidly increase your competence in sales, marketing, time management, and other key entrepreneurial skills that will dramatically affect the ultimate success of your business.

It's a pretty simple yet seldom discussed fact that competence in various disciplines of business brings success, lack of competence—failure.

If you have no money, then you most likely have never studied money, stocks, real estate, or the power of compound interest.

If you don't have enough customers, then you probably don't know enough about marketing.

If you have customers but aren't making enough money, then you probably don't know enough about sales.

If you are having trouble finding time, then you don't know enough about time management.

In my mid-twenties I discovered the amazing power of audio learning. I simply switched off the radio and swapped it for the power of great minds like Brian Tracy, Tom Hopkins,

Dan Kennedy, Jay Abraham, Zig Ziglar, Roger Dawson, Tony Robbins, and a host of others. I quickly learned more about the real world of business in my Audi GT than I had ever learned in school.

Learning in your car takes away the excuse that you don't have time and makes it painless. The car, of course, is not the only place you can rapidly gain knowledge. Books, DVDs, webinars, seminars, and teleconferences can all quickly add to your knowledge base. Focus first on the areas that you know will provide the largest payoff and continue from there.

You must commit a portion of your personal income, 3–5%, and a portion of your week to your own personal growth. If you are not growing, you are shrinking and if you are shrinking you are dying. You can start at www. CunninglyClever.com. There you will find an amazing collection of business information.

The more you know, the more you grow.

CHAPTER 109

What to Do Before Singing "Take This Job and Shove It!"

Twenty years from now you will be more disappointed by the things that you didn't do than by the ones you did do. So throw off the bowlines. Sail away from the safe harbor. Catch the trade winds in your sails.
Explore. Dream. Discover.
MARK TWAIN

Before you start whistling the classic country song "Take This Job and Shove It," be wise and test the waters. Figure out what you can do on a limited scale with your new venture before packing in your current job or wrapping up your existing business.

There are often ways to test a business idea inexpensively before you put all your eggs in one basket. Many karate school owners, yoga instructors, or dance school operators start out in a community center where they can teach classes a few times a week and build up a following before committing to renting a facility and doing it full time.

Many people dealing in antiques, records, books, or other products start out at the local swap meets before (if ever) expanding to a full-time location. The swap meet is an ideal and inexpensive way to test just about any retail concept. You can also try to consign things to existing stores, sell wholesale, and so on.

The Internet offers a host of very low-cost websites like eBay where you can test any product idea quickly to see if it merits more of a full-time effort.

Working for someone else is another great way to gain insight on both what to do and what not to do, even if you only do so for a few months.

Test the waters before committing all of your efforts to a new venture.

CHAPTER 110

Why Businesses Often Fail
When They Expand

If they don't fail outright, most businesses fail to
fully achieve their potential. That's because
the person who owns the business doesn't truly know
how to build a company that works without
him or her...which is the key.
MICHAEL GERBER

Other than the very obvious problems of stretching themselves too thin, both from a cash flow and talent point of view, the number-one reason that causes second locations to fail is simply the lack of business systems. When an owner opens up a second store, he or she naturally assumes that the second store will be run just like the first. The only problem is they forget that you can't be in two places at once.

Business methods and protocol that the owner takes for granted are not followed at the second store, or if the owner opens the second store, they soon go by the wayside at the first location. With systems, this cannot happen.

There is a general misconception about what is involved in creating a business system. Many business owners have some of the components but few manage to put them together and, to be honest, it's not easy. The upside is that once you have systems in place, running your business becomes ridiculously easy and expansion becomes possible. Without systems, expansion becomes a nightmare sooner or later.

A system must have:

1. a set of specific MEASURABLE results

2. a list of the tasks involved to attain the results

3. an orchestration of tasks so that they are done in the correct order

4. scripts

5. training

6. reporting

For example, let's take the mundane task of cleaning your business. First I will ask you the $64,000 question: What is clean? Your idea of clean and my idea of clean may be very different, so, first of all, we must define clean. For example:

- windows have no 5-year-old paw prints

- business smells like a new car, not a high school gym locker

- all trash receptacles are empty

- no cobwebs or dust

- all chairs and equipment are in designated places, etc.

How specific should this list be to QUALIFY as a real system? Well imagine for a moment that you left your Hyatt hotel room for the day and came back at night. How would you know the room had been cleaned?

How many things can you identify? 10? 20?

Okay, the beds have been made, there are fresh towels in the bathroom, and if it's a ritzy place, you might have a candy on the bed. That's three, how many more can you name?

The fact of the matter is, there are 127 different things that a maid in a Hyatt Hotel has to complete in order for the room to be defined as CLEAN! Imagine 127 different checks to make sure your room is clean—and I bet you didn't get past 20.

The remote must be in the right place. The Bible must be in the bedside table. The phone book, free soap, visitors' guides, and phones MUST ALL be in their designated places. Otherwise there would be inconsistency, and inconsistency creates more problems.

The first step to designing systems is to take every task in your business and DEFINE the outcome.

Once the outcome has been made clear, a list of tasks can be assembled to accomplish the outcome, followed by an orchestration of those tasks so that they happen in the right order (like dusting before you vacuum, not afterwards). Scripts can be put in place where needed, and training must be established so that everyone follows the system to the letter.

Finally, reporting must be put in place in the simplest form possible so every task is checked off. In the systems I designed for my business, the check boxes are just big enough for a yes or no, which means they are not big enough to write in an excuse.

McDonald's was so successful in expanding because every little detail was built into a system.

You NEED written systems to expand your business successfully.

CHAPTER 111

What Are Your Two Areas of Superiority?

*Many a small thing has been made large by the right
kind of advertising.*
MARK TWAIN

In order to have a widely successful business it's not necessary to be great at everything, but it is necessary that your business be superior in at least two of the following six areas. Once in a while you will see a superior product take the world by storm or a restaurant opens in the perfect location, but for the most part you need to be good in at least two of the following areas.

In order of importance:

1. Superior pricing or offer—Walmart

2. Superior location—Hotel de Paris, Monaco

3. Superior sales—IBM

4. Superior marketing—Nike

5. Superior product—iPhone

6. Superior service—The Ritz-Carlton

Before you start a business, make sure you know how your business will be superior on at least two of the above dimensions.

In the karate business, I did two things better than any of my competitors. My marketing was superior and I realized I wasn't in the karate business but the business of SELLING karate lessons.

In the golf business, I did two things better than my competition. I provided an easy-to-use "superior" product at a good price.

**You must be superior in at least
two key areas to succeed and more is better.**

CHAPTER 112

Ten Ways to Get the Cash You Need to Start or Grow Your Business

I'd say it's been my biggest problem all my life…
it's money. It takes a lot of money to make
these dreams come true.
WALT DISNEY

Here are ten ways that entrepreneurs get the money they need to finance a start-up or growth.

1. Bootstrapping. Sad and frustrating although it may seem, bootstrapping is very likely your best financing option. While it means growth will be slower than if you had cash on hand, you will be more careful how you spend it and more critical of the results. You will make your mistakes inexpensively and learn by doing. You will owe no one, keep all your equity, and lose none of your friends. I managed to build my first million-dollar business on this basis in about three years. While the hours were long and the effort hard, the satisfaction of doing it and owing no one was tremendous.

2. Credit Cards. I have done this twice and gotten away with it both times, once to the tune of $127,000 spread over nine credit cards. I do not advise you do this. The downside is potentially devastating, ruining your credit for seven years if you go bankrupt.

3. Grants. It's possible to get government, state, or local government grants to fund some or all of your business. They come in every shape and size depending on your geographical location and personal situation. The local SCORE, SBDC, or government pages of the Internet are a good place to start looking. You will, of course, need a business plan.

4. Business Loan. There is a wonderful plaque in the Ferrari museum in Modena, Italy that tells of Enzo Ferrari's dream:

You are very unlikely to be so lucky because banks as a rule really do only lend money to people who have money.

5. Home equity loan. I have used this strategy on a number of occasions, most recently to pay cash for an office building, thus really just trading one equity position for another. Using equity to trade for real estate that can be turned back into cash is one thing. Using it for cash flow is dangerous.

6. Loans from friends or family. Securing loans from friends and family is usually not that hard. In fact you may be surprised how willing people are to help a solid idea backed by a written business plan. The problems only start if the plan doesn't work. Remember, 95% of all first-time small businesses fold in the first few years. When people lose money, friendships get strained and often break entirely. Proceed with extreme caution.

7. Equity partners. Giving up equity means giving up control. Even minority partners can sue you at any time to get their money back. It can be easy to get equity partners; it can bring talent as well as cash. But the downside is huge if it doesn't work out.

8. Sellers. There are people looking to sell their businesses in just about every city in the world. For one reason or another— health, divorce, change of focus, etc.—they just want out. Very often there may be no viable market for the business and so the owner is forced to finance the purchase.

I bought several of my first few karate schools for no money down. In fact in a couple of cases I got the going business for absolutely nothing as the doctor who owned them had lost interest and just wanted his name off the lease. The businesses were barely breakeven but they were up and running and in a matter of months I had turned them around, having spent no money to do so.

9. Suppliers. There are many industries in which suppliers are willing to put up some or all of the money to make you a distributor of their product. For example it's typical in England for breweries to offer very generous loan terms to publicans looking to buy a pub, provided of course they commit to selling that brewery's brand. Dental supply houses will often finance new dental offices. Even if they won't lend you the money you will often find larger suppliers willing to give you their goods on the basis that you pay them when you sell them (consignment), which is another way of getting financed in retail..

10. Customers. By far the best way to find cash is to find it from your customers, either existing or future. How do you do that? You pre-sell memberships before you build your golf course. You pre-sell condos before you break ground. Pre-sell health club memberships before you open. You require payment up front to develop custom software. You sell options to buy your product, like say an exotic car. Recently I saw the Jim Russell Racing School offering a lifetime membership for $295,000. We did the same thing in the martial arts business, selling black belt programs 3-4 years up front for $3000 or more.

In fact if you think about it there are a lot more companies using this method of financing than you might have thought.

Bootstrapping, suppliers, sellers of businesses, or customers offer your best options for financing.

CHAPTER 113

How a Magazine I Published Lost $40,000 a Year and Was My Key to Making Millions

Don't let the opinions of the average man sway you.
Dream, and he thinks you're crazy. Succeed, and he
thinks you're lucky. Acquire wealth, and he thinks
you're greedy. Pay no attention.
He simply doesn't understand.
ROBERT G. ALLEN

There had been one or two attempts to publish a martial arts business magazine by the time I launched my first issue in 1992, but they were flawed attempts. Although the products were good, both attempts tried to survive on the classic magazine model of selling advertising. Other than a couple of major suppliers, there were simply not enough vendors to support a magazine through ads alone.

Despite publishing for five years with the long-term support of several vendors, my magazine never made a net profit from ads sales. What it did accomplish was far more important and far more profitable than ad sales alone could ever be.

First, publishing your own magazine to an industry of 15,000 or so schools was not as expensive as you might think — about $18,000 an issue — with ad sales picking up about 80% of the cost. This meant I essentially got into the magazine business with no money, as my advertisers had to pay in advance. (Good way to get financed.)

Despite losing an average of $4,000 per issue, the upside was huge: instant credibility. I was my own Randolph Hearst. I could say whatever I wanted about me, my competitors, and the various other suppliers in the industry. I could, in fact, influence a great many people.

1. I got to sell my own books, manuals, tapes, seminars, and my monthly $250 business-success package. This alone easily surpassed the $4,000 deficit from the magazine twenty times over.

2. I got to reward my clients by featuring them on the cover of the magazine (priceless). I mean do you have any idea what a kick it is to be on the cover of a magazine, even a small trade journal?

3. I had monthly branding of my business and services to the entire industry.

4. Last, and by no means least, I got to use the magazine's credibility, along with the accompanying association, to promote a massive annual trade and awards show that produced a six-figure profit.

The big money in any venture may not be in the most obvious or traditional places.

10

Solving Problems the Cunningly Clever Way

CHAPTER 114

Entrepreneurial Problem Solving

The pessimist sees difficulty in every opportunity. The optimist sees opportunity in every difficulty.
WINSTON CHURCHILL

Perhaps the greatest skill of most successful entrepreneurs is their ability to come up with creative solutions to the host of daily problems every business owner faces, be it lack of cash, competition, or employees. Rarely has anyone captured the essence of this trait better than George Bernard Shaw, who eloquently said, "Some men see things as they are and say why...I see things that never were and say why not." Innovation, creativity, the ability to dream things that never were, or change things that never should have been, are at the very heart of the *cunningly clever entrepreneur*.

Entrepreneurs are, by their very nature, legendary problem solvers. They learn early that one's position in life is very often measured in direct proportion to their ability to unravel difficulties. The better you become at problem solving, the more complex the problems you can graduate to in the future. If your issues are small and trivial and can be solved quickly and easily, or simply avoided altogether, then you probably have not gone very far in life. If, however, your problems are large, complex, or demand a great deal of thinking, time, and effort to solve, then you're probably well ahead of the pack in terms of power and position.

The ability to solve problems, especially your own, is a skill that is a key to success in life. The more quickly you solve existing problems, the sooner you can graduate to bigger challenges, and the sooner you can get back to dealing with the real issues that affect your business and your life.

On a practical basis, the better you become at problem solving, the higher you will go in your chosen field. Of course the higher you go, the more control you have over your future, the more influence you have on others and—incidentally—the more money you make. The payoff for being excellent at problem solving is both financial reward and personal fulfillment, so let's get to work and solve some problems.

Resolve to become a cunningly clever problem solver.

CHAPTER 115

Your Strategic Plan Must Serve as Your Guide for Solving Problems

*Be clear about your goal but be flexible about
the process of achieving it.*
BRIAN TRACY

There is a real tendency, even for smart and motivated people, to major in minor things. This in itself would not be much of a problem if the minor things added up to something bigger, something they could build upon, something that eventually would lead to success. However, most people who major in minor things don't have a vision of success, don't have a strategic plan, and don't have written goals with action plans and deadlines. As a result, they continually solve the same minor problems that, in terms of advancement, lead nowhere.

Cunningly clever entrepreneurs cannot afford to be caught in this trap. They must be selective in the problems they choose to solve. In order to move forward in your business and life by solving problems, it's imperative that you have a vision of where you want to be. That means having a strategic plan and specific goals. Without a strategic plan to guide you in your business decisions, you could end up solving hundreds of small problems, all of which add up to a great big nothing and lead you in the wrong direction completely.

So What's Your Problem?

Is it a real problem, or something you can easily dismiss or fix yourself? Is it a problem that relates to your strategic plan, or is it one that has absolutely no bearing on your future success? Is the problem one you can avoid? Is it a case of having to change old habits and adopt new, more powerful ones? Do you have a problem because somebody else has told you it's a problem, even though you may not perceive it as one?

Are you letting other people dictate your problems? For instance, as you learned in the customer service chapter, the customer is *not* always right. Or, have you ever bent over backwards for someone and found your efforts unappreciated? Perhaps you've given someone a special deal, only to find it comes back to haunt you later. Could it be you are creating your own problems?

Most, if not all, of these questions can only be answered if you have a strategic plan. If you don't have a clear, written, strategic plan, it's impossible to fix many of your day-to-day problems. It's certainly impossible to decide which are real problems, which should receive priority in your attention and resources, and which should not. The vision, strategic plan, and goals become your road map and companions in helping you make the right decisions.

Ultimately, you need to commit yourself to a single major goal to enjoy the most success. Only those dedicated to a single great purpose can have the focus, commitment, and time management skills to prioritize their problems and move forward as fast as possible. If you choose to focus on every problem that comes your way, you will never, ever have enough time for success. You must decide which problems to solve and which to ignore.

Focus on problems that are worth solving.

CHAPTER 116

Make Sure You Solve the Right Problem

Entrepreneurs are simply those who understand that there is little difference between obstacle and opportunity and are able to turn both to their advantage.
VICTOR KIAM

People often charge into action, only to discover they've set out to solve the wrong problem. Take the case of the major dog food manufacturer who introduced a new line of food at a cost of millions of dollars. Despite a high-profile marketing effort and plenty of shelf space at the local supermarket, the product just stuck to the shelves. Already worried after only a few weeks, the company rushed to solve the problem.

First they changed the packaging. "It must be the wrong color," said one. "It's the design," said another, while a third suggested the dogs in the picture weren't the right breed.

Back on the shelves it went with a bold new look and still nothing happened. Next, after brainstorming all kinds of wonderful ideas, they changed the name of the product to one that was sure to delight any canine lover. Still the product stayed on the shelves. Finally, the product team agreed it must be the price. It was, after all, at the higher end of the doggy food scale. After much debate, a new price was decided upon, significantly lower than the original introductory price. The product was rolled out once again, with new packaging, better looking hounds, a cuter name, and super pricing. It still didn't sell!

The CEO was so discouraged that he went personally to his local supermarket to observe buying habits in the pet food department. After a few minutes, a boy of eleven or twelve marched up to the dog food section and pulled down a large bag of competing chow. The CEO casually wandered over to the boy and politely inquired why he had chosen brand X instead of his brand. The boy cheerfully replied, "My dog hates the taste of that stuff. He just won't eat it."

Problem *solving* is often not as hard as problem *identification*! The first step in problem solving is to identify the real problem. Exactly what is the problem you are going to solve? Clearly define your problem on a piece of paper and list its individual components.

For example, say your business is not profitable. This is the first problem statement. Using a piece of paper, list all the components of the problem, or clearly write down what the problem is. Your business is not profitable because sales are down, the product is faulty, your accounting system doesn't track your expenditures, etc. The problem must be clearly identified if you expect to solve it.

It is important to note that many problems are very complex and thus need to be broken down into a series of smaller component problems. The trouble in solving most everyday problems is that they are often ill defined. The actual problem runs into another problem, and the desired outcome seems hazy at best. For example, I need more money. That is a vague problem that must be further defined into a specific amount — say $5,000. This gives you a clear problem with a clear outcome in mind. Now we can go about trying to solve the problem.

This step in clearly identifying the problem will ensure that you face the problem with the understanding necessary to solve it. A problem that is extremely complex and has multiple facets will only be a source of frustration because it is too large to tackle in one effort. Breaking the problem down to smaller, more manageable pieces will yield the desired effect...solving the problem.

As Peter Drucker said, "Once the facts are clear, the decisions jump out at you." Problems must be defined in detail and looked at from all angles and points of view before a problem statement is generated.

Examine the problem and define it clearly.

CHAPTER 117

Examine the Constraints

You play the hand you're dealt.
C.S. LEWIS

In any problem, business or personal, there will be some con-straints that are real and some that are perceived. Each must be examined and explored so that perceived but unreal constraints can be removed, permitting clear thinking on the real ones that remain.

Make sure the constraints you believe are in place really are.

List all such constraints that you believe are in place and carefully analyze them to make sure they are real. Often, when you take yourself through this part of the problem-solving process and look carefully at each constraint, you will expose false constraints that can be removed. This may offer quick and easy solutions on which you can act.

During testing for rank in my karate studio, I devised a simple problem that was seldom solved in hundreds of attempts by cus-tomers of all ages. I held a long wooden pole called a "bow staff" in my hand during the early part of the test. It was six feet long and about three inches in circumference. At the end of the test, I handed the staff to the students giving these simple instructions, "Use this staff to keep your feet off the ground for ten seconds."

I handed them the staff vertically and the students, young and old alike, would cheerfully plant the thin pole in the carpet and try to climb it and balance at the same time while they hung on like monkeys. Some made it up to a five count before they fell and their feet touched the ground again, but most never made it past two or three. I often repeated my instructions to keep their feet off the floor for ten seconds and gave them another chance to try their skill.

In all the years I used this test, only a handful of people took the staff, laid it lengthways across the floor and stood on it, thereby keeping their feet off the floor. They might have been just two inches off the floor, but it sure was a lot easier than climbing a thin pole and attempting to balance on it. The point is this: Many people make their problems far harder than they really are by not examining the constraints to see if they are really true. They focus so intently on what they perceive the problem and its constraints to be that they cannot solve it.

In ancient Asia, the Gordian Knot was said to hold the key to becoming the ruler of Asia. All who tried to untie the complicated knot failed until a young commander named Alexander, later to be called *The Great*, came upon the problem. After failing to find the starting point of the knot, he finally drew his sword and sliced the knot in half. Within a matter of months, all of Asia was his. He had simply removed the constraints all the others had felt they were under. With the constraints removed, the solution to the problem was ridiculously easy—and that's the way it often is.

Are the constraints you perceive real or can they simply be removed?

CHAPTER 118

Generating Creative Solutions

Everything new is really just an addition to or modification of something that already exists.
MICHAEL MICHALKO

Once the problem is actually defined and constraints have been examined, the next key is to gather your team and generate as many different solutions as possible. The more solutions you can generate, the greater your chance of finding the right one, the one that not only solves the problem, but perhaps even goes beyond it to create new opportunities. Before embarking your team on a no-holds-barred brainstorming session, a few simple rules should be followed to make such meetings of the minds effective.

Effective Brainstorming

Brainstorming is done a number of ways. However, too many sessions degenerate into simple discussions or "bull sessions."

Hold the session in an esthetically appealing place to stimulate creativity. Avoid distractions and interruptions.

The keys to brainstorming are:

- To generate lots of ideas. Encourage people to free associate with the goal or problem statement. Encourage them to adapt other people's ideas, to combine them, or to contradict them.

- All ideas are good ideas. Tell people you have thought of the normal solutions, what you're looking for is crazy, or outside-the-box ideas. There is NO criticism or discussion of ideas in this process.

  - There are no questions — the point is to make suggestions, not educate your group. Write down each suggestion without comment and post it on the wall. (Later you can evaluate and adapt ideas.)

- Keep the ideas focused on solving the problem at hand, not on unrelated issues.

Often in brainstorming, THE super, perfect solution will not be generated. That's fine. Usually the process stimulates new possibilities that can be combined with what is already known in later evaluation sessions.

The more solutions you create and explore through brainstorming, the better your chances of finding the perfect solution.

CHAPTER 119

Finding the Root Cause to Solve Your Problems

Shallow men believe in luck.
Strong men believe in cause and effect.
RALPH WALDO EMERSON

One of the first ways to look for solutions is by analyzing the root cause of your problem. In fully 25% of cases, simply looking at the causes of the problem will also provide you with a clear solution.

When I opened my first small karate school, many moons ago, my huge breakthrough came when I simply wrote down this question on a yellow legal pad.

"Why are you failing in this business?"

That was quickly followed by my answer, "Lack of customers."

The obvious follow-up question was, "Why are there not enough customers?"

Was this because the newspaper ads didn't work, my location was poor, or perhaps there was no market? I thought of all of these things but eventually concluded that the reason I had too few customers was simple. I did not understand customer acquisition—nor at that point did I have any idea about marketing. I resolved to read every book I could find on the subject and in a matter of three months turned my failing school into one of the most successful in the entire country.

It all started with that yellow pad and a series of questions to find the root cause of the problem.

If you find the root cause, you very often find the solution.

CHAPTER 120

Play the What-if Game

I am always doing that which I cannot do, in order that
I may learn how to do it.
PABLO PICASSO

When you are faced with a difficult problem to solve, it is important for you not to allow yourself to be governed by rigid or straight-line thinking. Most people think rigidly, because that is what they have been taught to do. You must allow your mind to wander in all directions and throw out any kind of wild and crazy solution that it cares to. You can then write down each idea as it comes. (This is like brainstorming without the group.)

When faced with a particular problem, take out a blank sheet of paper and write the problem at the top of the page. Then write down all the ways in which this problem could be solved. Do not think over your answers; just write all your thoughts and ideas down, no matter how silly or unlikely they seem. You can go back later and rate each on its particular merits.

A piece of paper headed with the problem "Lack of Capital," or more specifically, "Lack of $25,000," might include the following possible solutions:

- Get a loan from the bank.

- Ask Uncle Mort.

- Sell my car.

- Use my credit cards.

- Rob a bank.

- Win the lottery.

- Ask customers for money.

- Cash in my life insurance.

- Sell some of my stock.

- Get a partner for my venture.

The key is not to think about the validity of the ideas as you write. Just write freely. When you have filled the entire page with possibilities, then go back and cross off the ideas that are really off base. We will start by crossing off bank robbery and winning the lottery. The average bank robber nets only $4,000 and there is a 20-year jail term if you fail. Your chances of winning the lottery are slim to none. The bank won't lend money on such a venture, but after crossing off most of the solutions, we are left with getting a partner, soliciting customers, or asking Uncle Mort.

Now, take a second piece of paper and head it, "Finding a Partner." On this, you can list all your friends and relatives who are possible business associates. Then list other possibilities such as advertising in the newspaper for an investor. Better still, you could think of suppliers or customers who might aid you. By continuing this process at each stage, you will be amazed by the great ideas and solutions that you come up with. There is magic in letting your mind run free in What-if Land and writing your thoughts down in black and white.

Write down as many solutions as possible no matter how silly they seem at the moment.

CHAPTER 121

What Would Napoleon Do?

Impossible is a word found only in the
dictionary of fools.
NAPOLEON

What would Napoleon do if he were in your shoes? Or, what would Donald Trump do? What would your spouse or best friend do? What would your leading competitor do in this situation? Very often, when you change the perspective of the person charged with solving the problem, you will see the problem and the potential opportunities in a totally different light.

Years ago, a large banks ran a credit card promotion that awarded customers points based on the amount of money they charged each month. The points could be redeemed for gifts. One of the top prizes was a trip for two to Hawaii. I immediately set my sights on the trip and spent up a storm. I charged gas, meals, computer equipment, and anything else I could. At the end of the promotion, I had charged just enough points to make the trip.

I called to book my trip. The line was busy. I tried two or three times that day and the next with the same lack of success. After that, I kept the number and prize brochure on the corner of my desk and continued to call at irregular intervals. Finally, after about six months, someone answered the phone. They politely informed me that the time limit on ordering prizes had passed ten days ago. I explained that I could not get through. The operator said that the promotion had been far more successful than had been anticipated, and a lot of other people had the same complaint; however, she could do nothing. She suggested I write a letter to the head office.

I did this, fully expecting to get my trip and an apology for my inconvenience. Instead, I got a form letter telling me I was too late to qualify for my trip. I wrote again and received the same form letter. Now I was mad. I had spent over $40,000 to qualify for this trip and I wanted it.

I had called. I had written not one, but two, detailed letters and still no one took any action. At the time, I was running a small advertising agency and as I sat there contemplating my problem I thought, "Now what could I do if I were a large agency?" I could run a campaign telling people all over America what a rotten bunch they were. Yes, that was it. I could publicize their crime to everyone and stop people from using their bank. But I was small. What could I do against such a giant?

I typed out a letter on my agency stationary, which detailed the way I had been treated. I headed my letter "XZY Bank, A Customer Non-service Story." I enclosed with it a list of the magazines, newspapers, TV and radio stations to which I planned to send my ad. I then went to the post office to get the address of every bank branch in the state. Next, I went to the library to get the names and titles of every corporate officer I could find from the president on down. I mailed out my letter on Monday to over 200 people. By 9:30 am the following day, my problem was solved. I got my tickets and my trip to Hawaii. After trying to solve the problem by traditional means, I had looked at how to solve it from the perspective of someone else, and sure enough it worked.

Ask how others might tackle your problem.

CHAPTER 122

Go Beyond Your Normal Circles for Answers

To solve any problem, here are three questions to ask yourself: First, what could I do? Second, what could I read? And third, who could I ask?
JIM ROHN

An exclusive apartment building in New York had only one set of elevators, and there were growing complaints from the upscale tenants about the amount of time it took to get up and down in the building. Several engineers, consultants, and elevator specialists were called in to study the problem.

Lots of solutions were generated. Unfortunately, most dealt with adding more elevators, which in an old building was financially unfeasible. Some focused on trying to speed up the existing elevators with smart programming and so on, but this would still not increase the speed enough.

One of the tenants, who was in the television industry, heard about the attempts to solve the problem and put forward a solution of her own. Instead of messing around with the elevators, she simply suggested adding TVs around the elevator waiting area. She surmised the real problem wasn't the time it took for the elevator to travel up or down the building, rather it was that people had time to think about the wasted time while they waited for the elevator to actually arrive at their floors.

Suddenly people waiting for the elevator could watch the news while they waited and catch up on the day's events. Now that they had something interesting to do to pass the time, they actually thought the elevators had been speeded up!

Sometimes the best solutions will come from outside your organization.

CHAPTER 123

To Get Creative, Change Your Problem-Solving Environment

Drag your thoughts away from your troubles...by the
ears, by the heels, or any other way you can manage it.
MARK TWAIN

A change of problem-solving environment can have a remarkable effect on your ability to see a problem in a different light. A problem that seems insurmountable in your ten-by-ten office with the phone ringing and computer humming will take on a whole new light when you drive alone to the beach or the lake and look at it again. Very few offices are set up in a way that will stimulate creative thinking. They have no quiet rooms, only stock prints on the walls, and/or play elevator music 24 hours a day. It is very often necessary to take your problems out of this sterile environment and solve them elsewhere.

Take your problem to the ski slopes or take it fishing, away from the daily grind, and you may well discover new enthusiasm for attacking and solving a problem from a different angle. Fresh air, an ocean breeze, or the visual appeal of the mountains can have a profound effect on opening your mind. So, too, can physical activities like running. When you run, endorphins are released in the brain. This release of endorphins, or what is known as "runner's high" can help stimulate your thought processes.

I find very few of my major problems are solved in the office.

Instead, I solve many of my company's business problems, as well as my personal ones, when I jog with my two dogs to the lake near my home. Jogging in itself makes me feel good physically, and it relieves tension as I run. Fatigue and stress are two of the most stifling causes of uncreative thinking. By jogging or a similar activity, you are killing two birds with one stone, so to speak. You are improving your cardiovascular system and increasing your stamina while at the same time relieving stress.

Get away from your everyday environment to get more creative in solving problems.

CHAPTER 124

The Art of Entrepreneurial Deal Making, Creativity, and Making Things Happen

Creativity is a natural extension of our enthusiasm.
EARL NIGHTINGALE

Back in my martial arts days, my friend David Miller and I were looking for a software product for martial arts schools. He was in the martial arts supply business, I in the consulting business. Eventually we found a product that looked promising called Studio Manager. But when we talked to the owner, he had already agreed to sell the company to a martial arts billing company for $20,000.

We offered the same price plus offered to send a check instantly while the other company was going through its red tape. At first he said no, but a couple of days later he called back and said they were taking too long and we could have it.

What a coup, we thought!

As soon as the billing company, the largest in the industry, found out that we had the program instead of them, they were livid. The owner called me every name in the book and threatened to sue us all.

Once he had calmed down, I offered a solution. He had promised a bunch of his schools that his company would provide them with management software and he was willing to pay $20,000 to make that happen. I asked how many of the schools he had were ready to act and he said about 100. I proposed that we give him 100 copies at the greatly reduced price of $100 per license (it was selling for $400). He agreed at once and so we made back 50% of our purchase price in one day!

Over the next few months we quickly recouped all our costs, but suddenly the developer, who had promised to stand by us as he worked out everyday bugs, vanished. The bugs grew, the customers became unhappy, and with the original developer gone we simply couldn't fix things quickly or easily.

It soon became a nightmare of unhappy campers. Then to make matters even worse, a new company came out with a far better, although far more expensive, product. I had already made a small profit on the deal. All I wanted now was out. But I wanted out in a way that took care of the people I had sold the product to. We didn't want to give a total refund, we couldn't fix the code issues, and the phone kept on ringing with complaints.

After careful consideration, I approached the new company and asked if they would like an instant increase in customers. To their credit they were smart enough to realize the cost of acquiring the 300 plus users I had would far outweigh whatever short-term concessions they would have to give.

I asked for 50 free programs for my top clients and a $100 upgrade fee for the rest. (Their product was selling for $795.) They agreed and while not all my customers were happy, the great majority were. Best of all, the new company paid me a generous referral fee for new clients and a small commission every time a new upgrade came out. It turned a lose-lose situation into a win-win situation. Later the company even ran ads in one of my publications and sponsored some of my seminars.

**Very often your biggest problems become
your best opportunities.**

CHAPTER 125

Prioritize Solutions and Make the Right Decisions

I try to learn from the past, but I plan for
the future by focusing exclusively on the present.
That's where the fun is.
DONALD TRUMP

Once a series of solutions has been generated, the next step is to prioritize each possible solution based on vital factors, such as time, money, effort required, and resources available. Cunningly Clever Entrepreneurs have a unique ability to identify which idea will make the greatest possible difference, in the shortest possible time, using the least amount of resources, both financial and human.

Before making a final decision, ask the question "What's the worst thing that can happen if I make this decision?" Once satisfied that the rewards of your decision outweigh the risks, take ACTION! Do not procrastinate on making a decision; procrastination is very often the enemy. Few problems grow better with time, most grow in size and complexity.

Legendary entrepreneur Lee Iacocca came up with the idea of the Ford Mustang (one of the most successful cars ever) and later as Chrysler CEO, delivered that company from the brink of collapse. He said, "An average decision executed quickly will often outperform a perfect decision that takes months!" In his autobiography he also said if he had to sum up in one word what qualities make a successful manager, it would all boil down to *decisiveness*. "You can use the fanciest computers in the world, gather all the charts and numbers, but in the end you have to bring all the information together, set up a time table, and act."

It's vitally important that you make prompt decisions. Usually any decision is better than none. Execute your decision fully. Assign clear responsibility for carrying it out and then set a deadline for completion and review. A decision without a deadline is just a fruitless discussion.

The effectiveness of your decision is then observed, recorded, modified where necessary, and discarded without recriminations if it doesn't produce the desired results. Put another way, many people put off making decisions because they are afraid of mistakes. Entrepreneurs *expect* to make mistakes, learn from them, and move on to improved decisions.

Always act decisively.

CHAPTER 126

Always Have a Plan B

Focus on remedies, not faults.
Jack Nicklaus

S uccess is nothing more than the execution of your well-developed options. The clearer the options you have for solving problems and attaining your goals, the better your chances of success.

All great generals have a plan B. In fact, it was because of the famous German Admiral, Otto von Bismarck, that the phrase was coined. As general of your own army, even if it's a one-man army, you should always have a plan B. Normally, this is the second best choice in you list. For reasons of timing or available resources, what is the second choice option may, in a relatively short period of time, become the best option if your first choice is not available or working.

The key is to have developed a number of workable options and to retain the flexibility to change course when needed.

Your success will ultimately be determined by the quantity and quality of your well-developed options. Always have a plan B.

CHAPTER 127

Log All Problems and Solutions for Future Reference

The palest ink is better than the strongest memory.
CHINESE PROVERB

You can learn a lot from your own experience. Each time a problem rises to the surface and a solution is generated, both should be written down. Once logged, they should be made available to anyone in your organization for future use. I am amazed by the number of clients, who, after short periods, call me back with identical problems. Had they taken the brief time necessary to log both the problem and the solution, they could easily have used the resulting logs as their guide. Yesterday's solutions, even rejected solutions, may be the opportunities of tomorrow.

- Have all brainstorming results typed up, emailed to all participants, and placed on your office server for future use.

- Start an internal knowledge base so all of your staff can easily access solutions to common customer problems.

- Have all customer-centric problem solutions placed in the FAQ section of your Web site, preferably in a searchable database. This will save you a great deal of time and will provide a valuable tool for your customers.

History has a way of repeating itself, so be prepared with a solid database of problems and solutions.

Keeping a database of problems and solutions will save you a great deal of time and money.

CHAPTER 128

When You Can't Seem to Solve Your Problem, Change the Problem

*Experience taught me a few things. One is to
listen to your gut, no matter how good
something sounds on paper. The second is that
you're generally better off sticking with what you know.
And the third is that sometimes your
best investments are the ones you don't make.*
DONALD TRUMP

When all else fails to generate the innovative solutions you seek, your final line of defense against the most stubborn of problems is simply to change the problem.

For example, let's say you're not getting enough customers through the door. You have brainstormed this problem and come up with a host of less-than-ideal solutions, things that have been tried unsuccessfully before or cost too much money to implement. You can't come up with an acceptable solution, so the next step is to change the problem.

Instead of solving the problem of how to get more customers to come to you, set about solving the problem of how you could go to them, perhaps with a catalog, a website, or a mobile van. Maybe you could direct-sell your products like Mary Kay or

Amway. Perhaps you could generate leads at the local flea market or a sporting event where you know there will be thousands of people.

As you see, there are many possibilities for solving your problem by changing the focus entirely and putting your resources to work on a new and stimulating challenge.

How could you change a problem you now face to stimulate a whole new set of possibilities?

Creating Buzz

CHAPTER 129

The Key Media Strategy Any Small Business Owner Can Steal from Branson, Trump, and Jobs

A good ad which is not run never produces sales.
LEO BURNETT

Mega-entrepreneurs like Richard Branson, Donald Trump, and Steve Jobs are all masters of the media. Branson with his publicity stunts, Trump with his own TV show, and Jobs with his Apple product launches are all world famous.

The day Branson launched Virgin Airways, he climbed on top of a life-size model of arch rival British Airway's flagship Concorde parked outside Heathrow airport, dressed in a pirate outfit. Of course, all the British media had been alerted and were in attendance.

Herein lies the key: You don't have to be a major star or major player in your town or industry to create your own buzz—you just have to make the effort. The first law of BUZZ for the cunningly clever entrepreneur is that you can't leave it to chance—you have to create your own buzz.

Don't be bashful; don't be self-conscious; don't worry if you are good enough, know enough, have been doing what your are doing long enough to be regarded as an expert. Just do it!

It's been almost two decades since I lived in California but I still vividly remember The Crazy Greek Mattress Store and Don Worthington Ford. Both had outrageous ads. The crazy Greek ranted and raved about the unbelievably low pricing of his mattresses, while Don, always in his cowboy hat, frequently appeared with tigers or other outrageous props on his car lot.

And there's the professor with the Einstein hair and polka-dot suit and tie, screaming about all the money the government has to give away if you will only ask them.

You don't have to be a circus act to gain attention, but it doesn't hurt to be larger than life.

You can attract attention with community service projects— like the artist who paints the sides of abandoned buildings to brighten up the community. Or the karate school that organizes a "clean up the town" project every year, landing on the front page of the local newspaper, on the radio, and occasionally on TV.

As Virgil so aptly said, "Fortune favors the bold." Be bold about getting publicity.

Don't leave your buzz to the whims of the media—create your own!

CHAPTER 130

Creating a Larger-Than-Life Personality

Create your own visual style… let it be unique for yourself and yet identifiable for others.
ORSON WELLES

You might not like this chapter. You may find it sexist, clichéd, rude, and demeaning to women—perhaps even distasteful. BUT...whether you agree with my approach or not doesn't affect the laws of the REAL marketing universe YOUR company lives in, one bit...

Sex sells!

Let's not get off on the wrong foot here, with a lecture for me on political correctness or any of the above objections. Let's talk about something far more important—PROFITS.

YOUR profits are the very thing that keeps food on the table for you and all of your employees, especially in difficult times like these.

Recently we did a campaign for Pam's Ocean City Golf, a golf travel company badly hurt by the recession. The first question I asked was "Who is Pam?"

Whoever she was, she was long gone, so we gave the 25-year-old company a new look and a new personality. We gave them a color version of a new, sexy Pam. We gave them a new website with a tongue-in-cheek video sales pitch from Pam, a new catalog, and a new marketing message built around the top ten reasons to book through Pam's. Bookings went up 18% while the industry average in that area was off by 6%.

Reaction to the provocative campaign was mixed, but we created quite a buzz. There were a lot of positive comments, especially from the middle-aged guys who make up most of their clientèle. And there were some negative comments, from men and women alike, with the usual remarks about sexual stereotypes. But whether people liked or disliked the campaign is immaterial. What matters is that Pam's business went up 18% over the previous year and up 24% over their competition.

This simple fact is lost on most people in business. You shouldn't run marketing campaigns that everyone likes. You should run campaigns that ACTUALLY work.

**Personality sells and if that personality
is sexy, so much the better.**

CHAPTER 131

Consistency Breeds Confidence, Confidence Builds Brand

A brand for a company is like a reputation for a person.
You earn reputation by trying to do hard things well.
JEFF BEZOS

One thing that many small business owners overlook in building their brand is the simple power of consistency. Obviously, consistency of quality and service are important, but there are many other factors, big and small, that must be consistent to build your brand.

For example, a big consistency factor for restaurants is hours of operation. There are any number of restaurants in my area that close on Sunday. Some also close on Monday, especially in the summer (Florida's downtime), and many are even more erratic in the times they open. Some close because they are small, owner-run businesses. Inconsistent closing policies are bad for a brand. The problem is, I can never remember which ones close on what days. But I can tell you this, when I have showed up once or twice and been disappointed, I rarely show up again.

Even small consistencies are far more important than most businesses realize—consistency of colors, trucks, uniforms, logos, and names. That's why franchises have a much better track record of success than the typical small business.

One local business owner in the electrical business saw a massive increase in business when he invested $10,000 to have his four trucks painted bright yellow, with a huge logo and phone number visible from all four sides. Because they were so bright and recognizable, you seemed to see them everywhere. In fact, you would think he had 40 trucks, not four, so often did you recall seeing them.

Early in my marketing business, I choose orange as our color, not because it's my favorite color, but simply because at the time hardly any company used orange. We stood out at every trade show. Every time I spoke, I wore an orange shirt. Clients started sending gifts of shirts, ties, and sweaters in orange. In the golf business, when you see orange, you think of Legendary Marketing. The same is true of logos. Come up with a good one and stick with it. Don't have five different varieties or one for every season. Find one worth keeping and stick with it like Marlboro does with their cowboy, like Wells Fargo does with their stagecoach. Like Prudential Insurance does with their rock, or Nike their swoosh.

Consistency of unique selling proposition (USP) is paramount to branding success. Great brands stick with their USP and they stick with it for decades. Hertz is Number One, Avis is Number Two We Try Harder. Miller Lite – Tastes Great – Less Filling.

The more consistent your business is with hours, uniforms, colors, logos, personnel, UPS, and service, the more confidence you will produce in your customers, and the quicker your brand will grow. After all, a brand is simply about delivering on your promise.

Be consistent in all things, big and small, to quickly build your brand.

CHAPTER 132

The Total Experience Is Usually More Important Than the Actual Product

*We see our customers as invited guests to a party, and
we are the hosts. It's our job every day to
make every important aspect of the
customer experience a little bit better.*
JEFF BEZOS

Many businesses provide a total experience rather than just a product or service. These owners often get caught up in the technical aspects of their businesses—making sure the place is clean, the greens are cut, the coffee is hot, or whatever general standards are applicable to their types of businesses. In focusing on the technical aspects, they miss the boat in the more important *experiential* aspect of marketing their products or services.

Take restaurants for example. There are plenty of local restaurants near my home that sell good food: Casa Norma, The Rusty Duck, and Romano's come to mind, but none of these quite delivers when it comes to the total package. While each of these places has its own charm, they are not the type of modern, upscale bistro that you would find in a big city.

Then came the Crystal River Wine & Cheese Company. It was the total package: the type of place you would expect to find in Los Angeles or Manhattan, but not in Crystal River—which of course is what made it so special. The place was small, the menu a little quirky, but the food tasted great, the service was very friendly, the jazz band good, and the whole atmosphere produced a great evening's experience rather than simply dinner.

In this example, like so many in business today, it's often hard to put your finger on exactly why you like one place or one business more than the next. Good food is good food, good wine good wine, and music you like is…well, music you like. Actually, I'm not even much of a jazz fan, but the whole package combined worked.

The way your business, looks, feels, smells, and sounds can create an instant impression on your customer that he or she might not even be aware of, but that sets the tone for the experience that is about to commence. Colors can excite or calm people. Music from one particular era like the Fifties or Eighties can turn people on or turn people off. Even the clothes or uniforms you wear make some kind of impression. It's important that you pay attention to these less tangible aspects of your business or service if you want to create exactly the right type of experience for your customers.

The large restaurant chains like Outback, Applebee's, and others all pay very careful attention to these factors, but there is no reason why with a little thought and planning a small business could not do the same thing, only better. There are so many little things that you can do to enhance the experience your business gives customers and stand out from the crowd. Just pick a few and do them. The rewards are sure to follow.

Many businesses, like restaurants or clubs, should focus on delivering a total customer experience.

CHAPTER 133

Creating Instant Credibility

Give me enough ribbon and I will conquer the world.
NAPOLEON

Having quit school at 15 and never graduated college, I have never put much stock in certificates, diplomas, accreditation, or resumes of any kind. But just because I don't doesn't mean the rest of the world doesn't. In fact it astonishes me how much people crave such paperwork.

One of the easiest ways in the world to gain instant credibility is simply to form your own association. This practice was rampant in the martial arts world in which I once lived. As soon as an instructor felt he had gained enough knowledge from his master, he simply broke away and formed his own style and own association. King of his own nation and master of his own subjects in one fell swoop. This association would then offer membership and rank accreditation, generating membership and testing fees at every turn. The fact that the new master might only be 23 years old seemed to bother no one (other than his previous master). As long as his students had something more to learn from him, they gladly paid.

I started the Martial Arts Business Association as a trade group for martial arts schools. A former client started the Professional Martial Arts Association. Both offered certification in various business categories, held trade shows and seminars, and promoted business books and courses. Both started small and made a great deal of money quickly. There were several other companies, most notably the billing companies or martial arts supply companies who were in a unique position to pull this off, but they didn't simply because they didn't use an association as their marketing vehicles.

This idea works in just about any industry, and just because there are already ten people servicing your industry don't let it discourage you. Just like the 5th, 9th, and 27th Baptist church in your town, in a vertical market there will always be people who will join to obtain some sense of belonging.

The word "association" creates a magical, seemingly non-partisan effect that draws people to your cause. Associations can have members, hold banquets, and offer awards. In fact, I knew a guy in the martial arts business, whose association name eludes me, who made tens of thousands of dollars a year by simply handing out a massive plethora of awards at a $200 a plate VIP banquet each year. That was his only product.

You could start a horse-lovers association, a west-midlands funeral-home association. A "your town" entrepreneurs association. The possibilities are endless, the power huge, the credibility instant, and the start-up costs almost zero.

Starting your own association brings instant credibility and power.

CHAPTER 134

Harvey S. McLintock, Strongly Recommends Marketing Legend Andrew Wood in His New Book, *Desperately Seeking Members*

I expect history to view me very favorably… because that's the way I intend to write it.
Winston Churchill
(author of 93 books!)

There are very few things more powerful than writing a book in your chosen field for elevating your status and credibility. The one thing that is more powerful is *someone else* writing a book about you, or at least mentioning you positively in one.

One day I was sitting down writing my weekly newsletter for the golf industry when I realized that it had turned into an 18-page rant about incompetence in the industry. Realizing it was too long for a newsletter, I just kept writing until it became a book. The book is very funny, very factual, and has a practical solution, HIRE ME! The only thing I had to do to make it work was to have someone else write the book—so I invented Harvey S. McLintock as the fictional club manager and author.

After eight or nine chapters detailing the typical problems of a private golf club, and the ludicrous way boards attempt to solve them, Harvey starts sharing Andrew Wood's wisdom with the board.

A few weeks later, I got a call from a leading broker in the golf business on Saturday morning.

"Is this Andrew Wood?"

"Yes," I said

"*The* Andrew Wood," asked the caller.

"That's right."

"The marketing legend, Andrew Wood, who's in Harvey McLintock's book?"

I really thought someone was having a joke with me, but I kept playing the game.

"Yep, that's me" I assured him.

"Great," said the caller "I just wanted to make sure you were real, I wasn't sure, but my club really needs help."

I actually burst out laughing. After I shared the joke, so did the caller, but he had to say it was one of the most innovative marketing strategies he had ever seen. Best of all, he paid $24.95 for the privilege of being sold.

While I love to write, you don't need to be a great writer, or do anything more than showcase your knowledge to benefit from this strategy.

And with all the print-on-demand technology, it doesn't have to cost a fortune to self-publish your own book either.

The possibilities are endless and the upside to building your reputation huge.

- the restaurant owner's cookbook.

- the chiropractor's guide to stretching for health.

- the estate planner's simple guide to transferring wealth.

If you can write just two decent paragraphs per day, TWO —that's about 15 sentences—you will have a 180-page book by the end of the year. And even half that number is enough for a small book.

If you can't do a book, try starting with a 10-page booklet, or hire a decent ghostwriter.

Nothing builds your credibility like a book.

CHAPTER 135

Apple, Nike, and Your Town's Opinion Leaders

I must follow the people. Am I not their leader?
BENJAMIN DISRAELI

When Apple first started, they generated a huge amount of goodwill and a loyal customer base by donating millions of dollars of Apple products to schools. And when those school kids grew up, guess what type of computer they wanted?

When Nike got into the golf business, they did so only in a limited way and only with a blade product (favored only by top players). So in the first year, if you saw anyone using a Nike club, the chances are they were a good player.

Later, they started a program called Nike Staff, which was a bunch of amateurs all in positions of some influence in the golf business. They gave all of us free equipment.

Some golf clubs give free memberships to local sports stars. Real estate developers give land or a sweetheart deal to get a local personality in their community.

When I started my martial arts franchise, I focused my initial efforts on winning over two or three opinion leaders. One alone brought 100 schools with him, while a second brought twenty.

Which opinion leaders in your community would boost your brand if people knew they were doing business with you?

Use Social Media to Create Buzz and Brand

CHAPTER 136

Embracing Social Media and Web 2.0

Whoever controls the media—the images—
controls the culture.
ALLEN GINSBERG

In the last five years social media has exploded across the world. Billions of dollars have been made on the backs of social media's power, and there is an almost dizzying array of social media from which to choose: Twitter, Facebook, MySpace, LinkedIn, Fastpitch, blogging, and YouTube to name just a few.

It can be hard to know which are worth your time—and which are not—and harder still to figure out how you can profit from any investment of time or money in them.

In this section, I will try to cut through the clutter and give you the case for each of the major social media.

There are three questions that everyone wants to know the answers to in regards to social media:

- Why should I do it?

- What should I say?

- How often should I do it?

I'll answer the three questions, but first, whether we are talking e-newsletters, blogging, Facebook, tweeting, or any social media, there are three keys you must remember.

The Three E's of Social Media

Educate Your Customers. Your content must be of value and timely to your customers. If you are a florist, tell your readers what flowers they should be planting at this time of year. If you are a chef, tell your readers how to cook great food, pair wines, or invest in the right vintages. The more valuable your content, the more people will read it and pass it along to others, thus growing your list and your following.

Engage Your Customers. Be controversial, ask for opinions, tips, stories, pictures, feedback, and participation. Let your followers enter to win free prizes, discounts, and insider specials reserved only for them.

Entertain Your Customers. You MUST entertain your readers.

If your communications do each of these three E's, your readers will not mind that you have inserted a promotion or ad within the copy, just as they see in magazines. On the other hand, if all you do is bombard them with discount offers week after week without providing any of the above value, your lists and readership will shrink rapidly.

These three concepts are the mantras for social media. The basic idea is that you should communicate with customers and form a relationship with prospects and customers *before* trying to sell anything.

Educate, engage, and entertain your readers with your social media. Then, and only then, try to sell them something.

CHAPTER 137

Building Buzz and Brand by Blogging

A blog is merely a tool that lets you do anything from
change the world to share your shopping list.
ANONYMOUS

I have been blogging for a long time; it's easy for me because I love to write. Many people find blogging a hassle they can do without, judging by how few non-Internet businesses are using their blogs effectively to engage customers, build brand, and produce sales. Often I get people excited about starting a blog, only to find a few weeks later they have given up because they do "not have time" or because they did not get any instant feedback from their first few posts. Like most things in life, getting traction takes a little time.

A blog is important for several reasons.

1. A blog showcases your knowledge and positions you as an expert.

2. A blog gives your business a human face. Many customers may never have seen or heard from you or your key staff in person. A blog gives everyone the chance to connect with customers. A blog creates a feedback loop for customers and potential customers. They can comment, ask questions, and add to your posts. (NOTE: You get to review posts before they go up.)

3. A blog starts new relationships. A blog gives you a chance to attract new prospects and show them why a relationship with you would be valuable.

4. A blog strengthens existing relationships with customers. It gives existing customers a chance to bond with you. And featuring customers and how they use or benefit from your product or service on your blog or Facebook will increase their level of engagement with your business.

5. A blog increases links back to your website from other websites; this increases traffic.

6. A blog dramatically helps your search engine positioning. The more relevant content you have on your site, the higher your rankings. Google loves relevant content and inbound links.

7. A blog builds into a large and searchable database of useful information, entertainment, and opinion that can be accessed over time.

There is no doubt that blogging takes work but, if you commit to it, the upside is you'll have tons of content through which you can show your value to prospects and clients. You'll be able to use it on Facebook, Twitter, and other social media sites.

To blog or not to blog? Blog, I say, then blog some more.

CHAPTER 138

What to Blog About?

Bottomline of a successful blog is what else
but solid contents.
PARTHA BHATTACHARYA

The short answer to the question of what to blog about is anything that will engage, educate, or entertain your customers. This means things you know about and that your customers want to know about.

- If you are a day care center, share tips, pictures, and ideas about child rearing.

- If you own a garden center, share tips on the timing of various plantings.

- A golf professional should share golf instruction tips, travel tips, or comment on recent PGA Tour happening.

- The restaurant owner could blog about new wines, new recipes, or upcoming improvements to the facility, introduce new staff, etc.

- A lawyer can blog about how to avoid legal problems.

- Your blog could rally your business around a cause like prostrate or breast cancer.

- Share interesting pictures. Anything that will engage,

educate, entertain, or bring a smile is fine.

- Write on topics you or your staff are passionate about that customers and prospects may also enjoy.

- Share client success stories, case histories, and interviews.

I frequently write about things I see on my travels from a sales or marketing perspective. Ads I see in airline magazines, billboards, direct mail packages, and promotions are just some of the things I talk about on my marketing blog.

Check out some of my vertical blogs for additional ideas:

- http://smartsites.legendarymarketing.com/magazine_ blog

- http://www.cunninglyclevergolfoperator.com/word-press/

Blogging takes a commitment, but it's a commitment that will build your brand and help you increase business.

CHAPTER 139

The Big Blogging Secret
No One Told You About

The first thing you need to decide when you build your blog is what you want to accomplish with it, and what it can do if successful.
RON DAWSON

Here's a big secret that no one told you: Your blog doesn't have to be all that original to be interesting, engaging, and entertaining to your readers.

It helps if it is, BUT it doesn't have to be. For example:

- If you're a custom manufacturer, you can explain what new equipment can accomplish for your customers.

- If you are a golf club, September 10th is legendary golfer Arnold Palmer's birthday. Posting a great "Arnie" story would resonate with your readers.

- If you're an accountant, there's end of the year tax breaks and April 15th to write about.

Every profession has important dates, and every holiday has something you can tie your business to. Add a personal touch whenever you can, especially about generic holidays.

At the end of each post, I ask the reader to share the post with a friend. This drives additional traffic back to your website.

Use Humor in Your Blog Posts

Another easy way to spice up your blog is to share some humor. Fifteen minutes on Google will provide you with a year's supply of clean and entertaining jokes on any topic for dentists, lawyers, and more.

Are you a little weak on jokes? At the end of the post, I ask readers to share their best jokes. I get new material and have created an interaction with a reader. Remember, on your blog you get to approve what goes up and what doesn't.

Use Quotes In Your Blog, Your Tweets, and on Facebook

A few of your favorite quotes can be enough to engage your readers, make them smile, and perhaps pass on the link to your blog to a friend or two (viral marketing).

There are a million quotes online today on every topic. One of my favorites is supposed to be from Einstein: "The definition of insanity is doing the same thing over again and expecting a new result." Winston Churchill is always good for a quote. And in the golf area, try quotes from cynics like this one from Mark Twain: "Golf is a good walk spoiled."

Solicit engagement by asking readers to vote on their favorite quotes. Or ask them if they have a quote they'd like to share or a better quote on the topic.

Your quotes could also be used for Twitter posts or in conjunction with a Facebook post where you have more room to combine it with an offer. Finding online quotes is as quick and easy as a Google search. From search to blog, you can post in about two minutes flat.

For example, a Facebook golf course post might look like this:

Famous sportswriter Grantland Rice once said, "18 holes of match or medal play will teach you more about your foe than will 18 years of dealing with him across a desk."

Perhaps now would be a great time to invite that prospect you've been working on for a game? You never know what you might learn about him that could give you the edge.

For tee times click here.

A Twitter post (which is limited to 140 characters) might be:

18 holes of golf will teach you more about your foe than will 18 years of dealing with him across a desk. Grantland Rice. Call now 4 T-times.

The quote gives the reader a little value while also asking for action.

Video Clips

Video clips also make great Twitter, blog, email, and Facebook content since all you need is the link.

I have used a *Candid Camera* style clip of a man with a shotgun shooting down balls at a golf driving range to the astonishment of the golfers next to him. I shared this content through all of my social media and people just loved it. They re-tweeted it, gave it the "I Like" on Facebook, and passed it around via email. Exactly the type of response you want from your posts—something so engaging and entertaining it goes viral.

Use Social Media to Increase Downloads of Your Information

Offer your pdf downloads, special reports, brochures, and white papers from your social media. (This is a great way to build your opt-in email database.)

Use Blogs, Twitter, and Facebook to Promote Contests

Contests are a great way to get people involved with your social media. Give away prizes, discounts, promo items, vacations, and memberships. The bigger the prize, the bigger the response, and this is another easy way to build your database of prospects.

Use Guest Bloggers

You can always use guest bloggers when you are running dry or short on time.

Don't be afraid to use stock content for your blog as long as it's targeted to your audience.

CHAPTER 140

Don't Worry Too Much About Grammar, Spelling, Perfect English, or Emulating Mark Twain with Your Writing Skills

A man occupied with public or other important business cannot, and need not, attend to spelling.
NAPOLEON

I don't worry about spelling at all. I know this drives some people nuts, but at least it makes all those readers who are great at English feel good when they can point out my mistakes!

When readers point out my very common typos and other errors, I often send back this:

Typoglycemia

I cdnuolt blveiee taht I cluod aulaclty uesdnatnrd waht I was rdanieg The phaonmneal pweor of the hmuan mnid Aoccdrnig to a rscheearch at Cmabrigde Uinervtisy, it deosn't mttaer inwaht oredr the ltteers in a wrod are, the olny iprmoatnt tihng is taht the frist and lsat ltteer be in the rghit pclae. The rset can be a taotl mses and you can sitll raed it wouthit a porbelm. Tihs is bcuseae the huamn mnid deos not raed ervey lteter by istlef, but the wrod as a wlohe. Amzanig huh? yaeh and I awlyas thought slpeling was ipmorant.

All kidding aside, social media is informal; you don't need to be Ernest Hemingway or Mark Twain to get your message across. Sure, you can spell check it, but don't spend hours editing your blog. People are looking for content, ideas, entertainment, and education, not an English lesson. Twitter and Facebook practically have their own language that barely resembles English anyway.

Blog consistently, at least weekly, more often if possible. I like to get way ahead on my blogs in case something comes up I usually have five or more drafts already preloaded so I never miss a deadline.

Don't Expect Tons of Feedback Right Away

You *will* get feedback, but it takes time. In the hundreds of useful marketing posts I make a year. It's the two or three controversial ones that always produce the biggest response both positive and negative.

Sometimes to get the discussion going you need to plant your own posts, feedback, or questions to stimulate activity.

The Fastest Way to Create a Buzz Is to Stir Something Up

Be a little controversial or provocative if you want to get a response. Offer bold statements and clear views that demand comment.

DO NOT expect all the comments to be positive. You have to be thick skinned when using social media. For some reason people say things on blogs and other social media they would never say to your face. Don't worry about it. Remember the idea of social media is to create dialog—to educate, engage, and entertain.

Also remember that this sort of discussion is going on by your clients and prospects whether you listen to it and address it or not. Many business owners are scared of what people might post, but burying your head in the sand is not a good idea. You always maintain moderator control over your blog and so can choose not to approve distasteful comments.

You don't have to be perfect to generate a ton of business from your blog.
My spelling and grammar are appalling, and yet the response keeps coming.

CHAPTER 141

Thirteen Ways to Use Twitter Effectively

Oh, this is going to be so addictive.
DOM SAGOLLA,
Twitter co-creator

Twitter is a popular communication and engagement tool, but like any tool it must be used correctly to work. Too many businesses are either not using Twitter, not using it effectively, or trying it and giving up because they can't see the point.

Here is some of the value you can achieve for your business by maximizing your use of Twitter.

1. Connecting and Engaging With Your Customers and Prospects. This is the main reason why you should use Twitter for your business. The critical factor is to create compelling and interesting content to share with your customers and prospects, content that adds value to the relationship. The more personalized you can make that content the better. For example:

- I might mention a marketing book I am reading that I think will be of interest to my clients.

- I might pass on the address of a good marketing website.

- I could simply recommend a hotel or restaurant.

- I might post a reminder that the deadline is drawing near to sign up for my marketing bootcamp.

- I can congratulate Fred Smith on opening his new shop.

That's all personalized content that should resonate with the majority of your customers.

2. Branding and Building Your Authority. You don't have to be a big brand name like Nike or Virgin to brand yourself on Twitter. You can be an "average Joe" and brand yourself on Twitter to build awareness, trust, and loyalty. If you're using Twitter to discuss a particular niche within a bigger business, you can build your own authority within an organization by writing high-quality tweets. For instance, you might be the chef at a restaurant, the fitness instructor at the health club, or an employee in the local book store. Common ways to build your authority on Twitter are to send out links to useful resources, provide useful tips to your followers, give insight into relevant topics, answer questions, and engage in discussions with your followers.

3. Marketing. Perhaps the most obvious benefit of Twitter is generating traffic to your website, making the phone ring, and making money. You can:

- Tweet special offers and provide coupon codes to give your business a traffic boost. Businesses like food trucks tweet customers their locations and specials each day, with Twitter driving their businesses.

- Alert your followers to new blog posts, articles, or videos.

- Update followers on events, seminars, or meetings.

- Invite them to participate in contests.

- Give away free booklets packed with your best advice.

When you're connected with followers who care about you, they'll help spread your content by re-tweeting it to their friends. Now that the world has moved to smart phones, just about everyone can get your tweets on their cell phones just like a text message but without the cost.

Plus you don't have to worry about your message getting there like you do with email. Your Tweets won't have to deal with spam filters.

4. Customer Feedback. Once you have connected with your customers, you will get feedback. Some you will like, some you will not. Either way, listening to them will help you provide better service in the future.

People often use Twitter to express dissatisfaction.

> *Eating at XYZ restaurant, waiting for over an hour for entrée.*

Of course, they can also use it to spread a positive message virally and bring you business.

> *Eating at XYZ; best food in south county!*

Either way, follow the people who are following you or look at your mention tab to see what is being said about your business.

5. Learn Inside Industry News First. One of the best things about Twitter is that it keeps you up to date with all your industry news that often flies under the radar. By following the right people in your industry, you can always have the latest niche news that you can't find anywhere else. I tend to post new products, services, and ideas on Twitter and Facebook several days or even weeks ahead of announcing them through an e-blast.

For example, I posted about this book while I was still writing it, giving those people who follow me first chance to get the new information.

6. Spying on Your Competition. Twitter is a great way to spy on competition. You can track what competitors are doing and thinking (watch their tweets, who they're conversing with, and so forth). Gain insights. You can also read what customers are saying about your competition. Find out about issues and problems people are having with your competitors so you can capitalize on them, and perhaps even gain market share.

Just monitor the profiles and set alerts on the profiles of your competitors.

7. Reputation Management. Track your name to keep tabs on what people are saying about your organization at any given time. If it's a positive comment, you can re-tweet it as a third party endorsement. If it's negative, this information can be useful for fixing in-house problems and it can also help you eliminate any untrue rumors that might be spreading around. I'm a firm believer that every problem is an opportunity when viewed from the right perspective.

8. Finding Employees. Find good potential job candidates. Smart job seekers will follow the Tweets of the companies they wish to work for, knowing job opportunities will often be tweeted. This is a quick, easy, and free way to get resumes when you need them.

9. Market Research. Twitter is an ideal place to perform quick polls and research that will help you plan or implement your business strategy. Just Tweet your simple question and tally up the results.

Even a simple question like, "What's your favorite beer?" can get people interacting with you. Other questions such as which of your competitors they use can give you real marketing insight.

Be sure to offer rewards or a chance to win a prize for those who answer.

10. Solve Problems Quickly. Simply pose your question to the community and within minutes you'll have an array of responses from your followers. It could even spark a larger discussion that gets you some attention.

11. Building Customer Loyalty. Communicate with your connections in a direct and informative manner. Simply participating in conversations will push the needle of trust in your direction but you can do more than that. Suggest resources when there are questions or introduce connections to each other when a need arises. Loyalty comes from interaction, familiarity, and trust.

12. Meeting New People. You don't have to follow just the people you know. You can also make valuable new contacts with Twitter. Take the time to look through profiles, website links, and past tweets to determine if it's someone you'd be interested in following as a potential customer, employee, advisor, or friend.

Simply telling people where you are at a given time can create new relationships. Recently when in France, I tweeted I was there. I immediately got an invitation to visit a golf course near Paris from a golf professional who had bought my *Golf Marketing Bible* book. This started a new and interesting relationship full of possibilities, all from a single tweet.

Always invite others to follow your tweets. You can follow mine at CunninglyClever.com/tweet.

Build your twitter strategy around these key points and you will find it a very worthwhile tool.

CHAPTER 142

Building Buzz and Brand with Facebook

Facebook helps you connect and share with the people in your life.
FACEBOOK.COM

Facebook was the last of the social media I adopted after blogging, Linkedin, and Twitter yet probably it should have been the first. Its reach is long, its power for marketing your business undeniable, and its growth around the world truly staggering.

That power was clearly demonstrated to me when, after speaking at a martial arts convention for the first time in ten years, I hooked up with a few old clients and friends. One offered to help me grow my martial-arts-business following on Facebook. He recommended people "send a friend request" to me. Within a week I had over 1,000 professional martial arts instructors hooked up with me.

Imagine how long it would have taken you in the old days to build a targeted list of customers that large. That's the power of Facebook, the power to connect with a target audience and to get that audience helping you reach large numbers of other people quickly, easily, and at no cost.

Almost all of the points I have made about the value of other social media hold true for Facebook a well, so I am not going to repeat all of them in detail. I'll simply provide a bunch of practical examples to stimulate ideas for your business. Facebook allows you to find people, network, join groups, send updates, upload pictures and video, solicit feedback, make new friends, and more, all in one place. It's sort of like all the benefits of the other social sites rolled into one.

Facebook can be used in multiple ways to attract potential customers. Through communities on Facebook and invitations to users to link to your page you can potentially reach large numbers of prospects and customers. Just how large? Well let's look at the facts

Facts

- Facebook has more than 600 million active users.

- 50% of active users log on to Facebook on any given day.

- The average user has 130 friends.

- People spend over 700 billion minutes per month on Facebook.

- There are over 900 million objects (pages, groups, events, and community pages) that people interact with.

- The average user is connected to 80 community pages, groups, and events.

- The average user creates 90 pieces of content each month.

- More than 30 billion pieces of content (web links, news

stories, blog posts, notes, photo albums, etc.) are shared each month.

Global Reach

- More than 70 translations are available on the site.

- About 70% of Facebook users are outside the United States.

- Over 300,000 users helped translate the site through the translations application.

Mobile

- There are more than 150 million active users currently accessing Facebook through their mobile devices.

- People who use Facebook on their mobile devices are twice as active on Facebook as nonmobile users.

- There are more than 200 mobile operators in 60 countries working to deploy and promote Facebook mobile products.

You just can't ignore numbers like these. You must engage on Facebook.

CHAPTER 143

Profiting from Facebook

The opportunities to promote yourself and your products or services are extensive.
WWW.STARTUPNATION.COM

The first question to ask is "What's your business's goal for being on Facebook?" Ultimately the goal of most people will be twofold: to increase retention and sales by engaging existing customers, and to drive new business by finding additional customers. Like most marketing on the Internet, this will happen over a period of time and involve a number of phases.

The first step of your Facebook marketing campaign is to build brand awareness for your business and your Facebook page. People must know the general services you offer and that they can find out more about you on your Facebook page.

So how do you build awareness of your Facebook presence?

1. Your Exiting Website. Make sure you highlight your Facebook page on your existing website and let people know you are there as well as promoting all of your other social media.

2. Your Existing Email or Snail-Mail Databases. Use your existing email and snail-mail databases to let people know about your Facebook page. End every email with a promotion for your social media and make sure that all your ads and brochures carry your social media logos and addresses. It's Marketing 101 but you'd be amazed how many businesses forget to do this simple but powerful step.

3. SEO (search engine optimization). As you develop more content and links, your page will also help you develop better search engine rankings when people are looking for a business like yours.

4. Targeted Ads. Taking advantage of the Facebook advertising platform is also an option. The standard cost of a new fan for your Facebook Page is approximately $0.50. Ads are displayed to users based on their usage history. I get served up golf ads and also get a lot of exotic car related ads. Why? Because Facebook knows I like golf, cars, and marketing. It's very targeted.

5. Organic Growth. The very best way to grow your Facebook presence is organically. The golden rule of viral/organic growth online is *create great content that people will share*. It's honestly as simple as that. (See examples of great content in the blog section and on the following pages.)

There are lots of ways to use Facebook to market your business.

CHAPTER 144

Educating Your Facebook Visitors

Marketing should be education;
education should be marketing.
ANONYMOUS

For those visitors who already know your business, you may not need to do much education. For the rest, who are just beginning, or who are new to showing an interest in what you offer, the education process entails answering the following questions:

1. Who Are You? When I say "Who are you" I mean your identity that users can understand. Your business as a faceless organization cannot build relationships. As I tell people on a regular basis, you need to humanize your organization. Who is the manager, service staff, craftsmen? Who do you want as customers? By connecting with individuals on a personal level and letting them know that there are REAL PEOPLE behind the computer on the other end, you'll build a strong connection that will help the individual associate positive feelings with your business. Yes, you also need to let them know what your organization is, but the personal touch is much more important.

2. What Does Your Business Sell? This could be as simple as something within the information tab in your Facebook page that describes what your business offers in the way of products, services, memberships, and so on. You could also create an entire tab dedicated to describing your sales proposition.

3. Who's in Your Community? When a new visitor lands on your Facebook page, one of the first things they'll look at is the number of fans you have. You'll notice that as Facebook pages grow in size, they also tend to increase in the volume of new fans per day. This is because having a large number of fans turns you into a trusted authority.

Users will often browse through the members of your Facebook page to see who else is part of the community. They'll also view the comments people are posting to see if this is something they are interested in hearing about. Do you have brand advocates who are speaking up for you when you aren't around? Do you have fans who have something valuable to add to the conversation?

They say that you are who your friends are, and on Facebook, you are who your community is. Foster a valuable community and there's a greater chance you'll convert new visitors into fans.

4. Why Do I Want to Join? Finally, before becoming a fan the user will try to understand what benefits they are going to get from becoming a fan of your Facebook page. Make it easy for them. The benefit could simply be an opportunity to express their affiliation with your brand. Another benefit could be ongoing access to valuable content. If your Facebook page has nothing to offer the user, the only people who will become fans are those who are already your fans or those who are interested in existing community members. You want to also reach new customers so you'll need to present high value through your Facebook page.

Seek first to educate your customers and prospective customers.

CHAPTER 145

Engaging with Your Fans and Converting Them to Action

Relationship marketing [should have] the
characteristics of an interpersonal relationship.
THE MARKETING BOOK

Engagement has become the cornerstone of social marketing. The engagement process is critical to building a relationship with your fans and strengthening their personal feelings about your "brand." While some marketers criticize engagement for the inability to quantify it, every online marketer knows that engaging your customers is the new form of marketing. Rather than speaking at your customers, marketing has now become a two-way dialogue leaving many traditional advertisers feeling powerless and confused.

You aren't completely powerless though since you can control the environment in which much of the conversation takes place. While there are many other platforms for engaging your customer base, Facebook pages are a great environment for directly building relationships with a large portion of your customers and fans.

One thing to keep in mind is the impact that various forms of engagement have on the relationship with your customer:

- *Low Impact Activities*—There are a lot of low impact activities that a consumer can engage in. One example would be "liking" a status update in Facebook. ("Liking" is the feature in Facebook that lets you click "Like" under a feed story.)

- *Medium Impact Activities*—Commenting on a story could be one example of a medium impact activity.

- *High Impact Activities*—An individual or brand could turn a medium impact activity into a high-impact experience by providing one-on-one dialogue to turn the experience from a single comment to an ongoing conversation.

In contrast to search engine advertising, which involves prospects clicking on an ad and then (hopefully) taking some sort of action (e.g. filling out a form or purchasing a product), the Facebook sale normally involves building a relationship over time and eventually presenting opportunities to make a purchase, attend an event, book a tee time, call for an appointment, or to take some other form of measurable action. Most Facebook users are not ready to buy when they initially become a fan, which is why you need to present calls to action on a regular and ongoing basis.

Provide as many engagement opportunities as possible on your Facebook page.

CHAPTER 146

Your Facebook Profile Page

Who Are You?
How lovely to be somebody!
To tell your name the livelong day
To an admiring blog.
WITH APOLOGIES TO EMILY DICKINSON

The starting point for your presence on Facebook is your profile page. Your profile page is basically a landing page that you design in order to encourage your visitors to engage with you.

Not only is your profile the page that you have the most control over, it's the place where you can most deeply and authentically express your passion for the service, product, or business you want to promote. Your profile page is an opportunity to craft a credible, real-world story around the reasons you are the best in town. Take advantage of Personal Info, Work Info, Photos, and applications to tell bits and pieces of your narrative as it relates to your brand.

If you don't want to associate your personal identity with the product or service you're trying to promote, Facebook is not for you. Inherent in the current state of Facebook is a culture of transparency that values authenticity. If you're afraid to show the real people behind your business, that's okay — but save your time and money and go somewhere beside Facebook.

Most people don't realize how many page views profile pages

generate. One of the most common habits of Facebook users is browsing the profile pages of friends and "stalking" the profile pages of people they want to learn more about. By connecting to hundreds of partners, customers, associates, and friends on Facebook, you'll drive a TON of traffic to your profile page. Take advantage of that huge opportunity by making it a good one.

Fan Pages

You can have an unlimited number of fans. But there is a limit of 5,000 people with whom you can be *friends*, which is why many businesses and celebrities send people to their fan pages instead. Fan pages are also ideal for offshoot products or services (like my books). You might use fan pages off your main page for particular products or services to display their own voices and brands under your overall umbrella.

Use your Facebook profile page to advantage.

CHAPTER 147

What Should You Do on Facebook?

Posting on Facebook is a snap!
POPULARSCREENSAVERS.COM

The idea of using any new social media application can seem a bit daunting, but the interfaces are quite intuitive, and it's easy to jump right in.

- Start by inviting your friends to join you on Facebook.

- Then invite your customers.

- Then start looking at who they know and ask them to recommend you to their friends.

After these basics you need to think about what you can post on your page that will attract still more people.

1. Post Special Events. "Events" is a free application developed by Facebook that anyone can use to promote marketing events, sponsored parties, or even product launches, transactions, or company milestones. When you create an event, it gets a fully-featured page (much like a group) that includes a wall, discussion, photos, videos, and links. You can invite all of your friends to the event. Friends you invite will receive a special notification requesting their RSVP. You can also add admins to the event, who can also invite all of their friends and send messages to all who are attending the event. Facebook Events makes it easy to get the word out to hundreds of people, manage your guest list, and build community around your upcoming event.

2. Highlight Specific Services or Promotions. How many of your ongoing services and activities can be highlighted on your Facebook page? Charity events, open houses, lessons, new inventory, seafood night, happy hour, and so on are all things you should consider posting on your page.

3. Post Pictures of People Enjoying Your Services or Products. They say a picture is worth a 1000 words and when it comes to pictures of people enjoying your product or service they could be right. Make sure there are lots of pictures of any event you hold and get them up fast while the event is still newsworthy. Ask your fans to share picture of the event with their friends and all of a sudden you just went viral. Solicit pictures of your product in use from buyers. Take pictures of people who visit your office. You can get double duty out of these by posting them on Facebook and on your wall.

4. Post Videos. The more multimedia you can add to your Facebook page the more different people you are likely to attract. Post videos, audios, webinars, and slide shows.

5. Post Coupons and Ads. Intersperse regular promotions and specials in between your news, events photos, and links. You can do monthly, weekly, or even daily promotions provided that's not the only thing you do. Be sure to work real content in between your promotions and you will not risk offending your fans.

Remember the real beauty here is there are no spam filters or bad addresses. Everything you post will make it onto your fans wall. Use this power wisely.

CHAPTER 148

More Things to Post on Facebook

Many people are already in the habit of, "I have to go post to Facebook, I have to go see what's happening, I have to update my status."
SOUTHERN CALIFORNIA PUBLIC RADIO

Here are seven more types of information you can post on Facebook to generate interactions with fans.

1. Post Updates. People will appreciate knowing that your store is closed before getting in their car and driving twenty miles. Likewise it could be raining hard in Philly but sunny on the other side of the bridge in Jersey, thus giving you a great opportunity to get people to come out and play paintball with you if you tell them.

You can also post routine updates, explaining why or how certain things are being done and generally educate customers about your business.

2. Share Your History. Facebook is the place you can share your rich history. Pictures and stories from the past help to communicate the tradition and brand of your firm. You can show past and present pictures, discuss remodeling through the years, offer bios of the principles and prominent clients, and so forth.

3. Start Your Own Quick Poll. Get a quick feel of your customers' pulse with a poll on key issues. Answering will make them feel more involved with you which builds the relationship.

4. Promote Gift Certificates. Facebook is a great place to promote gift certificates. Your virtual presence on Facebook is open 24/7. Keep your buzz going while you sleep.

5. Post Links to Interesting Articles, Sites, or Videos. Use Facebook to bring attention to articles or reviews in other publications about you or your business. Use it to bring attention to other news and blogs on the Internet that you think your clients and prospects will find interesting or entertaining. While you may think it defeats the purpose to send your fans to other sites, the reverse is actually true. By providing your fans with quality content you become an authority and trusted source.

6. Post Interesting Facts and Testimonials. Facebook is the ideal place to solicit testimonials or re-post testimonials that have come in via email or snail mail. Re-post your recommendations from Linkedin and stream video or audio testimonials.

This gives you great third-party endorsements which are proven to significantly increase response in prospective customers.

7. Run Simple Quizzes to Encourage Engagement. Quizzes are a quick, easy way to get people interacting with your Facebook page and interaction is the KEY to building relationships.

Check out our Facebook page for more idea (http://www. facebook.com/CunninglyClever).

High-quality, high-content posts please fans and generate viral business.

CHAPTER 149

Maximizing Your Productivity on Facebook

The most important concept in interactive marketing
[may be] an experience that...helps the visitor
accomplish goals.
JIM NOVO

Here are several ways to increase your productivity on Facebook.

1. Incorporate the Tools You're Already Using into Your Profile. Do you blog? Do you tweet? Let's hope so after reading this section. Do you read feeds? There are Facebook apps available for all these services. If you already use these tools professionally, why not add them to your Facebook profile? After you add the respective app, you simply do what you were already doing and let the app do the work. You can see the Twitter updates from your Facebook contacts without necessarily following the updates on Twitter itself.

2. Join Groups Related to Your Business Interests. Many groups on Facebook are nonsense, but there are quite a few that can provide useful information and professional connections. Rather than trying to search for groups, watch the groups that your friends are joining. Often you will find them of interest for yourself. After all, they're in your contact list because you have something in common, right?

3. Add Apps Selectively. There are thousands of apps you can add to your Facebook profile. The temptation may be to try them all. Don't. Just because you can add love quotes to your profile, it doesn't mean you should if you want Facebook to be a professional tool for you. Think of your apps in two ways: 1) What do *you* want to see on your Facebook home page? and 2) What do you want the *world* to see that will appear on your profile?

Pick apps that won't waste your time when you visit your Facebook home page, so avoid those that involve playing games. Read the app description carefully. Know exactly what you're getting, and what the privacy settings are before you act. It helps to see how your contacts are using the app first. But never fear, if worst comes to worst you can remove an app as easily as you added it.

4. Limit Wasted Time on Facebook. Facebook can suck you in easily. It's very addictive once you get going—just ask any teenager. You, however, have important work to do. You won't help your business or career if you fall behind on projects because you were too busy playing in iLike! If you find that you're spending too much time reading Facebook message boards or reading about your friends' favorite book selections, then set limits for yourself. Check it only once or twice a day, switch off all the email notifications and ignore all the game requests.

5. Cross Marketing Your Social Media. The more you market the fact that you are active on social media, the more people you will connect with. Make sure you cross market at every opportunity. Everyone has their own favorite social media and it may not be the one you are most comfortable using.

Remember, there are a number of free apps you can use to make sure one social media posts seamlessly with another. Take advantage of them, they will save you a tons of time. That way when you tweet it will automatically post to your blog, Linkedin, and Facebook accounts and vice versa.

Also take advantage of smartphone tools like Echolon that allow you to tweet and Facebook from your iPhone.

Facebook can be a black hole; use it wisely or you might get lost.

CHAPTER 150

Using LinkedIn Productively

LinkedIn strengthens and extends your existing network
of trusted contacts.
LINKEDIN.COM

With over 60 million business users, LinkedIn is most popular with all types of business people: top executives, middle management, salespeople, business owners, consultants, entrepreneurs, and micro businesses. Some of them are the very people most likely to do business with you. In other words they can be your perfect prospects and contacts.

Understanding the importance of LinkedIn and how it can help you grow your business is an important part of your social media strategy. FastPitchNetworking.com is another fast-growing social site worth looking at with similar benefits to Linkedin but even more focused on business building.

LinkedIn can be used in many ways:

1. Boost Your Business. If you want to generate more customers, LinkedIn is a good place to start looking. The chances are very good that many potential clients are already on LinkedIn. Who are you trying to find, what company do you really want to land as a customer? Are you searching for a way in? LinkedIn is the answer. By using LinkedIn correctly, you can be introduced to the person you need to meet.

Let's say you have a business in Cincinnati and want to get the local BMW dealership's business. A quick search delivers Rick, who's also in charge of advertising.

2. Improve Your Google Results. Your LinkedIn profile will have a good Google page rank, so it should come up fairly high when people are looking for you by name on Google. Be sure and fill your profile with all the key information you want people to see.

3. Finding New Employees or Finding a Job Yourself. LinkedIn is a good place to look for new employees. Unlike all the major job search sites, it's free. When you post jobs you can attract both people actively looking for a job and people who are passively looking. Oftentimes LinkedIn job postings are forwarded by contacts because they think it might be a good fit. This creates a viral effect. LinkedIn is equally useful in finding suppliers and in finding a job when you are looking. **The key is to have your network well in place before you ever need a job.**

4. Checking References of Potential Hires or Suppliers. Trying to hire the perfect manager? You're not likely to find out about an applicant's sordid past mistakes by calling the references on their application. Do a search for others who worked at the same company at the same time, and get a better background check in minutes for free.

5. Research Companies and/or Business Opportunities. LinkedIn makes it easy to do extensive, business-related research all in one place. You'll have no trouble finding information about companies you may be considering dealing with or competing with. Through LinkedIn networking you may even learn about business opportunities of which you may have been previously unaware. Talk to employees or former employees of competitors. Former employees usually give more candid opinions about a business's prospects than someone who's still on board. You can also track "new" or "start up" businesses to find new opportunities for your business first.

6. Get and Give Professional Advice. LinkedIn Answers is a powerful resource you can use to get answers to your own business-related questions, while at the same time responding to others' questions based on your own areas of expertise. What do you need help with? Are you deciding between two POS software products for your business? Are you looking for the best marketing company for you? Need a graphic designer in London? Or a golf photographer in Leeds? All of these questions can be asked on LinkedIn and within minutes you will start receiving answers to help you make a good decision or direct you to a good resource. This give and take of questions, answers, and referrals can easily help forge mutually beneficial business relationships by creating a good dynamic between business peers.

7. Build Your Personal Network. Although I have my own CRM, iPhone, and Salesforce to keep all my information in "one" place, LinkedIn offers a clear advantage over all of them. When people move, change jobs, or start new ventures, they update their own contact information. This alone is worth the price of admission, saving the cost and hassle of updating your files yourself, and always giving you current contact information.

Build your network of connections, starting with friends, co-workers, suppliers, customers, and people you meet along the way. The larger your network and the more committed you are to engaging with it on a regular basis, the greater your success will be.

8. Increase Your Credibility and Build Your Brand. If you're trying to market yourself as an expert or develop credibility in your field, it looks good to have a strong presence with lots of connections on a network such as LinkedIn. If you answer questions with the knowledge of an expert in the Answers section, even better. Get active in the communities, groups, and forums within Linkedin

9. Find People. Looking for old friends or business associates who you want to re-establish a relationship with, former employers or employees, or someone you met at a cocktail party but can't find their card? Do a LinkedIn search. The local radio station just held an event at the business down the street and you'd like to host it next year. Try Linkedin first to find the right connection at the station.

Make it a point to build three new connections per day to create a large and targeted list of prospects in your area. If you don't know the contact directly, ask to be introduced from one of your existing contacts. Remember,**he with the biggest and best database wins. And nothing is better than a handcrafted one.**

10. Help Others. The best way to network is to help others succeed in their businesses or careers. This very often is the start of them trying to help you or your business. Use LinkedIn to help others — promote them, link to them, connect with them, recommend them, answer their questions, and so on. This includes friends, colleagues, suppliers, members, and clients.

11. Get Publicity. It can be hard to contact media or top bloggers. But many of them have a LinkedIn profile and you can contact them through these. I highly advise you not to spam them—but a press release or a polite email letting them know about something newsworthy at least will be noticed.

12. Build Business Referrals. People with whom you've done business in the past will be able to recommend you right on LinkedIn, and for those who don't you can politely solicit referrals from them. As you consistently expand your LinkedIn network by remaining active on the site, you should find your business on the receiving end of a growing number of referrals. Getting other people to say how great you are will attract more people.

13. Set LinkedIn Goals. Just like everything else in business, what gets measured gets done so it helps to set some simple goals to reach for. On LinkedIn your goals might be to connect with 10 more people per month, to recommend three people in your network, to receive five recommendations, or simply to meet with four connections this month on the phone or in person. Having goals is essential to insure you receive what you are looking for on LinkedIn.

LinkedIn is an excellent tool for business and personal networking, but you have to use it to get results.

CHAPTER 151

Delivering Social Proof

I never liked you, and I always will.
SAMUEL GOLDWYN

As I was traveling in France last summer, I used hotels.com, Vernere.com, TripAdvisor.com, and Bookings.com to locate and book rooms. Often, when the choice was not obvious from the limited information and photos provided, I looked at the guest reviews to help make my decision. In reality, this makes little sense since people's opinions are often different, even of the same experience. Nonetheless, I read them and was no doubt more influenced by them than I even know.

Ebay's reputation for safety was built in large part by customer ratings of the sellers. The same thing is true of buying a book on Amazon. Before they part with their hard earned money, people want social proof that the book will deliver the benefits or entertainment it promises. I'm proud of the quality of the readers' comments I have gotten for my books *Cunningly Clever Marketing, Cunningly Clever Selling,* and T*he Golf Marketing Bible*. I am sure they help sales stay strong.

What are people saying about your business?

Most people don't know what others are saying, but it's something you should check regularly. There may be one or two vocal people out there who could be badly damaging your online reputation.

People do look at and read these comments. They provide the social proof that your offer is what you say it is. Very often the negative comments about your business are unfair, but that doesn't make them any less harmful! They must be countered with a response, or with a stream of positive comments that relegates the negative ones to the dungeons of page ten!

A similar though different phenomenon of social proof occurred in our nightly quest for a great meal. There was a staggering number of restaurants from which to choose in every city during a recent visit.

How to choose? Well, generally not the one with no one in it (there must be a reason.) Most of the time, we chose busy, but not full, restaurants (we weren't inclined to wait). The fact that they were busy implied that others thought they were good—and in just about every case they were.

A further form of social proof is the positive comments others, (clients, staff, family, and friends to start) MUST be ENCOURAGED to provide on Facebook, Twitter, LinkedIn, Fast Pitch Networking, and MySpace to name just handful. If others are saying good things about you, it must be true!

Monitor and encourage, online and off-line, the social proof that tells the world your business is a winner.

CHAPTER 152

Exploit the Power of YouTube to Make Yourself a TV Star

Nothing is real unless it happens on television.
DANIEL J. BOORSTIN

YouTube is an amazingly cheap and powerful tool to create buzz. It basically gives you the ability to create you own TV show. If used correctly, that's serious power.

YouTube is the ideal place to share your expertise, highlight your products, and showcase your customers and results while you attract and entertain your existing and future clients. It's also a great way to go viral. It aids in generating web traffic and helps you climb up the search-engine rankings.

I use YouTube to showcase my sales and marketing expertise. Go to www.CunninglyClever.com to see samples or search Cunningly Clever directly on YouTube. Most of my shows are three to seven minutes in length and contain lots of meaty information, samples, and case histories.

At the end of each informative segment I direct viewers back to www.CunninglyClever.com to receive additional information. Once there, they can download additional free information, buy products, or sign up for ongoing access to my massive database of sales, marketing, and entrepreneurial information. The free shows in effect drive traffic back to the website, a percentage of which then become customers.

Many of the resorts I consult with use YouTube to showcase their golf courses, spaces, rooms, and other activities. Several restaurants I work with use YouTube to showcase different dishes they serve in the restaurant. Golf, karate, fitness, and instructors of all kinds use it to showcase their skills.

Then of course there are those businesses that put together funny skits that can quickly go viral. I did one such three-minute spot for a resort that featured Elvis playing golf, with Ozzy Osborne as his caddie, and Donald Trump playing through. It was watched by over 10,000 people in a single week. If you do "funny," make sure it somehow ties back into what you offer in order to be truly effective at building business as well as brand.

One important fact in marketing is that once you have produced a DVD and someone puts it in a machine and hits play, you are now on TV. The same is true of YouTube. It doesn't matter what it cost you to film it, you are up there just like Tom Cruise.

Being on that screen is an incredibly powerful tool in self-branding.

YouTube, is of course, not the only place you can upload your video content. Yahoo has a huge video section and there are another 30 or so mainstream sites and 125 additional ones that accept video content. That could be very time consuming. In fact, it was until I found Tube Mogul. There, for a small monthly fee if it's commercial and FREE if it's not, you can syndicate your content just like a big TV station to 30 or more key sites that accept video.

Don't wait for your chance at stardom; make yourself a star on YouTube!

Cunningly Clever
Selling for
Entrepreneurs

CHAPTER 153

Want Massive Growth? Then Train Your People How To Sell!

A minute's success pays the failure of years.
ROBERT BROWNING

Recently I had a call from a major resort asking what one idea I could give them to instantly improve revenue. The answer was easy and would have been the same had the caller wanted to sell more cars, computers, furniture, suits, consulting, or widgets: **Train your people how to sell!**

Nowhere in this entire book will you get faster results in terms of pure income than in this and the following section on how to sell. Few people in business genuinely "love" selling. Fewer still are good at it. In many ways, it's not surprising that most people don't like to sell. Selling not only has a bad image in many people's minds, *it often deserves it*. Telemarketing calls at dinner time, pushy salespeople who won't take no for an answer, and products and services that don't live up to their sales claims. These have all contributed to the bad image that sales has today.

In defense of sales, almost everyone sells in their everyday lives. Teachers need to sell students on the benefits of paying attention. Spouses sell their ideas to each other. Children sell their parents on staying up for that special TV show, and so on. Practice with sales will make it more comfortable if you have the right attitude.

Increasing your sales skills by even a few increments can dramatically increase your profits. Imagine if you closed two out of ten leads instead of one — you have just doubled sales at NO cost. Even small improvements in how you answer the phone, handle objections, and close can have massive impacts on your bottom line. Yet few businesses engage in the meaningful and ongoing sales training needed for entrepreneurial success.

A good sales training system must cover the following areas:

- how to get mentally ready to sell

- how to develop instant rapport

- how to qualify prospects

- how to give quality presentations

- how to handle objections

- how to close

- how to follow up

Having a documented sales training system for your business will be the best investment you ever make.

CHAPTER 154

Getting Mentally Ready to Sell— Conquering the Fears That Hold Back 99% of Salespeople from Being Superstars

It is not the mountain we conquer, but ourselves.
SIR EDMUND HILLARY

If you believe in what you are selling, your sincere attitude will communicate itself to your prospective customers. But you must have a positive attitude about the sales situation as well. If you or your staff feel uncomfortable selling, your prospect will feel uncomfortable buying from you no matter what you are selling.

Conquering the Two Great Fears

Before you can set off in pursuit of your quest for sales excellence, you must overcome the two great fears that hold back mere ordinary mortals. These fears exist in almost everyone, even great salespeople to a degree. They are:

- fear of money
- fear of failure

Until you have confronted these fears with your team and put them behind you forever, you will not achieve your true sales potential.

Fear of Money

Believe it or not, many salespeople are afraid to ask for money. Salespeople may be afraid to ask for large sums of money because they don't have enough money to buy the products they are selling. The fact that they are selling a product they themselves cannot afford may lead them to believe, at least subconsciously, that other people can't afford it either. Salespeople too often place a mental block on themselves and in doing so thwart their own efforts to obtain the success they deserve.

In my work with the PGA, I have found that despite the fact that golf professionals are working with some of the most affluent individuals in the country many of them are desperately afraid of asking for money. In this case, it's not because they don't make decent money themselves but because they don't want to be thought of as salespeople. What they don't seem to appreciate is that 90 percent of the people they deal with are businessmen or former businessmen who aren't offended by being asked for money. They expect it.

Overcoming Your Fear of Money

It's okay to make money selling. The more people you help to enjoy the benefits of what you offer, the more money you deserve to make. Whether or not *you* can afford to buy your product or service or wouldn't buy does not mean that others can't or won't. Whether or not you think it's expensive doesn't matter at all. Put your personal thoughts and prejudices away. Let your prospects decide whether or not they will spend their money. It's your job to give them the opportunity.

Fear of Failure or Rejection

Sometimes the problem that holds salespeople back is fear of failure or rejection. If salespeople had real faith in their products, they wouldn't feel rejected when prospects said no, but would sympathize with the prospects for not having the wisdom or money to take advantage of the opportunity they are being offered.

What's the worst that can happen?

When you make a phone call, greet an appointment, or welcome a "walk-in," what is the worst thing that can occur? I mean, after you have introduced yourself, made a presentation, and asked them to buy, what's the absolute worst thing that can happen to you? The prospect can hang up, walk out, call your mother names, or say no. That's it! Those are the worst things that can possibly happen. Compared to the millions of people who are dying every day, rejection is pretty minor!

Great. Now let's move on. There is one small problem we didn't mention—**EGO!** Our fragile human egos are such that when a person rejects our proposition, we take it as a personal affront. We feel humiliated, embarrassed, or even belittled. Rejection attacks our self-confidence and self-esteem.

Yet if you can let it go for what it is—a rejection of a sales proposition—you will have jumped a hurdle that many never cross.

Sales Is a Numbers Game

If you double the number of phone calls you make in a day, it will probably double your failure rate. But it will almost certainly double your sales at the same time. You know that when people don't buy your product or service they are *not* rejecting you. You know that when people REALLY can't afford your product they're *not* rejecting you. You know that when people are looking for a freebie gift rather than what you actually sell they're *not* rejecting you. How could it be personal when they don't even know *you*? Yes, it can *feel* like rejection; but come on, it's not!

Yes, many people will say no to you if you're doing a good sales job. But every no gets you closer to the person who wants to buy. And even the people who say no can give you referrals to friends who are more serious about doing business. So even if you *feel* like you're being rejected, you're NOT. You can't get over your feelings immediately, but you can begin. Take control of your feelings and move on to successful sales.

Fear of money and fear of rejection are two of the biggest hurdles most salespeople face. Deal with them and move on.

CHAPTER 155

Building Legendary Rapport

It's easy to fool the eye but it's hard to fool the heart.
AL PACINO

Rapport is the ability to bond with another person as you would with a friend, and, for a legendary salesperson, it is the most sought after of all conditions. Good rapport puts other people at their ease. They treat you as a person they are comfortable with, not a salesperson.

You start most sales relationships with one strike against you. People assume that you have *your* interests at heart rather than theirs. Thus, they naturally don't trust you until you can demonstrate that you are interested in them and can be helpful to them. Because of this negative conditioning, it is essential that you go the extra mile to be courteous, friendly, and professional as you start building rapport.

Calming Your Prospects' Fears

When people walk into your business to explore their options, it is very probable that they do so with some degree of trepidation. They are unsure of what to expect. Maybe you'll put a lot of pressure on them and it will be unpleasant. Maybe they won't be able to justify the purchase to their spouses. Maybe they won't feel that they fit in. One way to make most people more comfortable is to immediately tell them what will happen.

For instance, you could say something like:

> *Here's what I was planning to do in our time together: Ask you a few questions about your needs, tell you about our company, show you around, and answer your questions. Does that sound reasonable? Is there anything you want to know before we get started?*

Your foremost task in the initial sales contact is to make your prospect feel comfortable with you. Until this happens, it will be impossible for the prospect to make a buying decision.

Use the first few minutes of any sales encounter to remove your prospect's fear and help him or her to relax.

CHAPTER 156

If You Don't Sell Yourself First, You Won't Sell Anything

*Men in general judge far more from appearances than
from reality. All men have eyes,
but few have the gift of penetration.*
NICCOLO MACHIAVELLI

If prospects don't like you, they will not buy from you. That's pretty simple, isn't it? Consider for a moment. Do you buy products and services from people you don't like? No? Neither do most other people. Above all else, selling requires *selling yourself* to the prospect. If you don't do that, no sales technique in the world is going to save you.

The first few seconds of your contact with a prospect can determine your success in any sales interview. First impressions are lasting impressions and are usually the right impressions, at least as far as your prospect is concerned.

Your Appearance

The way you dress is very important in selling. Always be careful to strike a happy medium between *over*dressing and *under*dressing. Smartly attired people have an air of success about them. Without overpowering the audience you will be selling to, make an effort to improve your image by improving the quality of your clothing and tailoring. In the words of Henry Ward Beecher, "Clothes and manner do not make the man; but, when he is made, they greatly improve his appearance."

Is Your Office Destroying Rapport?

If you are selling from your own office or sales area, take heed. The way your office looks and feels can cost you sales. Be sure to avoid displaying anything that could create a negative response in a prospect or customer. The power of one negative image is almost ten times stronger than the power of one positive image. Your ultimate sales skill is to create in your prospect a powerful mental image of enjoying the benefits you offer. The best sales organizations in the world set up their offices in a very carefully thought-out way to inspire trust and positive feelings. They remove clutter and distraction so that the prospect's focus remains on the sales process. Testimonial letters from current happy customers are never out of place

Develop Winning Personal Traits

When asked what great secret he had found to influence people to his way of thinking, Abraham Lincoln replied, "If you would win a man over to your cause, first convince him that you are his sincere friend." To a great extent, the way people react to you depends on the little things—like smiling. When you are introduced to someone, always respond with a warm and friendly smile. Shake hands firmly because there are few things that turn people off quicker than a limp handshake. Stand up straight with your shoulders back and chest forward. Make good eye contact and generally let the other person know by your body language that you are a successful, professional, friendly, and confident individual who is genuinely glad to meet them.

How Do You Sound?

Next to your appearance, the tone of your voice and the way you deliver your words are the most important parts of making a good impression on the prospect. Make your conversation enthusiastic, friendly, and professional. If the prospect talks in a loud voice, raise yours slightly above its normal level. If the prospect speaks quietly, lower your voice a couple of decibels. Mirror your prospect's speech patterns by speaking a little slower or a little faster as appropriate. Remember, people establish the highest levels of rapport with others who are just like them. Your voice can indicate to prospects that you are indeed like them.

Body Language

The value of matching your prospect is equally true of basic body language. If the person you are dealing with has a military bearing and stands straight and tall, rather than lounging or slumping, it will definitely pay you to do the same. In your office, if the prospect leans forward, so should you. In short, mirroring your prospect's largely unconscious physical demeanor is one of the most effective ways to rapidly establish rapport. Be sure to use this technique in conjunction with the others mentioned in this chapter.

Compliments

Giving genuine compliments about your prospect or his possessions will almost certainly bring a favorable response. However, use caution in this area. Prospects easily detect false flattery. If you are insincere, you will lose their confidence, never to regain it. There are ways to make sure this never happens to you. Never make a compliment you do not mean and add a qualifying statement to all your compliments for added weight. For example, you might say to a women who walks into your place of business, "That's a beautiful sweater." Then immediately add a qualifier. "I gave one just like that to my wife last Christmas." You have demonstrated your sincerity. Why would you buy a sweater for your wife if you didn't find it attractive?

What's in a Name?

One of the surest ways to develop rapport is to remember a person's name. In his classic book, *How to Win friends and Influence People,* Dale Carnegie stated, "The sound of a person's name said correctly is one of the nicest sounds in the world, at least to them." Using someone's name is indeed one of the sincerest compliments you can pay a person. It builds self-esteem and lets him know you think he is important.

Sell yourself first to build rapport before trying to build credibility for your company or services.

CHAPTER 157

How to Open a Rapport-Building Conversation

After all, when you come right down to it, how many
people speak the same language, even when they speak
the same language?
RUSSELL HOBAN

In order to build rapport beyond the superficial stages, you have to get the prospect to talk to you. The best way to accomplish this is to ask open-ended questions. Open-ended questions are questions that can't be answered with a simple yes or no. They demand a more detailed response. Not only does this method build rapport, since you allow the customer to respond without interruption or contradiction, but it also provides you with valuable data for use in the sales presentation..

- Where are you from, Jack? [In states with rapidly expanding populations, like California, Florida, Arizona and Nevada, this is a good question, since the majority of people were born elsewhere.]

- What is the most important part of your job?

Move smoothly from basic questions to more specific lines of inquiry. It flatters people when you've done your homework. Don't ask questions that you should know the answers to from having looked at their website or social media pages

- How long have you lived here?

- That's an interesting occupation. How did you get into it?

- The more others talk about themselves, the more rapport you will be building, especially if you use active listening techniques.

Developing Active Listening Techniques to Increase Rapport

Active listening means showing the prospect that you are not only listening, but that you are interested in what he is saying.

Here are some of the ways you can do this:

- by holding eye contact and not looking around at anything else

- by nodding your head at appropriate points

- by raising an eyebrow (like Mr. Spock in Star Trek) to express surprise

- by laughing, smiling, and making occasional comments like, "Yes," "Uh-huh," or "I see" to show you are an active participant in the conversation, even though you aren't doing the talking

You will find that such active listening will draw people out and they will consider you an interesting person.

How People Process Information Affects Rapport

Essentially, people process information in one of three main ways—visually, aurally, and kinesthetically. Knowing which of these applies to a particular person can give you a much better chance of getting your point across. If a prospect asks to *see* the product or comments on the view from your office, he is almost certainly visual (and the majority of people fall into this category.) If he wants to *try* it for himself or comments on the *smell* of the trees, he is probably kinesthetic. If he asks you to *tell* him about your company, or *explain* the benefits of your product in detail, then he is probably auditory. In cases where someone displays a combination of two, or even all three of these forms, you can use multiple approaches, but one of them will usually be dominant. Understanding this human characteristic can be invaluable to your presentation by helping you to communicate better and faster with your prospect.

Asking a kinesthetic prospect to look at something is not nearly as valuable as having him do it himself. If you prevent a kinesthetic person from "feeling" things, you risk losing the sale. In the same way, if you simply talk to a visually oriented person you will soon lose his interest. If you can't tell which method your prospect uses to process information, try to use all three in your speech patterns. (It takes a little practice.) You will either find out what you need to know or at least will be sure that you have covered all the bases.

Use questions, active listening, and the communication orientation of your prospects to build rapport.

CHAPTER 158

Qualifying Your Prospects

*I never learn anything just by talking. I only
learn things when I ask questions.*
LOU HOLTZ

O nce rapport has been achieved, the next step in the sales process is to qualify your prospects. One of the biggest complaints by salespeople is that they are receiving "unqualified leads." The corresponding complaint from managers is that their salespeople can't close sales from the "great leads" they are given. To have success in any sales, you need to set up a system and then measure the results to demonstrate its effectiveness. You need to produce qualified leads, train your salespeople well, and measure performance.

What Is a Qualified Prospect?

Traditionally, a qualified prospect is someone who has a need for your product or service and the means to pay for it. If you are a garden center selling plants, any home owner in your area would be technically qualified. With plants, though, you're usually talking about a "want" rather than an actual "need."

If you are selling real estate, you will want further qualifications, such as high income. And you will need further information about their "means. " You need to find out how they would pay for it and if financing will be involved. And you need to find out how they will measure the value they receive for their investment. You also need to help them justify the purchase.

Some prospects are more equal than others!

The success of your sales program is based on generating the total number of leads needed to reach your goals. Successful programs recognize that leads come in varying qualities.

If you look at your prospects as a whole, you will get a very wide range of people — from those chomping at the bit to sign up to those with no intention of ever buying. Think of them as A, B, C, and D prospects.

- "A" leads include referrals, new people moving to the area, and customers of competitors unhappy with their current service.

- "B" leads include customers with no permanent supplier who can afford what you offer if they are shown the service and value they expect.

- "C" leads might be prospects or might not. They could be a source of future business and should be kept on a tickler program.

- "D" leads are simply not real prospects.

Referrals and people new to your area are often the best prospects. Direct mail leads offer the next best prospects since they can be prequalified by income, zip code, and other demographics. Telemarketing produces a wide range of leads but most tend to do better than average simply based on the professions that are targeted such as doctor, lawyers, and so forth. Web inquiries and telephone inquiries from newspaper or magazine ads tend to be far less qualified unless the ad was specifically written to discourage people from calling, which is an art in itself. (For instance, an ad might mention the financial qualifications needed to buy or you might have several qualifications as part of your online qualification.)

The bottom line is that all leads should be counted and standards created for the conversion of each kind. Referrals might sell at the rate of 1 in 2 or 3, while web leads might sell 1 in 20 or 30. You should measure an average return from each source.

Questions to Ask

You need to develop a series of questions that not only qualify people but go further to expand their thinking about their needs and your offer. For instance, confirming that prospects need your product and fit your income category isn't enough. You need to cover frequency of purchase, specific reasons they don't purchase from you more often, social influences, and so on. Prospects need to see you as helping them satisfy their needs, not selling to them to meet yours. The key qualifying questions you ask will depend on the nature of your business, your offer, and your location. Your questions need to be interesting to them. They need to enjoy the conversation. Here are some examples I use to qualify with my golf club and resort clients selling memberships:

- How often do you play?

- What's your handicap?

- Where do you play now? [If you know your market well, you should know if the answer is public or private, high-end or low-end, is the prospect looking to move up or down?]

- What three things do you enjoy most about playing?

- Does your spouse play?

- Do you have children? Do they play?

- What type of other activities does your family enjoy besides golf? (swimming, tennis, etc.)

- What type of work do you do?

- How often will you be visiting the area? (second memberships)

- Do you entertain clients on the course?

- What are the most important aspects of club membership for you? (get a game, great layout, convenient, etc.) Casually work the three or four most important questions you need into your initial conversation.

The more effectively you qualify your prospects the less time, money, and effort you will waste and the more sales you will make.

CHAPTER 159

Making an Effective Presentation

The lavish presentation appeals to me, and I've got to convince the others.
FREDDIE MERCURY

As you design your presentation, start by assuming that everyone who has qualified as a prospect wants to buy and buy *now*. This may eventually prove to be incorrect, but assume it anyway. Many people who are on the "edge" will make the decision to buy without your having to make a great deal of extra effort simply because you are so confident they want what you have to offer and today is the day they should buy.

Getting the Audience Involved in the Action

The more senses you can bring into play during the presentation, the better your chances of making a sale. Use sight, sound, feel, smell—anything you can to get prospects involved in your presentation.

Using Questions for Involvement

Questions can be an important part of your presentation by getting the prospects *involved* with your points. Prospects can't just sit back and pretend to listen when you ask them questions. And often, even if they wanted to remain detached, good questions will "hook" them into considering your proposition more seriously. Open-ended questions—questions that can't be answered yes or no—are best. Ask questions that get them talking about things that relate to features or benefits of your product or service.

The Points You Need to Cover

Many people think that giving a great presentation requires a gift of gab or a certain type of personality. Not so. There are many ways to give a winning presentation, the best of which is to write a script and practice it until you can deliver a legendary performance. A good presentation script will read a lot like a good direct mail letter. It will be full of features and benefits. While features are more objective, your emphasis should be on the benefits. There are usually more benefits than you think, and many of them are several levels deep.

List the features of your product or service that you want to cover in your presentation. Here is a good example from a country club to give you an idea of things you might include:

- history
- regional points of interest (for recent movers)
- types of members
- social activities
- the clubhouse
- the course(s)
- tournaments
- other facilities like tennis or swimming pool
- membership costs and financing programs

Now list the benefits that come from your features. (You may skip many features and go straight to benefits in your presentation.)

- family recreation and togetherness
- safe place for the kids
- relaxation
- new friends
- more social life
- exercise
- business contacts
- status
- meeting the "right" type of people
- a place to take customers
- money saved on vacations and entertainment

Simply spell out each benefit you want to convey on index cards or post it notes on your laptop and you have your basic presentation. Organize the cards from top to bottom with the lead benefits first (these may change depending on the prospect). Add a few testimonials from happy customers and you're well on your way to a great presentation. Time to start practicing.

Script your presentation just like a great movie. Develop the perfect script and the perfect delivery.

CHAPTER 160

Overcoming Objections

*An objection is not a rejection; it is simply a request for
more information.*
BO BENNETT

Objections are a necessary part of the sales process. Learn to
deal with them and you will close a much higher percentage of the prospects you meet. Unfortunately, many salespeople
take objections personally and their ability to complete the sale
is adversely influenced by this negativity.

**It's not personal. They are turning down buying, not turn-
ing down you.**

Think of objections not as rejections but as steps toward your
final goal. Rather than fearing objections, you need to ask good
questions to bring them out. An objection is not the *end* of the
sales process, it is the *beginning*.

Many objections mask a real or perceived problem. For
instance, if the prospect doesn't know your company, they will
hesitate to commit but may not bring up their lack of knowledge as
a reason. You should anticipate this issue and others such as cost,
and deal with them early by asking them if they have friends who
might use your services, assuring them that there are other people
like them, and so on. Hidden objections are often associated with
money. They will not want to admit that they are not qualified or
don't have decision authority.

Some objections arise as the result of nothing more serious than a lack of understanding. Your presentation didn't come across. In these cases it is necessary to further define and explain the benefits of your offer in clear and simple language. Use your sales material as the excellent business tool it should be. Put it in front of the prospect and check off the listed benefits, giving a short explanation of each benefit as you go. When features and benefits are there in black and white, any misunderstandings should soon vanish.

There are five important things to remember when you are dealing with objections:

1. Listen carefully to the objection. Resist the temptation to jump in before you have heard the full objection. Sometimes the prospect will talk himself out of it before you say a word.

2. The first thing you should do after an objection is thank them! This changes the tone of your interaction from adversarial to cooperative. It shows that you're not defensive or trying to avoid the objection. For instance, after you listen to an objection you could say, "I'm glad you brought that up." Or "Thanks for asking that question. It gives me the chance to explain…"

3. Never argue with a prospect. Remain calm and pleasant. They may just want you to listen to them.

4. If the objection is unclear, as in, "Well, I have to think about it," then ask more questions to isolate the real objection.

5. When you have the information you need, you can deal with the root of the objection. Convert objections to benefits. Remember, objections are not a surprise for you. And they should not lure you into an argumentative situation. After some study of this chapter, and consideration of your situation, you will know the issues that people will raise. Each concern they bring up gives you a chance to clarify a point and build further rapport.

Incorporate this five-step system into your sales process and you'll close more sales.

CHAPTER 161

The Feel-Felt-Found Solution

Brilliance without the capability to
communicate it is worth little in enterprise.
THOMAS LEACH

One of the most powerful objection busters in the business is the Feel-Felt-Found solution. That's why I gave it it's own chapter. It can be adapted to handle many different types of objections. When the prospect raises an objection, you listen attentively then follow up using these three steps:

1. "I understand how you FEEL." This statement avoids being argumentative and takes prospects' objections seriously. It tells them you were listening and shows that you do indeed have their best interests at heart.

2. Many of our clients FELT that way before they invested in our services. "For instance, Mr. Miller is in your line of work [church, age group, or other category]." This shows prospects that their concerns are valid and the fact that you name other customers they can relate to who had the same concern builds trust in you. "He worried about that but..."

3. What he FOUND was that... [your answer] there were lots of people with [concern]. However, his family enjoyed the club facilities, the contacts were valuable to his business, etc. Here are some examples that put all three steps together:

*I understand how you **feel** about our company having a $5,000 set-up fee while others do not. In fact, last year we were working with XYZ company from your state and their marketing director **felt** exactly the same way as you do. However, he **found** that being able to track the effectiveness of his ads by using our Marketing Commander solution saved him twice that much in the first month alone, and ten times that amount over the first year. As you know, no one else in the industry offers the ad- and phone-tracking features that we do. How much do you think you would save if by using our Marketing Commander technology you could cut out the 50-60% of your ads that are not effective?*

The feel-felt-found approach has been used successfully for over 50 years as a good way to respond to almost any objection. It allows you to take your winning story from current customers and create a personal solution that your prospect can identify with.

The feel-felt-found solution is one of the strongest techniques ever for dealing with objections. Add it to your repertoire.

CHAPTER 162

Anticipate Every Objection— Then Develop a Systematic Way to Deal with Each of Them

The best way to escape from a problem is to solve it.
BRENDAN FRANCIS

Many objections can be dealt with in the sales presentation by bringing them up before the prospect does and solving them. This neutralizes the objection before it is even voiced. Objections that can't be dealt with during the presentation should have been anticipated and a perfect answer scripted out as the response.

In a good sales system, there can only be one perfect answer to any objection. The answer to each should be carefully crafted to be the best answer possible, then learned and used exactly as scripted by everyone on staff. This is the type of approach used by Disney, Ritz-Carlton, and the world's best companies for a simple reason: It works. This may sound very rigid, but if you think about it, it's true at least 95% of the time. Sure, intuition and experience can come into play 5% of the time, but 95% of the time a well-orchestrated approach will produce better results. That's why movies have scripts. That's why comedians have scripts and practice delivering the lines so they don't sound like scripts—95% of the jokes you ever heard delivered, from Johnny

Carson to Jim Carrey, were scripted, rehearsed, practiced, and timed to be delivered to appear that they were told spontaneously.

Let me give you an example of a scripted response to an objection. Suppose a membership prospect at a golf club asks the simple question, "How long does it typically take to play a round of golf at your club?" (Four hours would be typical, but way slower than I like to play.)

Now let's look at how three different people could choose to answer that simple but deadly question.

    A)   It takes about 4 hours and 30 minutes.

    B)   It depends on what day you play: sometimes it's fast; sometimes it's slow.

    C)   We are committed to a pace-of-play policy that ensures maximum enjoyment for all of our members.

All of these are possible answers to the question but only one is actually the very best answer. The answer that does NOT turn off the prospect mentally IF he happens to be like me and hates slow play. The best answer, C, will produce better results for you every time than either of the other two answers or an off-the-cuff answer.

Here are some other examples where C is always the best answer of the three:

What kind of gas mileage does this car get?

    A)   18 in the city.

    B)   34 on the highways.

    C)   It gets the best mileage in it's class.

How long will it take me to lose twenty pounds?

A) 12 weeks.

B) 6 weeks.

C) Our program allows you to lose weight as fast or as slowly as you are comfortable with.

This doesn't mean that some people won't follow up with a more probing question that you have to answer more specifically, but 80% of them won't. What's more, you will make more sales by giving answers that do not exclude your prospects from buying because the specific answer was not what they wanted to hear.

Often many of the questions people ask are not that important; they ask so they seem like intelligent consumers. It's expected that they ask questions. Many are irrelevant to their main wants and needs, but answer them wrong and you blow the sale.

You can take a teenager and turn him into a sales genius by providing scripted answers to every question. If you are already a sales professional, this exercise can dramatically increase your income. But remember there is only ONE perfect answer to any question: Find it.

Here are a couple more examples:

Objection: The price is too high!

I understand. Prices today are certainly higher than they used to be in the past and will no doubt keep rising. This of course may work to your advantage for your investment.

Objection: I hear not all your customers are happy.

Really? I am surprised to hear you say that. In fact whenever I hear things like that floating around I often smile to myself as I think of the words Lincoln so aptly said, "Most people are about as happy as they make up their minds to be." Wouldn't you agree?

I love this one (made it up myself). I mean people might argue with you or me but who's going to argue with honest Abe?

You must anticipate every objection, and write the perfectly scripted answer for each.

CHAPTER 163

Legendary Closing

Well done is better than well said.
BENJAMIN FRANKLIN

Closing the sale is *the* key step in the sales process. All the money, time, sweat, and skill you've put into your sales effort mean nothing if you can't get the prospect to buy. Many salespeople get so caught up in their sales pitches that they fail to observe that the prospect is radiating all kinds of buying signals. The prospect is ready to buy, but the salesperson doesn't know when to be quiet and go for the close.

Dave Richardson, writing on InStoreMag.com has done unofficial surveys in jewelry stores to see if they will close the sale. He finds that more than half the salespeople won't ask for the sale. He notes that:

- Salespeople, on an average, miss 2.5 buying signals in every sale.

- Many salespeople wait to hear the customer say, I'll take it, and only then are they comfortable closing the sale.

One thing that epitomizes cunningly clever selling is knowing exactly when to stop presenting and start closing. The key to selling is getting the prospect excited about your offer. Once that has been accomplished, you must provide him with logical reasons why he must buy *today*. Then you must close. Continuing to talk after the prospect is ready to buy is overkill and often leads to a lost sale rather than successful closing. In fact, studies show that an astonishing 63 percent of all sales presentations are given without the salesperson actually asking the prospect to buy.

Close Early and Often

As you probably know by now, "closing" a sale means that your prospect has agreed to purchase. To be even more specific, they need to have signed the contract and given you a check (that clears the bank). Closing is *the purpose* of the sales process. Many people are uncomfortable actually asking for the sale. As mentioned earlier, most of us have a bad image of sales and don't want to seem "pushy." That's one reason people don't close enough. Another is that they think closing should come only *after* all the other steps in the sales process. In fact, sometimes the prospect is ready to be closed early. But you won't know this unless you try.

The prospect may be ready to buy when he walks in the door. You will make more sales if you ask for the sale early and often. Another benefit of trying to close early in the presentation is that it will get you over your discomfort about asking for the sale in general.

Early attempts to close the sale are called "trial closes." You don't necessarily expect them to work, but they sometimes do.

Here are a few examples:

When Mr. Miller walks into your office for your appointment, you might say: "Welcome Mr. Miller. Are you ready to invest in a new machine today or do you have some questions?"

While immediately asking for the sale is an unusual approach, you'd be surprised how often it can work. And you can see how it gives you more information, flatters the prospect, and focuses the interaction on the sale. In response to the first question, Mr. Miller might say yes, no, or maybe. Exactly what he says, and *how* he says it will give you information to better direct your sales presentation. For instance if he says "I might be interested if you can show me XYZ benefit," then you know what you need to start with.

Another point where you might try a trial close is when the person looks bored or distracted. You might say: You look as bored as my husband does when I'm telling him what he needs to do around the house. Is there something else you'd like me to cover, or are you ready to invest now?

If you don't feel comfortable using a humorous approach, you could say: It looks like you may not need more information on this point. Is there something else you'd like me to cover, or are you ready to buy now?

The exact words you say for these trial closes can vary. You need to adapt your script to your circumstances and personality. By asking early, you'll get more information about the prospect and his interests. You'll have a chance to better focus your presentation on what he wants to hear. Asking early and often makes closing a natural part of your presentation—not something you put off until the end when it may be too late to make adjustments. So ask—you never know when you'll get a pleasant yes.

Start trial closes early in your sales presentation; the prospect may actually want to buy!

CHAPTER 164

Spotting Closing Signals

Customers send out clear closing signals all the time,
yet most salespeople just don't register them.
INSTOREMAG.COM

L et's look at some common closing signals that will alert you
to when your prospect is ready to buy.

Verbal Closing Signals

Often you can tell that a prospect's level of interest has risen
by the type of questions or statements he makes. These suggest
that the prospect is now thinking like a customer.

- Do other [people like me] buy this model?

- Can I pay in three installments?

- I kind of like this one.

- Do you take credit cards?

- Do you have a guarantee?

- What type of special deals do you have?

Stay Focused on Closing

When the prospect asks questions like the ones just mentioned, try another trial close. Answer each question quickly and professionally in accordance with the answers in your presentation and objections scripts and then go directly for the close—ask for the sale.

Do not allow yourself to become distracted from selling by answering a series of questions that do not lead to the close. Always draw your prospect's attention back to closing (or your presentation if necessary). If the prospect persists in a series of distracting questions, excuse yourself and leave the room for a moment. This will help you regain control of the conversation. When you return, sit down and get right back into your closing sequence or structured presentation. Lead and remain in charge, but never be "pushy." Just because someone asks a question doesn't mean you have to answer it immediately, or even at all.

For instance, you could say, "I'll be getting to that point a bit later." You are in charge of the situation. It's up to you to dictate the pace and control the interaction. When a prospect asks if he can pay in three installments, don't say yes. Instead, say, "Are you ready to invest if I can arrange a three-part payment?" The answer will tell you if it was an idle question (or one trying to distract you), or if the prospect is ready to go.

Nonverbal Closing Signals

You must not only listen to what your prospect *says*, but watch his body language as well. The majority of communication is *not* based on *what* your prospect says. Below are some of the clues you may observe that will help you pick the right moment to close.

- nodding in agreement

- making more frequent eye contact

- leaning towards you

- picking up your sales literature and intently studying it

Be alert for such signals. When you observe any of them, bring your presentation to a pause point and try a trial close. You will find your sales volume increases significantly when you raise your level of alertness to nonverbal signals.

Getting to the Close

In order to ask for the sale smoothly, you need to set it up in advance. The way to do this is with your trial closes. As just mentioned, usually you'll attempt a trial close after the prospect has shown buying signals. If the close works, great. If not, follow the procedures in the objections section to isolate and answer any concerns and then go back to your presentation or float another trial close.

Be alert for verbal and nonverbal closing signals to find the best time to close.

CHAPTER 165

Legendary Closes

One of the reasons mature people stop learning is they
become less and less willing to risk failure.
JOHN GARDNER

The professional salesperson knows that every prospect has a close that fits him or her—one that appeals to him on a most personal level. The secret is to find out which one will resonate most deeply with your prospect so you can obtain a favorable response and make the sale.

There are several closes below that have been successful for decades in selling. Although you might know some of them by other names, anyone who has been in sales for even a short period of time will recognize many of them. Others may be new to you. You might like some of them; you might hate others. It's important to be completely comfortable with the closes that work best for your style and personality. As you go through the following closes, adapt them to match your style and selling situation. Whichever closes you choose to adopt, practice them, role play them, and perfect them. The more you practice, the more they will flow naturally. The one thing that is certain is that if you don't ask prospects to buy, they won't.

Closing on an Objection or Question

Very often a prospect's question or objection gives you the perfect segue into closing the sale and you must be alert for such opportunities. This is also called the conditional sale because it sets a condition that if met results in a closed sale.

For example:

Prospect: *How quickly will I learn French with your program?*

Salesperson: *How quickly do you want to learn it? Obviously the sooner you start, the sooner you will begin enjoying the benefits. Let's get things going now.*

* * * * *

Prospect: *Do you have it in red?*

Salesperson: *If I can find a red one, do you want to take it with you?*

The Straightforward Close

> *Mr. Miller, based on what you have seen, do you think that Legendary Country Club is the type of club where you would like to become a member?*

The Assumptive Close

Always assume that the prospect is going to buy. The assumptive close handles the sales interaction as if you were certain that the prospect would buy.

> *Mr. Miller, based on our conversation it seems like this solution meets most of your criteria. Would you like to start using it at once before the price increase?*

The Alternative Close

The alternative close is perhaps the best known of all closing techniques and has many variations, depending on the exact circumstances. Another common name for it is the "either-or" close. This close gives the prospect the choice between buying and buying, between yes and yes.

Shall we put an offer in on this property, or the first property we looked at today?

* * * * *

Would you like to start your dance classes tonight, or would tomorrow night be more convenient for you?

When you give the prospect a choice of free benefits, it is much more difficult to say no:

Would you like the free gift or the free month of service?"

When your prospect is on the verge of making a buying decision, the most direct way of closing the sale is to ask how he intends to pay for it. This approach can best be used when a prospect has made the decision to buy, but is asking unrelated questions—the kind that prevent him from giving you the order. At this point, "Will you be using a credit card or cash?" is the best way to take control of the sale and complete it.

Each one of the previous alternative closes offers the prospect a choice. No matter which one they choose, they will feel committed to buy once they have made the choice.

The Action Close

In the action close you ask the prospect to *do* something to accelerate the process and help them make a positive decision.

Shall we head over to the design center and pick your carpets?

* * * * *

Shall I get the car detailed for you while we finish the paperwork?

The Minute-or-Cents Close

If you have a prospect who is stuck on price, the way to handle it is to break it down to ridiculous proportions. This is how life insurance has been sold for decades, but this type of close works just as well selling any mid- to high-end product, especially to value-oriented prospects. When you show people how little your service will cost them on a daily basis, it makes it much easier for them to justify, or rationalize, the purchase.

Due to the efficiency of this machine, your copies will only cost about one cent per copy. I am sure you will agree the savings this offers easily justifies the investment.

* * * * *

This website, with all the features and benefits it offers, comes to just $9.95 a day."

* * * * *

Membership in our health club is just a dollar a day. Isn't your health worth a dollar a day?"

The Puppy-Dog Close

This close is often used when a prospect is hesitant to purchase because of price. The "giveaway" close, or puppy-dog close as it is often called, allows the prospect to enjoy your product or service for a period of time before making a final decision on whether to buy. Once the prospect has experienced the product in a risk-free way and been treated well by your staff, he will almost always buy. He'd almost be embarrassed not to.

Here's an example of a close with a copier machine playing the role of the puppy:

> *Ms. Prospect, we have already agreed that you need this new copier. The speed and sorting capabilities will enhance your business. With your permission, I am going to have a machine delivered to you on Monday and let you see first hand just how valuable it will prove to be for your business. If at the end of two weeks the advantages are not readily apparent to you, I will remove it with no questions asked. Shall we go ahead and set that trial period in motion for you now?*

There are almost an unlimited number of ways to close a sale. I've covered just a few of most successful ones here. Try them, say them out loud, and role play them with your staff.

Find the closes that seem most natural for you and put them into action at once.

CHAPTER 166

Legendary Follow-Up

Instead of loving your enemies, treat your friends a little better.
ED HOWE

Someone once said, *"It takes less effort to keep an old customer satisfied than to get a new customer interested."* The final element of a great sales system is the follow-up. No matter what you are selling, your job doesn't end the instant the client completes the purchase. You want your relationship with the customer to continue and grow stronger, so he will buy from you again and recommend you to friends.

Reinforce the Buying Decision

After you have made a sale, reinforce the buying decision immediately. Compliment the buyer's choice by saying, very sincerely, something like, "Based on what you have told me, I'm sure your new exercise machine is exactly what you need to get in great shape. I know you are going to be very happy with it." In other words, reassure your customer that the decision to buy your product, rather than one offered by anyone else, is an excellent one. Be sure to thank them for their business; they had a choice and they chose you.

Reward the Customer for Buying Your Product

Consider rewarding your new customers with a little something extra that they didn't expect. A coffee mug with your logo on it, a T-shirt displaying your company's name, or some other inexpensive gift can help get your relationship with them off to a great start. The value of the reward would, of course, be commensurate with the amount of the purchase or size of the sale. You are giving the customer something more than you promised during your presentation.

Send a Thank You Note or at Least An Email

Send your customer a thank you note. Usually the only letters a customer gets from people with whom he does business are bills or ads for additional products. Let your customers know you are different; you have a touch of class. People love to be thanked. The same is true of staying in touch with *your* clients. If you wait for Christmas or a birthday to come around before you mail them a card, you may well find you have to send them a "Where did you go?" card, instead of the greeting card you had planned. As Harvey Mackay said, "Little things don't mean a lot; they mean everything."

Follow Up with Calls to Insure Satisfaction, Upsell, and Ask for Referrals

In any type of larger sale, or in any type of service business, you should always follow up with a courtesy call. There are three excellent reasons for doing this.

First, to insure satisfaction with the product or service. If there's no problem, that's fine. If anything is wrong, fix it at once and you'll get a repeat customer.

Second, you will often get the chance for an add-on or upsell once the customer has started to use the product.

Third, you can uncover new leads and referrals. For example, you call Bob and ask him how he likes his new Jaguar. Specifically you ask him what his neighbors said when they saw him in it. He tells you that Tom, his next door neighbor, is green with envy, and he wouldn't be surprised if Tom came in to look at a new Jag in the near future. You, of course, cannot rely on such a chance encounter, and inquire if you might have Tom's phone number, so you can give him the same great deal and service.

Retention

The fastest and best way to build total sales volume is to keep your present customers as you are adding new ones to your list. The easiest and most effective way to do so, is to constantly communicate that you care about them, both on and off the job. Take time to follow up in a way that will mean something to your clients. Don't cut corners by taking the easy way out. You will find the extra effort you expend will pay big dividends in the future.

Develop Your Sales System

You should develop a system that you apply to your sales. They are the life blood of any business. Your sales presentation should be carefully scripted. However, you don't need any special gift of gab to be a cunningly clever salesperson. You just need to involve your prospect and explain your benefits in a credible way.

Overcoming objections to your presentations is one of the most challenging parts of the sales process. Yet if you believe in your value, you help people to see the benefits more clearly. As you learn to deal better with objections, you will also improve your qualifying, presenting, and closing. The sales system works together to make you more effective. Just remember, your benefits can overcome any objections for the right prospects. Look for them, find them, and help them see how your offer meets their needs.

Develop a follow-up system to build and enhance relationships with customers.

Best Sales Tip of All—Buy This Book or Listen to These Audios

In this section I have provided you with some of my most valuable sales concepts, but since I can only devote one chapter to this critical function you must go further. You must invest in *Cunningly Clever Selling*. Yes, it's a shameless ad for another one of my books in this one. (I did not include this page in the page count.) But it's a book you will thank me for a million times over once you read it and instantly profit from it's advice. The audios make for a great staff training program. Your staff can become sales superstars in the comfort of their cars!

Visit www.CunninglyCleverSelling.com.

Critical Factors to Overcoming Business Adversity and Making Millions

CHAPTER 167

Vanquish Business Failure by Studying Success

Our greatest glory is not in never falling,
but in rising every time we fall.
CONFUCIUS

I didn't have to figure out how to be a successful entrepreneur by myself. I am fortunate to have learned about business from a great many of my friends, the majority of whom are self-made millionaires and entrepreneurs in an amazing variety of businesses. Scott Jaffe in the financial services business. Marcus Adolfson in Internet retail. Alan Sutherland in environmental services. Pat and Linda Parelli in the horse training business. Russ Hatle and Pete Rosberg in real estate development. Bill Clark and a host of others in the martial arts business. David Frost, PGA Tour player and vineyard owner. Robert Lynch in the carpet business. All started with little or nothing and grew their enterprises into multimillion-dollar businesses.

Ever since I was a bag boy at the Wellington Country Club, back in the 1980s, I made a habit of asking people how they made their money. What did they do to become successful in the hairdressing business, the jewelry business, or the printing business? I was still doing it fifteen years later after I made my first million. My new friends in California were a completely different crowd, including rock stars and band promoters, art gallery owners, and mortgage brokers. The answers I got were surprisingly similar.

Beyond my own circle of friends and acquaintances, I have studied the biographies of a great many of the world's most successful entrepreneurs—Richard Branson, Donald Trump, Felix Dennis, and many more. Whether their success ended up in millions or billions, there are common factors to all entrepreneurial success, factors that allow some people to succeed at an astonishing level while others only eke out a living.

Between my study of famous entrepreneurs, the observation of my friends, my constant questioning of every successful person I have ever met, and my own meandering experiences, I have come up with 12 factors that really make the difference between entrepreneurial success and failure.

Read these success factors;
believe them;
live them.

CHAPTER 168

The Persistence Factor:
The Turning Point to Greatness

Success consists of going from failure to failure
without loss of enthusiasm.
WINSTON CHURCHILL

Running a small business is never easy. It comes with long hours, red tape, unreliable staff or suppliers, and finicky customers. It can be a seemingly never-ending roller coaster ride of emotional and financial highs and lows. Just about every business struggles for survival at some point in its life. In fact, the average self-made millionaire has been broke, bankrupt, or financially destitute 3.7 times before becoming a financial success.

My first karate school was running on air for months before I cracked the code and eventually turned it into a chain of 400 schools. Along the way, my savings vanished, my house was mortgaged beyond its worth, and I had $127,000 spread over an ever-expanding collection of credit cards.

On its first day of operation, with a fleet of air freighters flying in from all over the country to its Memphis headquarters, the ground crews of Federal Express waited expectantly. As the planes landed one after another and rolled up to the unloading dock, the crews scurried around like ants picking up packages from each plane and taking them to the central distribution center. When they had completed this task, they found a total of 16 packages had arrived! Today FedEx is synonymous with overnight delivery, and a major worldwide success story.

Colonel Sanders, of KFC fame, was 65 years old sitting on the front porch of his failing motel when his social security check of $105 arrived to see him through the month. Disgusted and with little hope of increasing his motel business since the new Interstate had stolen all his traffic, he thought hard about what he could do well. The only thing that came to mind was his fried chicken, people went crazy over it. Armed with nothing more than a handwritten recipe, this senior citizen hit the road and visited *1010* roadside restaurants before one agreed to buy his chicken recipe and pay him a 5% residual fee on the sales. That person went on to be a multimillionaire—as of course did the Colonel. By 1964, Colonel Sanders had 600 franchises selling his trademark chicken. At this time, he sold his company for $2 million dollars but remained as a spokesperson. In 1976, the Colonel was ranked as the world's second most recognizable celebrity.

McDonald's founder, Ray Kroc, was once on the verge of bankruptcy, even with 200 stores in operation. Baron Hilton (founder of Hilton Hotels) was so desperate for cash to meet payroll at one point that he kept his hotel chain going with a loan from a bellboy of just $300. In the 1980s, former heavyweight boxing champion George Foreman was on the verge of bankruptcy. In Foreman's case, fear of financial ruin proved to be a good thing because it drove him to re-enter the boxing ring at age 45 and regain his heavyweight title against Michael Moorer in 1994. This second chance at success enabled him to pay off millions of dollars of debt and launch a new career as an entrepreneur hawking George Foreman Grills. Millions have been sold; in fact, I think we have two.

Donald Trump, the business mogul who's known for his reality series *The Apprentice* and his tagline, "You're fired!" probably should've fired himself after two bankruptcies. The first bankruptcy of his hotel/casino empire occurred in the early nineties to the tune of hundreds of millions of dollars. His second business bankruptcy occurred in 2004, this time to the tune of $1.8 billion. In 2005, Trump stepped down as CEO of Trump Entertainment Resorts, Inc. Meanwhile he has a hit TV show, *The Apprentice,* and is aggressively rebuilding his real estate and entertainment empire yet again.

Before Rich DeVos and Jay Van Andel struck diamonds by founding the Amway Corporation, they sold products for Nutralite. Nutralite was a California company that marketed products through direct sales in much the same way as Amway would later do. Shortly after embarking upon their new venture, they held what was to be a large meeting to try to attract distributors.

They ran radio and newspaper ads, handed out flyers, and scoured the town, telling everyone about the meeting and the excellent business opportunity they would be offering. They believed wholeheartedly in the products and the income potential they offered to other distributors. Because they felt so good about the product, they felt sure the hall would be filled to capacity with people eager to hear what they had to say. That night, despite their huge promotional effort, only two people showed up in a room set up for several hundred people.

They gave their sales pitch as best as they could to these two people and then drove home through the night because they couldn't afford a motel room. Looking back and laughing at the incident, DeVos said, "We could have done one of two things. Either we could give up, or we could persist. We persisted." Later, as Amway became a billion-dollar corporation, they bought the Nutralite company they had once represented.

It is truly amazing how many turning points in the lives of

most entrepreneurs come down to the same decision. Should we try again, or should we throw in the towel and settle down to a life of peace and security, such as it is. There is absolutely no better long-term solution to business success than single-minded, bulldog determination. There must, of course, be a capacity for making changes to deal with fluctuations in market conditions. Constant attention must be paid to implementing necessary changes in strategy, marketing, and sales, but the long-term goals remain the same.

Persistence is the ingredient that truly separates those at the top from the also-rans and wannabes. Like all the other ingredients, it can be easily learned, and putting it into action is as easy as deciding to just do it! Out of the greatest disasters come the greatest redemptions. As legendary radio commentator Paul Harvey so aptly put it, "In times like these, it pays to remember there have always been times like these."

The desire and determination to succeed must never waver.

CHAPTER 169

The Experience Factor
and the Power of Failure

*If you're not failing every now and again, it's a sign
you're not doing anything very innovative.*
Woody Allen

*Experience is what you get when you are looking for some-
thing else.* I read that quote by Mark Twain on the back of a
matchbox when I was a child. I quoted it widely whenever anyone told me what a great experience it was to play in a big golf
tournament, even if you played like a dog. In a nutshell, gaining
experience is often very disappointing.

Many of the entrepreneurial giants of history have had
to experience the ignominy of failure many times over. The
difference is in how these great people viewed their failures.
Many refused to look upon them as failures at all. Rather, they
considered them, as did Edison in his thousands of unsuccessful
attempts to design a light bulb, as successfully demonstrating
how *not* to accomplish a particular task. By eliminating another
idea that didn't work, the path to success became clearer. This is
a classic example of positive re-framing.

Almost all business building involves a painful process of
fixing problems, thus eliminating things that don't work in the
hope of eventually finding something that does. Learn to treat
each setback you encounter as another way not to reach your

goals. You'll never have to waste time doing things this particular way again. Instead, you will regroup and try a different approach, knowing you are now closer to your goal. By genuinely learning from your experiences, you can see how your setbacks are necessary steps on the path to success.

There is a famous tale of an IBM employee who blew a $10-million deal and offered company president Tom Watson his resignation. Watson, who had hired the man, looked at him as if astonished and said, "I can't possibly let you go. I've just spent $10 million dollars training you!" The employee, armed with an increased sense of loyalty and trust, went on to a long and mutually profitable career with Big Blue.

Watson understood the principle of experience and tried to teach it to others. "Would you like me to give you a formula for success?" asked Watson in a speech. "Double your rate of failure... You're thinking of failure as the enemy of success. But it isn't at all. Go ahead and make mistakes. Make all you can. Because, remember, that's where you'll find success — on the far side of failure."

Cunningly clever entrepreneurs have a way of turning weeds into roses, in part to guard against severely bruising their self-confidence and hurting their resolve. Cunningly clever entrepreneurs learn to redirect any situation in their favor by using the experience factor.

One reason so many people never become persistent is because they take every rejection, setback, or failure personally. They somehow equate their idea, product, or service with their personal self-esteem and worth. In this type of negative thinking, each business setback means the person is a failure and a loser in life, and will never get ahead. Think back to past setbacks. Are they really a reflection of you as a person? Of course not.

Give Yourself a Break

Get out of the habit of beating yourself up mentally when things go wrong. There are plenty of other people out there who are only too willing to do it for you! By focusing on blaming yourself, you are breaking down your own persistence and resolve like a wrecking ball. By all means, analyze what went wrong, but don't take the rap personally, even if it was your fault. Simply focus on a new angle of attack and use your mental energy to come up with a new solution.

Remember, the past does not reflect what will happen in the future.

The Disney Company, now recognized around the world, has annual revenues of $35 billion. But life wasn't always so good for founder Walt Disney. His early company producing Laugh-O-Grams for Newman cinemas in the Kansas City area was unable to generate enough income to cover the animators' high salaries. It went bankrupt... and Walt went to Hollywood. That might be the best lesson to learn from his bankruptcy: a failure doesn't have to be the end of the story. In fact, it might just provide the experience needed to create the next big success.

There is no success in anything without some failure along the way. The key is to fail fast, admit bad decisions quickly, and kill them fast. As W.C. Fields once said, "If at first you don't succeed, quit. There is no use being a damn fool about it!" What he forgot to add was, "Learn from your experience and quickly move on with more productive strategies."

Use your experience to turn
defeats into victories.

CHAPTER 170

The Reality Factor

Face reality as it is, not as it was or
as you wish it to be.
JACK WELCH

In his book, *The 50th Law,* co-authored with Robert Greene (*48 Laws of Power*), rap star and entrepreneurial multimillionaire Curtis Jackson, aka 50 Cent, says the first key to success is to live in reality.

See things for what they are—intense realism. Reality can be rather harsh. Your days are numbered. It takes constant effort to carve a place for yourself in this ruthlessly competitive world and hold on to it. People can be treacherous. They bring endless battles into your life. Your task is to resist the temptation to wish it were all different; instead, you must fearlessly accept these circumstances, even embrace them. By focusing your attention on what is going on around you, you will gain a sharp appreciation for what makes some people advance and others fall behind. The firmer your grasp on reality, the more power you will have to alter it for your purpose.

For two weeks I have been pitching a really big website account with a national company based in Orlando. They really want to hire me. I have proved that I can do the job. I have shown them examples of what I have done for other companies like them, and yet after three trips to Orlando and three weeks I still do not have the account. (I should have quit after two meetings.)

The reason for this is simple and quite beyond my control. By hiring me to do the job, someone at the company has to admit that their previous attempt to do what they want me to do FAILED!

Not only did it fail, but they wasted well over $200,000 and hired the wrong guy. A triple WHAMMY failure. Everyone connected with the project knows this is the case. BUT instead of just admitting the reality of the situation, everyone is trying to get me to work with what they have already got in place—bad though it is–simply to protect their fragile egos.

They want us to work in the programming language they have committed to but that's woefully outdated.

They want us to work within a template web system that is not suited to the quality of work they profess to want.

They want me to somehow use the guy who has already failed to produce on the project. They tell me this is very important. I say, "Fine, how do you want me to fit him in? He can't write copy, has limited graphic skills, and is not familiar with the programming language we use, so how?"

They don't know. Can't I think of something? I have explained that no matter how they wish to change the parameters of the job, the cost will not go down. In fact, it may well go up. Despite this, and despite the fact that they want me to accomplish in 45 days what they have failed to do in almost two years, they still can't quite pull the trigger because **someone has to justify all that failure.**

This is a large company and therefore you almost expect this sort of thing. Yet many smaller companies follow this same philosophy of hindering their future success by ignoring reality.

A business owner rents twice as much space as he really needs, yet doesn't want to downsize because it would "look bad."

A potential client has invested $5000, $10,000, even $50,000 in a bad website that has never produced a dime. Because of this, he refuses to believe the web can help him, or even if he does, he won't fix the problems in his website because the first $10,000 he invested was wasted.

A former top salesman has struck out for six months in a row. He's drinking heavily and has problems at home, but you keep him on because of his past performance. It does you no favors, the rest of the company no favors, and even the salesman himself no favors—but it's easier than facing reality. He's washed up and YOU have to fire him.

Are you making good business decisions based on reality or are you hanging onto bad business decisions or strategies just because you have so much time and money invested in them that it SEEMS too painful to quit and try to reach your goals in another way?

Remember the greatest skill of top leaders is not the ability to make good decisions, but the ability and courage to admit bad decisions and cut their losses.

If you had to start last year all over again. what would you NOT have done? Where would you have saved more money? Where should you have invested more money?

Do not protect yourself from bad decisions or the outright admission of "short-term" failure to protect your ego. Live in reality, make your decisions based on reality, and you will greatly reduce the time and effort it takes to succeed.

Dream big but live in reality.
Accept the reality of unproductive situations,
make changes, and move on.

CHAPTER 171

The Goals Factor

A man has to have goals—for a day, for a lifetime.
Mine was to have people say, "There goes Ted Wil-
liams, the greatest hitter who ever lived."
TED WILLIAMS

While I know plenty of successful entrepreneurs who made it without written goals, they've been very helpful for me. Ever since I first heard Brian Tracy say, twenty years ago, that "goal setting was the master skill of success," I have written and rewritten my goals on a regular basis. Keeping goals in front of you at all times helps keep you focused, helps you make good decisions, helps you keep score, and ultimately helps you connect work with reward.

Using the SMART Goals System

Here is a short and simple course on goal setting using the SMART system. (If you want the full Monty on getting ahead in life using goals, read *Cunningly Clever Achievement*.) Goals must be:

S mart
M otivational
A ttainable
R elevant
T rackable

Goals must be *specific* in order to be of any use — you can't just say you want things to be better. "Better" is not specific. Pick a specific number for profits, sales, or quantity of product sold as a goal. You must also pick a date and break goals down into manageable increments. For example:

This year I will sign up 60 new clients who will place an order of at least $2,000 each. I will sign up five new clients a month, one a week.

- This would be followed by detailed strategies for achievement of these goals, quantified and with due dates. For instance:

- Increase the number of sales calls you make by three per week.

- Add a new focus on gaining a referral from every existing customer with a minimum of five per week.

- Put in an extra effort to reconnect with one past customer per day.

Goals must be *motivational.* This means they are challenging, and they must have the emotional power to excite you enough to expend the time and effort necessary to achieve them. Even when you have goals and are doing something that you like, performing the same tasks day in and day out can become a grind. You need to reward yourself for your continuing efforts and results.

Sales goals are measured in money — what will you do specifically with your share of the profits? Each time you make a sale, you make a specific amount of money. What will you do with it? Will you take a vacation? How about buying that new car you have been promising yourself? Will you put the money down on a new house? Will you pay off your credit cards?

Whatever your goal, come up with a clear and specific use

for the money you will make from each new sale. Now as you make an appointment or pick up the phone to call back a prospect, visualize how spending that money will feel. Think how nice it will be to show up at work in a new car, bought in part by your new clients, Mr. Smith and Mr. Jones. What an easy but effective way to motivate yourself toward higher sales. Just connect the end result of each sale to a personal item you want in your life.

Also motivate yourself in small ways, like taking a coffee break after so many calls, or taking the afternoon off for golf after closing a big deal.

Goals can be ambitious, but they must be grounded in reality. They must be *attainable*. Setting a goal like, "Someday, somehow, I want to be president of a major corporation," does not meet the requirement of attainability. A goal that says, "I want to make $100,000 this year by gaining 60 new customers," is specific, motivational, and attainable.

Goals must be *relevant* to your ultimate goal. For example, "I want to gain 60 new customers this year and increase my income by 30%." This works with the bigger goal of having 200 customers in three years and generating one million in revenue with a 20% profit margin.

Your goals must be *trackable*. You must be able to measure progress as you go along. If your goals are not trackable, you don't know what progress you've made on the road to your goal. Ideally, you should track your goals yearly, monthly, weekly, and daily.

Keep your goals close at hand, review them daily, and continue expanding their scope. **Break them down from large goals into simple steps that you KNOW will aid you in reaching them**. Use your goals to develop a sense of urgency and each day you will quickly accomplish more of the simple little tasks, the sum of which adds up to giant success.

Remember, each and every day you have choices in the things you do. Some of these choices will move you forward, just as surely as others will move you backward. You are responsible for your choices. Having written goals and clear steps in front of you makes those choices much easier to make.

For more details on the power of goal setting go to www.CunninglyClever.com.

Set big goals, make detailed plans, and chart your progress daily.

CHAPTER 172

The Motivation Factor

Strength does not come from physical capacity. It comes from an indomitable will.
MAHATMA GANDHI

Mark Twain once said that the key to his success in life was "... that I was born excited." Most entrepreneurs I have met feel exactly the same way. That doesn't mean they don't need a little boost along the way or the tools to translate their excitement into motivating others on their team into action.

Very often when people think of successful entrepreneurs, the first thing that jumps into their minds is motivation. It's a fact that your ability to motivate yourself and others will ultimately determine how successful you are in business and life. The more motivated you and your team are, the more you will accomplish. Motivation destroys procrastination, encourages positive action, boosts energy, and increases performance at every level of any organization.

The cunningly clever entrepreneur knows that few great achievements are the work of a single person. As a leader, you must serve as a catalyst for others so great things get done. It is your ability to perceive the need for motivation, recognize what kind of motivation will serve best, and reward motivated individuals, that ultimately leads to team success.

One of my favorite motivational stories is that of Charles

Schwab, legendary leader of U.S. Steel under Andrew Carnegie and the first man ever to be paid a million dollars a year. He was a master motivator. Schwab had a mill manager whose people weren't producing their quota of work. "How is it," Schwab asked him, "that a manager as capable as you can't make this mill produce what it should?"

"I don't know." the manager replied. "I've coaxed the men, I've pushed them, I've sworn and cussed, I've threatened them with damnation and being fired. But nothing works. They just won't produce."

The conversation took place at the end of the day, just before the night shift came on. Schwab asked the manager for a piece of chalk, then, turning to the nearest man, asked: "How many heats did your shift make today?"

"Six," replied the man.

Without another word, Schwab chalked a big figure six on the floor, and walked away.

When the night shift came in, they saw the chalked number "6" on the floor and asked what it meant.

"The big boss was in here today," the day people said. "He asked us how many heats we made, and we told him six. He chalked it down on the floor."

The next morning Schwab walked through the mill again. The night shift had rubbed out "6" and replaced it with a big "7."

When the day shift reported for work the next morning, they saw a big "7" chalked on the floor. So the night shift thought they were better than the day shift, did they? Well, they would show the night shift a thing or two. The crew pitched in with enthusiasm, and when they quit that night, they left behind them an enormous, swaggering "10." Things were stepping up.

The competition continued at a ferocious pace until the output of steel from a single shift was the best in the entire chain of plants. This resulted in millions of additional dollars—not by technology, pay raises, promises, or threats, but by the power of a two-cent piece of chalk (and the brain behind it).

The Five Prerequisites for Motivation

In order for motivation to work effectively in any organization, big or small, there are five prerequisite conditions:

1. **The goals you are striving for must be clear and well-defined.** Nothing is less motivating than a nebulous goal like "Let's make customer service better." Make the target easy to see.

2. **There must be a way of keeping score so you and your team know how you are doing:** sales, weight loss, collection of funds, runs scored, production of widgets. Whatever it is, improvement must be trackable.

3. **The tools, resources, and (if necessary) the process of achieving the goal must be identified,** explained by you, and understood by your team.

4. **Information, training, and mentoring must be available.** Often when you take on a major project, you or your team may not have all the knowledge you need to complete it. When this is the case, you must be committed to finding the information and engaging in any necessary training.

5. **There must be something in it for them.** At the end of the day, there must be a payoff of some kind. The bigger and better the payoff, the stronger the

motivation, although that may not always be money. For many people, time off and peer recognition are stronger motivations than cash.

Understand what motivates you. Seek to discover what motivates others. For more ideas on how to motivate your team, go to www.CunninglyClever.com.

Being able to motivate others is a fundamental factor in all great successes.

CHAPTER 173

The Preparation Factor:
Stack the Deck in Your favor

Success depends upon previous preparation, and with-
out such preparation there is sure to be failure.
CONFUCIUS

Napoleon was once asked if he believed in luck in warfare. He replied, "Yes, I believe in luck. I believe in bad luck, and I believe that I will always have it. I therefore plan accordingly."

I often joke that the two reasons for all failure are lack of talent and poor planning. Both are fixable. You can take lessons, coaching, and seminars to improve your talent, while poor planning is even easier to fix.

Start each endeavor with a deck stacked in your favor. Know your goals, vision, and strategic plan inside out. Know your product, know your staff, know your resources, know your customers, and know your competition. Anticipate objections, eliminate roadblocks, and be overarmed with solutions.

The clearer you are about your goals and objectives, the harder it will be to sidetrack you and slow your progress. The clearer you are about your vision, the easier it will be to enlist support and take action, especially in times of trouble.

The better you know your organization, managers, and employees, the better you can gauge their unique strengths and weaknesses in helping you with the task at hand. This avoids a host of problems associated with hiring, or asking, the wrong person to do the job.

The better you know your competition, the more likely you are to anticipate their next moves and plan your strategy accordingly. You are therefore less likely to be blindsided by a pricing, marketing, or technological breakthrough.

Finally, the better you know your customers, donors, or partners, the better you can anticipate their wants and needs and adjust your strategy accordingly. The importance of good preparation cannot be overstressed.

As Abraham Lincoln said, "I shall prepare and one day my time will come." This statement is never truer than in the face of every adversity that confronts every entrepreneur.

Always be overprepared, not underprepared.

CHAPTER 174

The Action Factor

Never confuse motion with action.
BENJAMIN FRANKLIN

Successful entrepreneurs have a strong propensity towards action. Those who don't, tend to not make it.

At the end of my very first seminar for small business owners, five people came up to me to tell me how much they had enjoyed it. Each then proceeded to tell me in detail how they had been planning for several years to do exactly what I was doing. Two of the five even suggested I could improve the quality of my seminar if I allowed them to help me. I asked both to send me a letter detailing their basic ideas: neither letter ever arrived.

At my next seminar several weeks later, a similar thing happened. Only this time, six people approached me either immediately after the seminar or in private later that evening. Since then, hardly a seminar goes by where at least one person doesn't tell me exactly the same thing. "I have been thinking about doing seminars or starting a consulting business on such and such," they say.

"Are you an expert on that subject?" I ask.

"Oh yes," they say. "I have been involved in that subject for twenty years."

"Then why don't you go ahead?" I ask.

It is at this point that people seem to get truly creative. If most people put half as much effort into figuring out creative solutions to their problems as they do in coming up with reasons to procrastinate, there would be absolutely no chance of failure. To my knowledge, none of the people who told me about their plans have ever actually gone ahead with them.

Have you ever been sitting in a coffee shop or a restaurant and overheard two people talking about all the things they were going to do just as soon as they:

- had more money?
- found extra time?
- quit their lousy job?
- get a lucky break?
- find someone else to help them?

There simply is no more fatal disease for the successful entrepreneur than procrastination. Cancerous little statements like these kill:

- I was tired.
- I will do it later.
- When I finish this course, then I will be ready to get going.
- I will get to it next week, next month, next year.
- I will do it when I save up more money.

You can find these and 1,001 other excuses just like them on the lips of the millions who are not happy with their positions in life. They are the *wannabes* trapped in a mediocre life they really want to leave. Unfortunately for them, it seems they are not unhappy enough to destroy their tendency toward procrastination.

You can always find reasons why you should *not* start something right now. But if you give your brain equal time to think *how*, you can find just as many reasons to do it *now*. Go! Start! Lights, camera, ACTION! You cannot reach your goals without taking direct and massive action to get you there.

So Why Do People Procrastinate?

What is stopping you from taking action toward your dreams? Dreams don't change the world; actions change the world. Procrastination really goes back to poor planning and fear of failure. If you have correctly laid out your goals and the actions needed to achieve them, there should be no reason not to move forward. You have clearly identified the things you wish to achieve and the steps needed to accomplish them. You have set a timetable, a checkup system, and a reward system for reaching your short-term goals. You have no reason not to take action except fear of failure. And as I've already covered, there is no failure if you are learning and working toward a goal.

People who have completed their planning stages step boldly forward into the blackness. They expect holes, but they are confident they will know how to deal with them when they come. They know what is on the other side of the tunnel, and they know it is worth reaching. They know the pain of not reaching these wonderful goals is far too great to stand around and do nothing. They also know the rewards are great and if they stick to their plan, in the long run there is no chance of permanent failure.

Have You Written Down Your Goals Yet?

Have you written down a list of people you need to meet? Have you written down a list of actions and the dates by which they should be accomplished?

If the answer is no to any of these questions, then there is a very good chance you may not be ready to take the action needed to propel you to the top. It is amazing how the simple act of defining a clear plan and strategy will improve your business instantly. As I write this book and put down my thoughts on paper, I am filled with an immense feeling of excitement. By writing about the techniques I have used, it heightens my awareness of them and makes my own goals and strategies crystal clear. A strong picture of your ultimate goal and the actions needed to achieve it will allow you to triumph over procrastination.

I often quote the well-known words of Francis Bacon, "Knowledge is power." However, knowledge is only *potential* power until it is actualized. A person with the knowledge to succeed who takes no action is no better off than a person with no knowledge at all.

All action in the right direction—no matter how small—makes a difference. In life, everything counts. Every single time you take action toward your goals, you are reducing the time you will have to wait before your ultimate reward. Conversely, every time you decide to turn on the TV or put off daily action for another time, you are ensuring that you will have to wait longer for your ultimate prize.

Taking action creates a "magnetic" force that draws opportunity into your path even at the simplest level. Always try to create more opportunity for yourself by taking action rather than by avoiding it.

Action creates opportunity; procrastination is the enemy.

CHAPTER 175

The Method Factor— The Critical Importance of Finding a Duplicable System

Almost all quality improvement comes via simplification of design, manufacturing… layout, processes, and procedures.
TOM PETERS

If you look at the success of most major companies, like McDonald's, Federal Express, The Body Shop, or Gold's Gym, the most common factor is a methodology, a unique and systematized way of doing business. They create a method that permeates every level of the organization and indoctrinates every employee to the cause.

Apple has a highly systematized way of launching its products. KFC has a highly systematized way of cooking and serving its chicken. FedEx has a highly sophisticated way of initiating picking up, tracking and delivering packages. It's not necessary to be a multimillion-dollar business to make massive gains in your operation by copying this concept.

For example, are your sales presentations written and orchestrated so no two salespeople will answer the same question differently? There is only one perfect way to answer most sales objections. If your people are ad-libbing, they could be winning and losing at random. It's highly unlikely they will get the same sales results using different scripts. Find the answer that fits best and make that the script everyone uses–without exception. This is the process that makes companies like Disney and The Ritz-Carlton so consistent and so successful.

You need a method for every part of your business. You need a predictable method of generating leads. You need a predictable method of training new staff. You need a predictable method of delivering and servicing your product. You need a predictable method of forecasting revenue, paying your bills, and reporting on results. Such revenue items should be done on a set day, every week or every month, not when you have time or feel like it.

The more you write down, orchestrate, and share with your staff your method and unique way of doing business, the more successful your business will become.

The more methodical you make each part of your business, the more predictable your results will become.

CHAPTER 176

The Discipline Factor: Time, Focus, and the Power of the Pareto Principle

It's easy to have faith in yourself and have discipline
when you're a winner, when you're number one.
What you've got to have is faith and discipline
when you're not a winner.
VINCE LOMBARDI

Your strategic plan and goals must be your guide in how you use your time. They should clearly tell what to focus your efforts on, and what will bring you the greatest possible return. There is an old Cuban proverb that says, "When the sun rises, it rises for everyone." We all start with 24 hours in a day, but top performers seem to get more out of each and every day.

The key to getting more out of your day is time management and that means having the self-discipline to say "No." You must be ruthless in cutting out (or at least cutting down) those activities that do not propel you forward. When at work, don't waste time reading the sports page. Save it instead for reading at home that night. Spend your lunch hour improving your skills business skills by reading or listening to audio programs as you eat. Have lunch with a prospective customer or an associate with whom you must speak, thereby killing two birds with one stone. Say no when employees or friends try to distract you from finishing the task at hand.

In short, when you make your time count by setting and reaching short-term goals, your long-term goals will quickly be achieved. Take massive action by first taking smaller actions to get you going. How much time is wasted in the workplace every day by trying to do a multitude of tasks at the same time and failing to satisfactorily complete many–if any–of them? How many times have you felt overwhelmed by the tasks that lie ahead because you try to confront all of them at the same time, instead of picking one and working on it to a successful conclusion?

Concentration on achieving a single, distinct purpose has been the key to many a business success. As B.C. Forbes (of *Forbes* magazine) said, "One worthwhile task, carried to a successful conclusion, is better than a hundred half-finished tasks." Too often in today's fast-paced world of meetings, phone calls, emails, and everyday problems, we are distracted from the job at hand. It's not unusual to be busy all day without finishing a single important task. You come home, your spouse asks what you did today, and you're so frazzled you say, "I don't really know." This problem can quickly derail progress and successful people take steps to avoid it.

The world's most successful people start every day with a to-do list. Work on the first item, and only go to the second when you have completed the first, unless you have to wait for material needed for completion of the first. When you must tackle a tedious task, do it first and get it out of the way.

The Pareto principle, also known as the 80/20 rule, says that 80% of your results will come from 20% of your activities. For instance, 80% of your income will come from just 20% of your customers. Having the self-discipline to focus the majority of your efforts on the important 20% of your activities at the expense of the rest has been the turning point for many entrepreneurs. Focus your time, money, and efforts ONLY in those places where you know you will get the highest returns.

In life, every minute counts.
Have the self-discipline to use your time to
maximize your business.

CHAPTER 177

The Passion Factor

Without passion you don't have energy,
without energy you have nothing.
DONALD TRUMP

The power of passion was recognized years ago by the famous advertising guru, David Ogilvy, who built the most successful ad agency in history from the ground up. After designing campaigns for most of the megacorporations over the last 50 years, he came to the conclusion that only one thing could give a company the edge over the long haul. He found the key to success for any company was its ability to create an emotional bond with its customers that went far beyond the nature of the product the company was actually selling.

To paraphrase Ogilvy's words slightly:

> *A company competing on the basis of price can always be undercut. A company competing on the basis of uniqueness can always be copied. A company competing on the basis of a technical advantage can always be caught. A company competing on the basis of value can always be matched. But a company with passion cannot be touched.*

The long-term success of your business will be dictated not so much by the products and the value you provide, but by the emotional bonds you build with your customers. Those companies that fail to create such a bond, a feeling of something greater than the widget or service they happen to be selling, will not be able to compete at the top for any length of time.

Think:

- Ferrari

- Apple

- Virgin Atlantic

- Starbucks

- Dallas Cowboys or Manchester United

All are passion-charged brands with motivational CEOs and fanatical followers. All are brands that extend way beyond the people who use their product or have ever actually been to the stadium. This passion factor is by no means limited to megacorporations. I only use them as examples because you'll recognize them. In fact, this is one area where the small business owner has a real advantage. You start with few enough customers to create real bonds with them.

- It's the Italian restaurant on the corner of the street with great food and singing waiters.

- It's the hairdressing salon that treats you like a queen, greets you with champagne, and listens to your problems better than Oprah.

- It's the local golf pro who adopts your son as if he were the next Tiger Woods.

- It's the model shop that offers workshops with time-saving advice and tips.

- It's the bar that knows your name, knows your drink, and knows your mood.

Most of all it's the energy, enthusiasm, knowledge, experience, and passion you put into your business that extends out through your employees and in turn is absorbed and embraced by your customers.

Find tangible ways to transfer your passion into your business and you will always have an unbeatable edge.

CHAPTER 178

The Score Factor

*Checking the results of a decision against its
expectations shows executives what their strengths
are, where they need to improve, and where they lack
knowledge or information.*
PETER DRUCKER

Top entrepreneurs play to win. To play to win you have to keep score. While the P&L statement will be your ultimate record of success, the more different ways you can find to keep score along the way, the faster you will get there.

Keep score on:

- your leads
- number of outbound calls made by your salespeople
- your sales
- salesperson closing rates
- customer acquisition costs
- sales costs
- number of contacts in your database
- number of customers
- market share
- your web traffic

- your email open rates
- your response rates to individual offers
- media mentions
- number of friends, fans, and followers on your social media pages
- number of inbound calls you receive
- number of orchids (praise)
- number of onions (complaints)
- number of referrals
- lifetime value of a customer
- your profits
- employee turnover
- lowering your debt
- increasing your net worth
- progress toward you personal goals

The more factors you can list to keep score on in your business to help you measure incremental improvement, the more effective your business will be in doing the things necessary to grow rapidly. Study these numbers weekly and take necessary actions on the results at least monthly. Most entrepreneurs don't start out as "numbers people," but almost all successful ones become that way. As Churchill once said, "However beautiful the strategy, you should occasionally look at the results."

**If you don't keep score,
you are really not playing to win.**

CHAPTER 179

The Change Factor

When you're finished changing, you're finished.
BENJAMIN FRANKLIN

Of all the things that will test your patience and resolve, change is perhaps the hardest to deal with. Yet change is the one thing in business that is constant. Change will always affect your business, be it changing tastes, changes in competition, changes in technology, or changes in the general economy. Sometimes that change may help your business, other times it will hurt it.

Imagine being in the video rental business in, say, 1984.

Gold Mine!! You could open a video store on any street corner for the cost of the videos and be profitable by the end of the month.

Imagine being in it in 2014.

In less than thirty years, the corner video store has come, succeeded, declined, and will ultimately vanish like the dodo bird as everybody downloads their favorite movies from Netflix, iTunes®, or similar outfits.

Things change and change fast. You must always be on the lookout for changes in YOUR business environment. Too many people expect their businesses to simply keep on doing what they've always done while outside forces eat away at their very foundations.

Sometimes the winds of change or twists of fate happen so fast they catch even the most astute entrepreneurs off guard. Unforeseen and unpredictable events like 9/11 or stock market and real estate crashes can bring emotional and financial calamity to an entire company.

Cunningly clever entrepreneurs do their best to counter this danger by being constantly aware that market conditions can sometimes change rapidly. They prepare contingency plans to deal with the worst-case scenarios and they are always on the lookout for new horizons that offer expanded opportunities. Good advance planning and the willingness to change direction quickly and effectively help minimize damage to their market shares, reputations, and incomes. They waste no time in self-pity or recriminations, but concentrate on setting new goals and moving forward. They treat each new set of market changes as opportunities to improve their positions, vis-à-vis their competitors and to profit from their own visions and preparedness.

As soon as you see, or better still, predict changes in your marketplace, you must take action!

To innovate and deal with change before you HAVE to change, never stop asking these questions:

- How can we do it faster?

- How can we add value? What features can we add?

- How can we sell more? Keep customers longer? Increase referrals?

- What does the competition do better than us?

- Where is the future growth going to be geographically?

- What are they doing in other industries that we could import to ours?

- How are others connecting with customers using new media?

- How can we spread our risk by being in more than one market or adding additional revenue streams?

It pays to remember that change scares most people, especially employees, partners, and suppliers. People will fight tooth and nail to maintain the status quo. But you, like all great entrepreneurs, must continually challenge it.

Embrace change, seek it out. Besides death and taxes, it's the only thing you can count on.

Index

WOW Your Audience with the Energy and Wisdom of a Real-World Sales, Marketing & Entrepreneurial Legend!

Andrew Wood Speaks...

If you really want your group to learn firsthand how to improve their sales, marketing or business strategy from someone who has **really done it** at every level of the business world, there is no better choice than, Andrew Wood. Author of over 20 books on sales and marketing, he's an entrepreneur, who built a national franchise of 400 units and a multimillion dollar ad agency from scratch. He's a real-world marketing legend who continually astonishes clients with unheard of results from Internet, direct mail, and his out-of-the-box marketing campaigns.

-Andrew will electrify and entertain your audience with his business stories and cuttin edge strategies that attendees can instantly use to increase profits no matter what their business. From two-day marketing boot camps to 60 minute keynotes, Andrew covers all aspects of sales, marketing and entrepreneurial business growth in his presentations.

The highest-rated speaker at every event he has ever addressed, it's best to let Andrew's audiences support his claim as the pre-eminent marketing speaker in the world!

Visit www.LegendarySpeaker.com for details of Andrew's speaking and consulting programs incuding keynotes, half-day, full-day, and multi-day sessions on sales, marketing, and entrepreneurial leadership. Or contact him direct at 352-266-2099 or Andrew@CunninglyClever.com.

Cunningly Clever Marketing
The Inside Secrets of a Marketing Legend
By Andrew Wood

Out Market Everyone!

Nothing is more important to your business, career and, indeed, survival than to make <u>your marketing astonishingly more effective than any of your competitors!</u> Read ***Cunningly Clever Marketing*** and watch your **marketing's performance soar with innovative strategies for turning an ordinary business into an extraordinary business and immunizing yourself from recession**. It's over 400 stimulating pages jam-packed with powerful ideas, tactics and strategies to **quickly and ethically double**, even triple **your sales**, through superior marketing!

A fast, easy read full of graphics, examples and stories; you'll find **it fun, entertaining, practical and PROVEN!** Get inside secrets from a battle-tested marketing legend along with a bulletproof blueprint for superior marketing success. **Make every dime you spend on marketing count!**

*"**Cunningly Clever Marketing** made me laugh, wince, nod in agreement, howl, point out a statement to my wife, and become wiser in the ways of both marketing and reality.*
A superb read!"

Jay Conrad Levinson,
Author, "Guerrilla Marketing"
Over 20 million sold!

ou'll Discover:

- **Why entertaining marketing produces astonishing response, but only if it's done right!**

- Why Bruce Lipshitz can sell $200 blue jeans you couldn't sell for $50!

- **The outrageous marketing campaign that generated millions in new business for a Michigan resort!**

- The $7 million dollar sales letter that works in any industry to open doors!

- **The secret to getting other companies to promote your business to their customers for free!**

- Why your company's current Web strategy is almost certainly wrong... and costing you millions in lost revenue!

- **Ninja marketing – for stealing business from your competitors!**

- **How to quickly generate $250,000 without a loan, a rich uncle, or a gun!**

- The changing face of email marketing- how to boost your delivery rates!

- **The important art of Getting Paid!** Generating a stunning response from your **collection letters!**

nningly Clever Marketing reveals the inside rets Andrew Wood has accumulated over a time of studying and practicing what works in real world when his own money is at stake. My npany is using his ideas—and seeing results. I hly recommend it!"
Tom Hopkins, author of *How to Master The of Selling*, Scottsdale, AZ

- **How an ad in the LA Times, for motivational guru Anthony Robbins made me $18,000 in less than a minute!**

- Building your million-dollar mailing list in six weeks or less!

- Getting inside your prospects' heads with your marketing message!

- **How I made $75,000 in three days from an 11-page email no one read!**

- Selling Ferraris on eBay and the power of the damaging admission!

- **Thunderbolt Marketing, the world's most devastatingly effective marketing strategy!**

- The unknown and/or largely ignored secrets of effective Website design!

- **Irresistible offers and ironclad guarantees – are your secret weapon in the battle for massive response!**

- There are only three ways to grow a business... any business!

- Preach to the choir – don't try to convert the Muslims!

- **Are you wasting your marketing money? Most companies have no idea! But you will know your response to the penny!**

- *And much more...*

*"This **amazing cunningly clever series** is loaded with practical, proven methods and techniques to attract more customers and make more sales than you will be able to handle!"*
—**Brian Tracy, world-famous sales and motivational author of over 45 books**

Cunningly Clever
Selling
Outsell Everyone!

Easily & Ethically

🦊 *Andrew Wood*

Discover how even a small change in how you answer the phone or handle an objection can have a major IMPACT ON YOUR SALES SUCCESS!

- Inside sales secrets from hollywood that will out sell every other method by 330%!

- **The incredible two-second sales presentation power test.**

- The relentless follow-up campaign that takes less than a minute to execute!

- The fine and profitable art of painting with words so every prospect gets the message.

- How to create a sales experience that's so enjoyable price doesn't matter!

- **The secrets to turning lost sales into serious cash, by using the power of psychic debt!**

- Converting shop-around prospects to loyal customers in seconds, without discounting.

- Developing Instant Credibility Using the Power of the Damaging Omission.

- Instant rapport with every prospect to massively increase your sales potential.

- Painless prospecting: attracting a constant, and automated, RIVER of qualified leads!

- Selling to salesman, skeptics and other tough cookies.

- **Presenting so the prospect NEVER, ever says, "I have to think about it!"**

- Cunningly Clever presentations to disarm every objection, before they even come up!

- Tripling the value of every sale with a single sentence!

- Staying motivated, even on Mondays.

- **The incredible power of sales stories – crafting yours for astonishing results!**

- Breaking mental barriers for record sales.

• • • • •

"A must read for anyone selling anything who's looking for a rapid increase in sales!"
**Dermot Dalton, CEO,
Golf Services, Dublin, Ireland**

- **Destroying "The price is too high" and other money objections!**

- Guaranteed referrals from every sale!

- Turning suspects into sales even if they walk in because they're LOST!

- The world's best, battle-tested closing techniques, revisited, refined and re-charged!

- **Stephen King's astonishing secret to creating stories (presentations) that sell!**

- Why 98% of all retail sales are killed in just four words!

- Why raising your price often brings sales success—strange but true!

- **Hundreds of proven qualifying, presenting, closing and objection scripts!**

- Cunningly Clever techniques for breaking out of sales resistance.

- How to get 48 hours out of every sales day.

- Why switching job descriptions to position agreements can triple your team's sales performance overnight.

- **Killing your competition professionally with Cunningly Clever innuendo!**

Plus Much More...

"As a sales manager who's read ALL the sales books, listened to all the audios, and been to all the seminars, I still found the new and practical concepts in this book BRILLIANT!"
Kevin Strom, Sales Manager, FL

• • • • •

"Brilliant, readable, practical, entertaining and enlighten – even for an accountant!"
**Mike Steventon, Senior Partner,
KPMG, London, UK**

• • • • •

*"The best sales book ever written and the only one you'll ever need. **Cunningly Clever Selling** is packed full of wonderful ideas to make MORE sales happen, NOW!"*
Barry Owens, CEO, Treetops Resort, MI

CunninglyClever.com
Out Market, Out Manage, Out Sell Everyone!

CunninglyClever.com is a unique website dedicated to providing you with proven **inspiration, ideas, and answers to quickly maximize your business and enhance your life!** No textbook stuff here; it's all street-smart strategies and firsthand advice that actually works. The very information you need to maximize your profits and enjoy your life without the heartache of making all the mistakes yourself!

Our site is divided into the five main categories of success:

- Marketing
- Sales
- Entrepreneurial skills
- Leadership
- Personal Development.

These are the key master skills, needed to grow any business or advance any career!

Fresh and innovative content is provided weekly by top experts in the form of articles, special reports, audio seminars, and video streams. Use whichever method best fits your lifestyle to keep you on the cutting edge.

Just 5 minutes a day on CunninglyClever.com can change your world!

Speed is a strategy—that's why we have all the potent information and strategies you need to succeed in searchable, bite-size nuggets of information.